T0293887

THE WILD ATLANTIC WAY
AND WESTERN IRELAND

THE WILD ATLANTIC WAY AND WESTERN IRELAND

6 CYCLE TOURS ALONG IRELAND'S WEST COAST

by Tom Cooper

JUNIPER HOUSE, MURLEY MOSS,
OXENHOLME ROAD, KENDAL, CUMBRIA LA9 7RL
www.cicerone.co.uk

© Tom Cooper 2018
Second edition 2018
ISBN: 978 1 85284 909 2
Reprinted 2021, 2024 (with updates)
First edition 2010

Printed in Singapore by KHL Printing on responsibly sourced paper

A catalogue record for this book is available from the British Library.
All photographs are by the author unless otherwise stated.

Acknowledgements

Thanks to my parents for the enduring gift of a love of the outdoors, and to Charlotte for her help with the text and enthusiasm for the project.

Updates to this Guide

While every effort is made by our authors to ensure the accuracy of guidebooks as they go to print, changes can occur during the lifetime of an edition. Any updates that we know of for this guide will be on the Cicerone website (www.cicerone.co.uk/909/updates), so please check before planning your trip. We also advise that you check information about such things as transport, accommodation and shops locally. Even rights of way can be altered over time. We are always grateful for information about any discrepancies between a guidebook and the facts on the ground, sent by email to updates@cicerone.co.uk or by post to Cicerone, Juniper House, Murley Moss, Oxenholme Road, Kendal, LA9 7RL.

Register your book: To sign up to receive free updates, special offers and GPX files where available, create a Cicerone account and register your purchase via the 'My Account' tab at www.cicerone.co.uk.

Front cover: Author off the beaten track approaching Cleggan (Route 3, Stage 4)

CONTENTS

Achill Island from Minaun is one of the finest views you can ride to in Ireland (Route 6, Stage 2

Bantry Bay from the Sheep's Head peninsula (Route 6, Stage 3)

THE WILD ATLANTIC WAY CYCLE ROUTE

This table lists the stages from the six cycle tours devised for this guide (see 'Six cycle tours in western Ireland') that make up the route of the Wild Atlantic Way. Details of any variations from the official WAW driving route are set out in Appendix C.

Section	From	To	Route/ stages	Days	Distance (km)
1	Derry/Londonderry	Donegal Town	1	9	503.8
2	Donegal Town	Westport	2/1–6, 7 (part), 7A	7	463.3
3	Westport	Galway	3/1–7	7	291.0
4	Galway	Tarbert	4/1–7A	8	440.6
5	Tarbert	Kenmare	5/1–7	7	389.7
6	Kenmare	Cork	6	6	359.3
Total	**Derry/Londonderry**	**Cork**		**44**	**2449.8**

SIX CYCLE TOURS IN WESTERN IRELAND

Route	Start/Finish	Stages	Total distance (km)	Average stage (km)	Longest stage (km)	Ascent (m)	Highest point (m)
1	Derry (Londonderry)/ Donegal Town	9	503.8	70.0	81.4	6903	280
2	Donegal Town/ Sligo	8	559.9	70.0	99.9	6142	200
3	Westport/ Westport	9	405.5	45.3	68.1	4354	110
4	Galway/ Limerick	7	381.2	54.4	130.6	4053	190
5	Tarbert/Tralee	9	468.4	52.0	69.7	6323	410
6	Kenmare/Cork	6	359.3	59.9	94.4	6107	160

Six cycle tours in Western Ireland

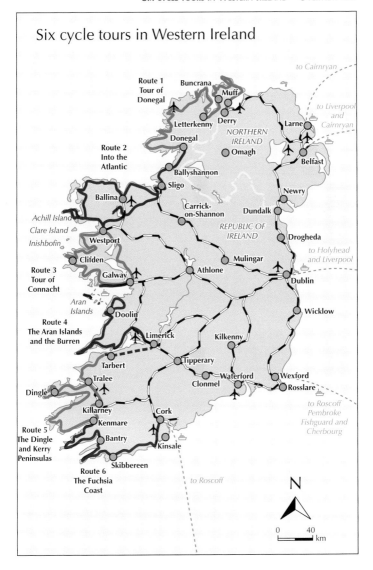

Route 1
Tour of
Donegal

Buncrana

Muff

Letterkenny

Derry

Larne

to Cairnryan

*to Liverpool
and
Cairnryan*

Donegal

NORTHERN
IRELAND

Omagh

Belfast

Route 2
Into the
Atlantic

Ballyshannon

Sligo

Newry

Ballina

Carrick-
on-Shannon

Dundalk

Achill Island
Clare Island
Inishbofin

Westport

REPUBLIC OF
IRELAND

Drogheda

*to Holyhead
and Liverpool*

Clifden

Route 3
Tour of
Connacht

Galway

Athlone

Mulingar

Dublin

Aran
Islands

Doolin

Wicklow

Route 4
The Aran Islands
and the Burren

Limerick

Kilkenny

Tarbert

Tipperary

Tralee

Clonmel

Waterford

Wexford

Dingle

Rosslare

*to Roscoff
Pembroke
Fishguard and
Cherbourg*

Killarney

Cork

Route 5
The Dingle
and Kerry
Peninsulas

Kenmare

Bantry

Kinsale

Skibbereen

Route 6
The Fuchsia
Coast

to Roscoff

N

0   40
km

Greencastle Harbour, County Donegal (Route 1, Stage 1)

INTRODUCTION

Sunset at Strandhills (Route 2, Stage 3)

Officially launched in 2014, the Wild Atlantic Way winds along more than 2000km of coastline at Europe's far northwestern shore. Here, breakers rolling in from the Americas have shaped ancient rocks into a land of special beauty. The people, too, have forged a distinct cultural identity. Gaelic is still spoken along the Atlantic coast and the island's story is etched into the landscape in prehistoric remnants, early Christian architecture, castles, grand 18th century houses and contemporary Nationalist murals. From Derry/Londonderry and Malin Head in the north to Mizen Head and Cork in the southwest, fine beaches, harbours and towering cliffs await the turn of your pedals.

This guide adopts and adapts the Wild Atlantic Way to suit the cycle tourist. The official Wild Atlantic Way is a driving route. As such it includes long stretches of main road when quieter and more scenic alternatives are close at hand for cyclists. The 'Way' also skips two excellent cycling spots – the Aran Islands, where there are no car ferries, and Killarney, which is a sublime day-ride away from the coast. (See Appendix C for a detailed breakdown of the ways in which the route described in this guide differs from the WAW driving route.)

Since not everyone has seven weeks to spare for a full Wild Atlantic Way tour, this guide offers six self-contained tours based on sections of the Wild Atlantic Way, each of which can be fitted into one week or two. For the full Wild Atlantic Way experience, the distinct routes link together into a 44-stage, 2400km trip along Ireland's west coast.

The beauty of Ireland's Atlantic coastline is based on its geological foundations. The island's oldest rocks are found in the north and west. For a large part of its geologic history these parts of Ireland were part of the continent of Laurentia, the bigger part of which is now part of Canada and the northern United States. These rocks remain as the foundations of the island to the north and west of the fabulously named Iapetus Suture which runs from the Shannon estuary to Clogherhead, north of Dublin on the east coast. Ireland's oldest exposed rocks are the 1.8 billion-year-old granitic gneisses of Inishtrahull, an island visible from Malin Head in the far north west. Further south along the Wild Atlantic Way you will find the 200m high Cliffs of Mohr, made of Namurian slates and sandstones about 320 million years old. Close by are the rock pavements of the Aran Islands, and the neighbouring Burren, shaped from slightly older Carboniferous limestone.

The bays and peninsulas of Kerry and Cork were shaped into their east–west alignment by movements some 270 million years ago (known as Armorican folding), while in the north and west the mountains follow the northwest–southeast alignment of the far earlier Caledonian stage of

Fine glaciated features at the Poisoned Glen, Dunlewey (Route 1, Stage 6)

mountain building, some 500 million years ago.

During the most recent ice age much of what is now Ireland was covered by ice, and the landscape retains some of the finest glacial scenery in Europe. Doo Lough Glen in County Mayo and the Poisoned Glen in County Donegal are glacial valleys of the highest order. Two glacial landforms, the esker and the drumlin, take their English names from Irish words. Drumlins are low, whale-backed hills deposited under the ice, while eskers are long sinuous ridges believed to result from water flowing under the ice.

WILDLIFE AND FLOWERS

The development boom of the 'Celtic Tiger' economy increased the pressures on Ireland's wild places, but as a cycle trip along the Wild Atlantic Way will reveal, Ireland remains predominantly rural.

Ireland's plant and animal populations are typical for a northwest European country. The main points of interest are some absences – Ireland has a slightly impoverished flora and fauna compared to mainland Europe and Britain – and a handful of unexpected species. Of the absences on the animal side, most notable are the snakes which, according to legend, St Patrick banished from Ireland in the fifth century.

The few unexpected residents mostly fall into the category of Lusitanian species – which are more commonly found in northern Spain and Portugal and are absent from Britain. There is no conclusive explanation for these disjunct populations. The most visible Lusitanian species to the casual observer is the strawberry tree (*Arbutus unedo*) of West Cork, Kerry and Sligo, which produces spiky bright-red fruits from September to December. A similar curiosity in the animal kingdom is the spotted Kerry slug, which is found in only three sites in Ireland – including the Killarney National Park – although it also occurs on the Iberian peninsula.

Ireland is an important bird habitat. The long coastline and position at the northwest corner of the Eurasian landmass attract countless seabirds. Little Skellig Island off the Kerry coast is home to some 70,000 gannets – one of the largest colonies in the world. Puffins also breed here and at other sites along the Atlantic coast including the Cliffs of Mohr.

HISTORY

Ireland's history has been turbulent right up until the recent past. For many centuries, the island was ruled by England, later Great Britain, and much of Ireland's more recent history has been consumed by tensions relating to that colonial legacy.

The island of Ireland is divided into two political units. All but a few kilometres of the routes in this book are in the sovereign country of

Ross Errilly Friary has a well-preserved cloister (Route 3, Stage 8)

Ireland – the term Republic of Ireland (RoI) is sometimes used to distinguish this state from the totality of the geographical island, also called Ireland. The remainder of the island is taken up by Northern Ireland, part of the United Kingdom of Great Britain and Northern Ireland. The political division of the island reflects a complex and at times violent history with periods of tension continuing through to the present day.

Early times
Christianity is thought to have come to Ireland in the fifth century, or even earlier. By tradition this was at the hand of St Patrick who landed in 432. In what was a relatively stable land, Christian scholarship and ministry flourished as the rest of Europe descended into chaos with the fall of the Roman Empire. Irish monks then contributed greatly to the spread of Christianity throughout Britain and the rest of Europe with, for example, Columbanus establishing monasteries in France and Bobbio in Italy, where he died in 615.

From the late eighth century onwards Irish settlements and monasteries became targets of Viking coastal raiders. The Vikings established permanent bases in Dublin, Wexford, Waterford, Cork and Limerick which went on to become the first significant towns in Ireland.

Politically, Ireland had been ruled, since prehistoric times, as a series of regional kingdoms with, occasionally, one king emerging as more powerful than his rivals and claiming suzerainty. Ireland's first High King, Brian Boru, was crowned in 1002. He is credited with bringing stability to the island, supressing the Viking threat and restoring some of the damage inflicted on the monasteries during the preceding century.

English invasion and religious division

The Anglo Norman invasion of 1169 began a process of the slow seizure of power from the traditional Gaelic rulers of Ireland. But the Gaelic political and social order that had flourished since prehistoric times persisted into the 17th century in much of Ireland.

English interest in Ireland waxed and waned periodically after the initial invasion, before reawakening in earnest during the 16th century. The first of the British rulers to claim the title of King of Ireland was King Henry VIII of England in 1541. Much of the conflict in Britain and Europe over the following two centuries stemmed from Henry's decision to split the church in England away from the Catholic church, alongside the wider ructions of the Reformation. It became Ireland's destiny to be proxy battleground for wider disputes between England and other European powers.

In 1594 a full-on Irish rebellion against English rule broke out. What is now called the Nine Years' War ended in 1603 following the defeat of the Irish, and an invading Spanish force, by the English at Kinsale. In 1607 the Ulster chieftains sailed out of Lough Swilly on the Donegal coast and into exile in France. This 'Flight of the Earls' marks the end of the power of the traditional Irish dynasties on the island.

Derrynane House is the ancestral home of Daniel 'the Liberator' O'Connell (Route 5, Stage 6)

English-backed Protestant settlement of Ireland soon began in earnest. This, together with authoritarian attempts to impose the Reformation, set in place a religious divide that grew wider with the enacting of laws that discriminated against Catholics – who tended to be native Irish – and cemented the power of a ruling Protestant gentry. A period of open warfare, and a brief flowering of Catholic power, came to a brutal end in 1649 at the hand of England's Lord Protector Oliver Cromwell. More than a quarter of the island was then handed to Cromwell's followers. The century ended in more tumult as the conflict between the deposed Catholic King of England James II and his Protestant successor William of Orange was fought out in Ireland. James was defeated at the Battle of the Boyne in 1690 foreshadowing another century of oppression of Catholics.

The United Irishmen Rebellion of 1798 – inspired by revolutions in North America and France – tried to unite Catholics and Protestants behind the cause of Irish freedom. But it prompted a backlash from Britain, not least because it was supported by a small-scale French invasion of Ireland. In the aftermath, the Irish Parliament was dissolved and Ireland was absorbed into the new Kingdom of Great Britain and Ireland, governed from Westminster.

During the 19th century, the tide began to turn against anti-Catholic oppression. Daniel 'the Liberator' O'Connell was elected to the Westminster parliament in 1828 as the member for County Clare but, initially, the Catholic Kerry-born barrister was not allowed to take his seat. The law was changed, not least because of fears of a Catholic uprising, and O'Connell took his place in parliament in 1830.

The Great Famine

Before the Great Famine of 1845-52 Ireland was one of the most densely populated countries in Europe. The tenant farmers eked out an impoverished existence on land owned by a largely absent aristocracy. There was widespread dependency on potatoes as a subsistence crop, and when blight struck in 1845 the British government was disastrously slow to respond to the unfolding crisis. The ensuing famine saw some one million deaths with a further million emigrating, mostly to the United States, although estimates vary widely.

The Famine was a watershed in Irish history and has become a rallying point for Irish nationalists and totemic of English exploitation and suppression in Ireland. The following years saw some small victories in improving land rights but a Bill that would have returned an Irish parliament to Dublin was continually blocked by the upper chamber of the British parliament, the House of Lords. An awakening of Irish culture was also underway with, for example, the Gaelic League founded

THE GREAT FAMINE

The potato fungal disease *Phytophthora infestaris* first struck in Ireland in 1845. There had already been warnings that there was an over-dependence on potatoes but it was when the blight returned in 1846 that the full horror of the Great Famine began to unfold. The disease did not appear in 1847, although by this stage there was a lack of seed potatoes and the crop was low. The blight then returned in 1848 and 1849, and had run its course by 1850. Contemporary political ideas put faith in markets to deal with short-ages and private charities and landlords to deal with the immediate crisis. It was not until 1847 that the British government changed tack and began actively feeding the population – but by then Ireland was already the scene of harrowing starvation and disease was rampant. Estimates of the total num-ber of deaths vary, but they amounted to at least a million. Some of the accounts recorded at the Skibbereen Heritage Centre (Route 6, Stage 4) are truly shocking, but it is in the silence of the Abbeystrowry famine graveyard, where 8000–10,000 unidentified people are buried, that the true scale of the tragedy can start to be comprehended.

in 1893 to promote the everyday use of the Irish language.

The Easter Rising and beyond
The prospect, in 1912, of an Irish Home Rule Bill finally being forced past the recalcitrant Lords galvanised unionist groups in favour of close ties with Britain, and both Irish national-ist and unionists began to gather arms. The Home Rule Act was given royal assent in 1914, but then suspended when Britain was drawn into World War I.

The nationalist Easter Rising of 1916 saw the taking of strategic sites in Dublin, including the General Post Office, and the proclamation of an independent Irish republic. The British government, then engulfed in a life-or-death conflict with Germany, had no qualms about using troops diverted from the Western Front and heavy armaments in central Dublin. Many of the rebels were executed as traitors – a heavy-handed approach that boosted support for Irish nation-alism. Future president of Ireland, Éamon de Valera, was originally given a death sentence which was later commuted to life in prison.

In the post-war election of 1919, the nationalist Sinn Féin party won the majority of Irish seats (in the Westminster parliament). The mem-bers then declared Ireland independ-ent and formed the Dáil Éireann (Irish Assembly). The Irish War of Independence followed, ending in 1921 with the Anglo-Irish Treaty

*A Victorian post box overstamped
with the 'SE' Irish Free State mark*

from guerrilla warfare laid a poor foundation for a fledgling independent nation.

Ireland remained neutral during World War II. Its next major landmark came in 1973 as the country joined what was then the European Economic Community (now the EU) at the same time as its single largest trading partner the United Kingdom. By then 'The Troubles' had already broken out in Northern Ireland, where British troops were engaged and paramilitaries from pro-Republican and pro-British factions were on the streets. The Good Friday Agreement of 1998, ratified by all sides, brought an end to the violence, but political conflict and socio-political division remain.

Eye of the tiger

In the south of the island, economic growth had at best been stuttering since independence, while unrest in the north had blighted investment there since the 1970s. Historically, many of Ireland's best and brightest left to pursue careers in Britain or further afield. At the start of the 1990s Ireland was a poor country by Western European standards but, driven by EU investment, low taxation, pro-business policies and the availability of a well-educated workforce, the economy entered a boom phase. The economy grew at over 9 per cent a year between 1995 and 2000 and continued to expand at up to 6 per cent a year until the global credit crisis began to hit in 2007-8.

that established the Irish Free State. The treaty allowed six of the northern counties of Ulster – mostly still in favour of union with Britain – to opt out of the Free State, a right they promptly exercised.

The Treaty was, however, divisive among nationalists, many of whom objected to the partition of Ireland. The Free State's status as a dominion, albeit autonomous, of the hated British Empire also rankled. The subsequent Irish Civil War of 1922-23 between pro- and anti-Treaty forces petered out into a de facto victory for those backing the deal. However, the loss of lives – including charismatic and high-profile figures such as Michael Collins – and the damage

Ireland was by then dubbed the 'Celtic Tiger' as one of the few European economies to match the growth in the Asian Tiger economies at the time. Companies such as Microsoft and Facebook had chosen Ireland as a European base. Land prices had ballooned and new housing estates littered the Irish landscape. But the good times ended abruptly with the 'credit crunch' of 2008. A calamitous downturn followed and, as a Eurozone economy, Ireland suffered the indignity of intervention from the EU, the European Central Bank and the International Monetary Fund.

By the early part of the second decade of the century Ireland's economy returned to growth. Dublin booms again although the growth is less visible in the west of the island. Tourism, for a long time a reliable contributor to the Irish economy, is stirring after suffering (at least by comparison with other sectors) during the Tiger period. Luring visitors away from Dublin and traditional hotspots such as Killarney is a policy goal: projects such as the Wild Atlantic Way are seeing significant investment and improvement in accommodation, places to eat and visitor facilities, some of which seemed destined to moulder away during the boom years.

WHAT'S IN A NAME?

Because of the history of the island, most places in Ireland have both Irish and Anglicised names. Visitors to Ireland generally find the Anglicised names easier to recognise, read and pronounce – something which could be crucial when following or asking

Dawros Bay is ringed with small beaches such as this one at Rossbeg (Route 1, Stage 8)

for directions. Purely for pragmatic reasons, therefore, this guide tends to use the Anglicised versions.

Appendix B gives a few of the original Gaelic placenames with an explanation of their meanings.

BUILT HERITAGE AND ARCHITECTURE

Ireland has megalithic structures and other prehistoric remains of the highest order. The Iron Age ring fort of Dun Aengus on the Aran Islands is one of the star attractions, but there are countless other interesting and well-preserved sites.

Ireland is also blessed with some fine early Christian architecture. Skellig Michael monastery is one of the best preserved early Christian sites in Europe. A feature unique to Ireland are its round towers, dating from the 9th to 12th centuries and usually part of a monastic settlement. These thin stone towers, commonly 25–30m high with a conical roof, served as bell towers and places of storage as well as a lookout. There is a fine example at Killala in County Mayo.

The later Christian architecture of Ireland is also impressive. Muckross Abbey, County Kerry, and Ross Errilly Friary, County Galway, remain as particularly fine monastic ruins.

A fortification to look for from an earlier period is the crannog. These lake island fortifications date from the Iron Age through to medieval times. There are particularly good examples

Round towers such as this one at Killala are a distinctly Irish medieval form of ecclesiastical architecture (Route 2, Stage 4)

at Kiltooris Lough (Route 1, Stage 8) and on Achill Island (Route 2, Stage 6).

Fast-forwarding to the 18th century, Ireland has more than its fair share of grand houses. Bantry House in County Cork dates from this period. There is also some fine 19th-century Gothic Revival architecture in Ireland.

At a more prosaic level, although the traditional whitewashed thatched Irish cottage is slowly succumbing to modernisation, some good examples still survive, particularly in Donegal.

CULTURE

Literature

Ireland has a great tradition of Gaelic literature, much of it hailing from the Atlantic coast. Good translations are, however, hard to find. You could try Máirtín Ó Cadhain's 1949 novel *Cré na Cille* which has new translations as *Graveyard Clay* and *The Dirty Dust*. For poetry, try Máirtín Ó Direáin's *Tacar Danta/Selected Poems*. Perhaps more accessible is the Irish contribution to literature in English. The island has produced four Nobel Laureates for literature: William Butler Yeats – who had strong ties with the Sligo area, George Bernard Shaw, Samuel Beckett and Seamus Heaney. Another great of Irish literature with ties to the Atlantic coast is John Millington Synge whose one-act play *Riders to the Sea*, set in the Aran Islands, was first performed in 1904. For a more contemporary perspective, the trials and tribulations of life in Ireland since the financial downturn of 2008 have sparked a revival in novels and short stories. Writers such as Sarah Baume, Kevin Barry and their contemporaries are an effective antidote to any over-romantic view of life in Ireland.

Appendix D contains some suggestions for reading before, during and after your trip.

Gaelic sports

Gaelic football and hurling are the two most popular sports in Ireland. Both are fast and skilful games where endurance also counts. Gaelic football is a little like a cross between

Gorse flowers on the hills above Lough Swilly (Route 1, Stage 4)

rugby and soccer, played on a pitch with H-shaped goals. Hurling is a stick-and-ball game played on the same pitch. The hurling stick is axe-shaped and the game far more aerial and physical than games like hockey.

Irish music

For visitors, the most common place to hear Irish traditional music is the pub. In fact some areas, such as Doolin in County Clare, seem to be building a tourist industry based almost entirely on pub music. It always pays to ask for local advice about the best venues.

GETTING THERE

By air

The major international airports are Dublin, Shannon (near Limerick) and Belfast (Belfast International and Belfast City). Shannon is within a few kilometres of the routes in this book. Of the smaller airports, Derry/Londonderry, Cork, Knock in County Mayo, and Kerry airport offer good access to the Wild Atlantic Way. Donegal also has an airport, at Carrickfinn, near Dungloe, which currently has a handful of flights per day, mainly to Dublin.

Flying with a bike throws up no difficulties peculiar to Ireland. Most airlines will charge a special baggage fee for a bike, which will usually have to be paid at the time of booking. The bare minimum to pack a bike for flying is to take off or reverse the pedals, turn the handlebars sideways, let down the tyres, and lower the seat and handlebar stem. The bike will have to be packed, at the very least, in something to protect other baggage from the oily parts – such as an all-enclosing plastic bag. A bike-sized cardboard box (these are freely given

Packed and ready to fly – George Best International Airport; Irish mainline trains have cycle spaces that should be booked in advance

Ferry crossings			
Route	Frequency	Length of crossing	Operator
From England			
Liverpool–Dublin	12 per week	7h30m–8h30m	P&O Ferries
Liverpool Birkenhead–Belfast	13 per week	8h	Stena Line
From Wales			
Holyhead–Dublin Port	5 per day	1h50m	Irish Ferries
Holyhead–Dublin Port	4 per day	3h15m	Stena Line
Pembroke–Rosslare	14 per week	4h	Irish Ferries
Fishguard–Rosslare	14 per week	3h30m	Stena Line
From Scotland			
Cairnryan (Stranraer)–Larne	7 per day	2h	P&O Ferries
Cairnryan (Stranraer)–Belfast	5 per day	2h15m	Stena Line
From France			
Cherbourg–Rosslare	1 per week	16h	Brittany Ferries
Cherbourg–Rosslare	6 per week	18h	Stena Line
Roscoff–Rosslare	1 per week	13h	Brittany Ferries
Roscoff–Cork	2 per week	12h	Brittany Ferries

away at most bike shops) can be used for better protection. Check ahead with the airline for packing requirements. Then arrive early, be relaxed and friendly with the check-in staff, whatever happens, and – just in case of a mishap – be insured.

Dublin airport is some 10km north of the city centre. The ride into town is along busy main roads and requires extreme care, especially if you are tired after a long flight. It is also not currently well signed for cyclists but the situation should improve. Check the Transport for Ireland journey planner for up-to-date directions (www.transportforireland. ie/plan-a-journey).

By sea
Ferries can be a practical and economical way of getting to the Emerald Isle but the only ferry port with good access to the Wild Atlantic Way is Cork and that is currently only served with ferries from France. However, there are rail connections from both Dublin and Belfast (see below). The easiest way to get from Dublin Port to the heart of the city is to ride – follow

the city centre signs until you reach the north shore of the Liffey where you can pick up the cycle path.

For ferry company contact details, see Appendix A.

Getting to the Wild Atlantic Way
If you arrive in Dublin there are direct rail connections to Cork, Galway, Sligo and Westport. A change of trains may be needed to reach Limerick, Tralee or Ballina in County Mayo. If arriving in Belfast there are regular rail services to Derry/Londonderry. Dublin has two main railway stations. If you are heading to Cork, Limerick, Tralee, Killarney, Galway, Westport or Ballina you will need to go to Dublin Heuston, which is a couple of kilometres west of the town centre on the south bank of the river Liffey. For services to Sligo or Belfast (with onward connections to Derry/Londonderry) go the more central Connolly Station, on the north side of the river a few hundred metres inland from the landmark Customs House.

Public transport options around the capital are limited if you have a bike with you. Only folded cycles are allowed on suburban tram system (the Luas) and on city buses. You can take a cycle on the suburban train network (DART) between 10am and 4pm on weekdays and any time at weekends.

Visas
At the time of writing, citizens of European Union countries and most Western countries do not require a visa to enter Ireland or Northern

Ireland. Non-UK or non-Irish nationals do require a passport or national identity card. But all these arrangements are subject to change following the UK's 2016 decision to leave the EU. UK citizens currently do not, strictly speaking, need a passport to enter the Republic of Ireland (Northern Ireland is part of the UK in any case), but most carriers (air and sea) insist on valid photographic ID for security reasons.
• Northern Ireland Visa Information: www.gov.uk/check-uk-visa
• Republic of Ireland Visa Information: www.dfa.ie/travel/visas

GETTING AROUND
See Appendix A for contact information for public transport operators.

Trains
In the Irish Republic, booked bicycles are carried free on nearly all inter-city rail services (with some peak-time restrictions) although there is limited space (usually three or four cycles). Cycle reservations should be made at the same time as buying passenger tickets on the Irish Rail website (www.irishrail.ie). For the latest information follow the 'Travel Information' then 'Bicycle Information' links from the Irish Rail home page.

In Northern Ireland, public transport comes under the Translink banner. On trains, cycles are carried free on all services after 9.30am.

The Spanish Armada ship La Trinidad Valencera was wrecked off Kinnagoe Bay on 16 September 1588 (Route 1, Stage 1)

Buses

In the Republic, Bus Éireann will carry bicycles in the bus luggage compartment if there is space. If you are leaving from a bus station, buy a ticket before boarding, as well as a separate ticket for the bike. In rural areas, during the day and during the week, many services are nearly empty. If there is just one or two of you, a bus hop is a practical way of extending your range, and the network is comprehensive.

In Northern Ireland, buses also come under the Translink umbrella. Up to two cycles can be carried in the luggage bay of express services (called Goldline Express) after 9.30am, but again this is subject to space. There are no reservations.

WHEN TO GO

My favourite months for cycling in Ireland are May, June and September. Experience and the statistics suggest that May and June, especially in the north, are as dry as, if not drier than, the rest of the summer, while September is a golden month in which to watch the harvest and notice the first colours of autumn in the trees.

The Irish tourist season effectively runs from Easter to the end of September, and that is the practical limit for cycle touring too. Outside these months, the weather is too cold and unreliable, the days too short, and campsites and some other types of accommodation close.

Tourist numbers peak during July and August. Travelling at peak times is not a problem – it just pays to plan ahead a little more, as accommodation can fill up.

ACCOMMODATION

Hostels

Official Irish youth hostels are run by An Óige. A membership card is not required, although a card from an affiliated youth hostel association usually secures a small discount. Many youth hostels have closed in recent years, and there are gaps in the network, but independent hostels have stepped into the breach.

There is an association of independent hostels in Ireland: the Independent Holiday Hostels of Ireland (IHH). An Óige and this group publish very useful maps of their hostels. The IHH map covers all of Ireland, and the An Óige map includes the Hostelling International Northern Ireland (HINI) hostels as well as the RoI ones. Look for a copy at the first hostel you stay at, or get it from a tourist office. Dormitory beds cost on average about €30, with private rooms typically about €35–45 per person.

Some of the hostels allow camping, which saves a bit of money (this varies) and allows you to still use the hostel's facilities.

Camping

Ireland has a scattering of official campsites. Generally, sites are more plentiful as you head south and west. The best source of information is the

Castletownberehaven was once a Royal Navy port (Route 6, Stage 2)

Irish Camping and Caravan Council. Most touring sites are members and they are listed on the council website and in their annual *Caravan, Camping and Motorhome Guide*. Copies are available from tourist offices or you can order one online for a small fee. Supplementing this list is a handful of local authority-run sites and forest parks as well as unaffiliated sites.

Sites usually charge per person, not per tent, and cyclists are usually charged €11–15 each. Sometimes there is a €1 charge for a token for a hot shower.

There is no right to wild camp anywhere on the island. Seeking permission from landowners is not easy, as in remote areas it is hard to find someone to ask. But in some of the quieter corners of Ireland where there are no official sites, such as Donegal and perhaps Connemara, wild camping on or near the beach or in the high country is possible. Ordnance Survey maps (1:50,000) are good for ferreting out potential places. Setting up as it gets dark and leaving early are both a good idea. Be exceptionally clean, well behaved, and, if you do meet anyone, polite. 'No Camping' signs are getting more common, so don't ruin the few wild possibilities remaining.

Bed and breakfast
If there is an open tourist office in town, they will often find you a bed and breakfast, for a booking fee (about €5), but it is best to be prepared with at least a few numbers to call yourself. The official B&B Ireland website includes a searchable map and a booking portal as well as special Wild Atlantic Way sections.

Expect to pay €35–40 per person sharing, and €50–60 for a single. Some pubs also offer bed and breakfast accommodation – look for signs.

See Appendix A for some useful websites for finding accommodation.

HEALTH AND SAFETY

Emergencies
Dialling 112 or 999 will put you through to the emergency services – fire, police, ambulance or mountain rescue.

Crime
The police in the Republic of Ireland are the Gardaí (pronounced 'gardee', sometimes known colloquially as 'the guards'), or, in the singular, Garda – but if you ask for the police, people will usually know what you mean. For non-emergency police matters, contact the nearest Garda station, or in Northern Ireland, police station. In the Republic, the nationwide free Irish Tourist Assistance Service aims to help with the practical and emotional aftermath of crime (01 6669354, www.itas.ie).

When travelling in Ireland it is sensible to take reasonable precautions against crime, without being paranoid.

Barleycove beach (Route 6, Stage 3)

Healthcare and insurance

Both the Republic of Ireland and Northern Ireland have public healthcare systems, but access to free treatment is by no means guaranteed for visitors. Since costs such as property loss or damage, legal expenses, repatriation costs and alternative travel arrangements may also be incurred, visitors to Ireland should take out travel insurance.

Some insurers do not include cycle touring in their basic level of cover, so check this. Most insurers will expect you to access public healthcare where possible. European Union residents should obtain a European Health Insurance Card (EHIC) before travelling. UK residents should obtain a free GHIC card (Global Health Insurance Card), which has replaced the EHIC with the UK's exit from the EU. The EHIC/GHIC will give access to the public system for treatment that becomes necessary during your stay. In both Ireland and Northern Ireland this is a good level of free treatment, although you may have to pay prescription charges. Do expect to pay for dental treatment. Some other countries have bi-lateral arrangements, which may give access to either free or below-cost healthcare. Without an EHIC/GHIC or access to these bilateral schemes, expect to pay the full cost of any treatment.

Pharmacists are a good first point of contact for non-emergency problems. As well as being able to supply some medications without a prescription, the pharmacist can advise and point the way to a doctor or hospital if necessary. To access free care in the Republic, it is important to see a GP contracted under the Primary Care Reimbursement Service (PCRS) scheme. If you can't find one, the local Health Service Office (www.hse.ie) will have numbers. In Northern Ireland there are fewer doctors working privately, but in all cases it is worthwhile mentioning you want to be treated under the EHIC/GHIC arrangements.

When appropriate you can go to the accident and emergency (A&E) department of a public hospital, and this is probably where an ambulance will bring you in the event of an accident. EHIC/GHIC holder or otherwise, if you end up in this situation, the most important thing is to get better and not be worrying about charges, so be insured, keep the details on your person, and get a friend to contact the insurer's helpline for advice.

TAKE

- EHIC/GHIC
- copy of insurance policy and contact card
- copy of prescriptions
- reasonable supply of regular medication
- spare spectacles/contact lenses and an optical prescription

FOOD AND DRINK

Maintaining a healthy diet with a good calorific intake should be a priority on any extended tour.

If the plan is to eat out, the bigger centres generally have a choice of restaurants where a three-course meal will set you back a minimum of €45. Pubs offer cheaper food, although the quality is mixed, and especially in rural areas some pubs only serve food on certain days, or don't serve food at all. At cafés and pubs you can usually pick up a meal for upwards of €10.

In terms of specialities, the seafood is worth a try anywhere on the Wild Atlantic Way. Bed and breakfasts usually offer a 'full Irish' breakfast. The core ingredients are bacon, eggs and toast, while sausages, beans, potato cakes, soda bread, black and white puddings and other fare is often included. Ireland is not a paradise for vegetarians – count on having to look around when eating out.

Most small towns have a takeaway and if you stick to the busy ones you won't go far wrong. Some of the international franchises such as McDonald's have made it to the larger towns.

For food on the road there is no reason to not eat plenty of fresh fruit, breads and cheeses – these are available everywhere. Fresh vegetables are widely available, and, together with staples such as pasta and rice, a big nutritious evening meal can be made for as little as €10.

Ireland's national drink is Guinness, but there are other similar dark stout beers available – Beamish and Murphy's are two alternatives. Ireland is also known for its whiskies.

LANGUAGE

Irish is the first official language of the Republic of Ireland, and, according to the 2016 census, 40 per cent of the population can speak it. This figure is considerably higher in the Gaeltacht – areas where Irish is recognised as the predominant language. The main Gaeltacht areas are all along the Wild Atlantic Way. These include much of northern and western Donegal, the north and west of County Mayo, including Achill Island, a large part of southern Galway plus Connemara and the Aran Islands, the Dingle peninsula and southern and central sections of the Inveragh peninsula (the 'Ring of Kerry'). In all these places it is common to hear Gaelic spoken in streets, shops and pubs.

In the Gaeltacht the Irish language traffic signs might confuse you a little at first but the intent is usually clear. In other areas, both the Irish and Anglicised names are usually signed. Most maps have both versions of the name.

Visitors for whom English is not a first language find the Irish accent difficult to begin with – but this passes quite quickly. Similarly, speakers of English as spoken in England, the US and elsewhere, might initially have to try to speak clearly to be well understood.

See Appendix B for a useful Gaelic–English glossary and some phrases to try in Gaelic.

In the Irish-speaking parts of Ireland expect signs in Irish Gaelic

MONEY

Cash

The currency in the Republic of Ireland is the euro. Northern Ireland uses the pound sterling. In border areas, many businesses will take notes in either currency, but you will tend to get change in the local denomination.

Cash is still the most convenient way to pay for small transactions on the island. Paying cash will also keep down foreign currency transaction charges – if your card-issuer levies them.

Fort Dunree stands guard over the entrance to Lough Swilly (Route 1, Stage 3)

Cash points are still rare enough in rural areas to make running out of cash a real possibility. Carrying enough money for at least the next four or five days is advisable. Service stations and shops often have ATMs, as do local branches of banks, although these are increasingly rare. The Plus/Visa and Cirrus/Mastercard-linked ATMs are the widespread ones, and UK travellers generally have no problems accessing cash from their home accounts through debit cards.

Whatever card you have, check the charges your bank will levy, and at the same time, check your card will be accepted in ATMs. If travelling both sides of the border, it is worth emphasising when you enquire that you need the card to work in both Ireland and the UK.

Credit and debit cards

Visa and Mastercard credit and debit cards are widely accepted in shops and hotels. Hostels almost always take cards, and sometimes ask for a card number to secure a booking. B&Bs and campsites are more likely to prefer cash.

Budgets

If you are extremely frugal, it is just possible to tour the Republic of Ireland for €40–50 a day if camping or €70 a day in hostels. This is an absolute minimum, and assumes you self-cater and stay away from fast food. Since B&Bs will cost from €35 (per person sharing), and you will also have to buy an evening meal and food during the day, €95 is a more realistic absolute minimum daily budget for

35

The traditional Irish farmhouse is increasingly hard to find (Route 1, Stage 2)

B&B travellers. If you are staying in hotels and eating out you might just get away with €150 per day each if you share a room. A double room in a modern hotel during the summer will cost around €160. A single room will not be much cheaper. At smaller, usually older, hotels you may find double rooms from €90 or so.

POST, PHONES AND INTERNET

Post

The rural post office network is clinging on in rural Ireland although opening hours are often short and sometimes only a couple of days a week. On most days you will pass through at least one small town with a post office: look for a 'Post' sign on a green background.

For postal rates see www.anpost.ie or www.royalmail.com for Northern Ireland.

Phones

- Ireland: international code +353
- Northern Ireland: international code +44
- international prefix (north and south) 00

The Irish phone system is complicated by the fact you are dealing with two countries with two international codes. The numbers in the text assume you are calling from within the country in question – for example Republic of Ireland from Republic of Ireland. When dialling from the Republic of Ireland to a fixed line in Northern Ireland, the 028 code is replaced with 048. This does not work calling mobiles – use the full international code and prefix. When calling from Northern Ireland to the Republic, dial the full international prefix and code.

Calling Republic of Ireland numbers
The Dublin Visitor Centre's number is 01 8980700, so:
- from Northern Ireland or elsewhere in UK dial 00 353 1 8980700
- from the Republic of Ireland dial 01 8980700
- from overseas dial local international prefix + 353 1 8980700.

Calling Northern Ireland numbers
For example, the Belfast Welcome Centre number is 028 90246609, so:
- from Northern Ireland or elsewhere in UK dial 028 90246609
- from the Republic of Ireland dial 048 90246609
- from overseas dial local international prefix +44 28 90246609.

Mobile phones
A mobile phone is the most convenient and often the cheapest way to stay in touch when in Ireland. In the Republic the major networks are eir, Three and Vodafone. Coverage is almost universal although there are a few blank spots on hill-bound coasts. Northern Ireland is covered by UK operators. If you are bringing a phone from overseas check it is compatible with Irish networks. Some US network phones, for example, will not work.

Mobile phone rates are now capped for EU travellers travelling within the EU but beware that if your home network is outside of Europe these EU-imposed limits for call and data charges may not apply.

Getting your phone unlocked, to work on any network, before you travel gives you the option of buying a SIM card in Ireland. Check out the prices and do the sums, but for most UK and EU travellers their existing phone/SIM will be the best option.

Don't forget mobile charger and plug adaptor if you need it – all of Ireland has UK-style three-pin plug sockets.

Payphones
Phone boxes have almost completely disappeared from Ireland but If you happen to pass one, calls cost €2 minimum.

Internet
4G mobile data services are assured in most towns. In some rural areas coverage is patchy. 5G services are available in major cities and towns. WiFi hotspots are easy to find in major centres with cafés, restaurants and transport hubs often having free access. Most tourist accommodation will also have free or cheap WiFi access. Internet cafés have almost completely disappeared so take some sort of device – a laptop, mobile or tablet – with you if you want to be sure you can connect to make, for example, travel bookings.

CYCLING IN IRELAND

Traffic and driving

Ireland has speed limits and distance signs in kilometres. The start of Route 1 is in Northern Ireland which uses miles. The signage scheme is different in the two countries, but similar enough to not cause any confusion.

In both countries, motorways have an M prefix and cycles are not allowed on these roads.

In the Republic there are national 'N' roads (100km/h limit), regional 'R' roads (80km/h) and local roads (also 80km/h). There is a general limit of 50km/h in built-up areas and other limits are signed. Speed limits are widely ignored unless there is a chance of getting caught. N roads are divided into primary and secondary routes, with a figure higher than 50 (eg N87) indicating a secondary route.

Cycling on N roads can be quick, but there is generally too much fast, heavy traffic to make this a comfortable experience. Some of the R roads are just as bad. The few N road sections in this book are either in quiet areas, or are short, unavoidable stretches.

The routes in this book are built, where possible, around local roads. Typically these are not quite wide enough for two cars to pass without slowing down. They are sealed (tarmac) roads. The quality of the surface varies considerably. Irish roads often break up or suffer subsidence on their edges. Always keep an eye out for potholes, especially on steep descents – if you hit them at speed they can throw you off your bike.

Author riding a new stretch of cycle track between Dungloe and Lettermacaward (Route 1, Stage 7)

OFFICIAL CYCLE ROUTES IN IRELAND

The Kingfisher Trail (NCN91) was Ireland's first signed long-distance cycle route and, crossing as it does between Northern Ireland and the Republic, was symbolic of improved cross-border relations in the wake of the Good Friday agreement. It is a figure of eight route following over 360km (230 miles) of minor roads through the border counties of Fermanagh, Leitrim, Cavan, Donegal and Monaghan and can be joined at Beleek, 8km inland from Ballyshannon (on Route 2).

A map of this route and other long-distance routes in Northern Ireland is available from Sustrans (www.sustrans.org.uk).

Smaller roads all over Ireland are generally not well graded (that is, they have many short and steep climbs). In some areas this can make for roller-coaster roads, and very slow progress.

Dedicated cycle tracks are most often encountered leading into towns and cities but these are often only separated from the traffic with a painted line. Cycle tracks are generally marked with a cycle symbol painted on the road or pavement surface or, less commonly, with a round blue sign with a white cycle symbol.

Greenways are a new arrival on the Irish cycling scene. These are traffic-free routes for cyclists, pedestrians and other users which typically follow the routes of former railway lines. Route 2, Stages 5 and 7 follow the Great Western Greenway to and from Achill Island in County Mayo.

Hazards
Thorn hedges are common in Ireland, particularly in the northern parts. Puncture-resistant tyres are essential – see below. On narrow roads watch

KEY POINTS

- Cycling and driving are on the left.
- A cycle must have a working bell and a rear reflector.
- Stay away from N roads if you can – the ones in this book are unavoidable or not too bad.
- Cycling is not allowed on motorways.
- Distances and limits are in km in Ireland, miles in Northern Ireland. This book uses km throughout.

For the full rules go to www.rsa.ie and search for 'Rules of the Road'.

out for stray undergrowth catching your legs, arms or, more seriously, your face and eyes. In summer the odd stinging insect might lodge in your clothing, but generally Ireland is pretty low risk for things that bite.

Safety points

- Helmets are not compulsory, but are a good idea.
- Bright colours are a good idea but there is no need to be fluorescent. It's a fashion!
- Keep left-ish, but staying 1–2m in from the edge of the road will give you a safer road surface and encourage cars to manoeuvre around you.
- If cycling at night, lights must be used and it is advisable to wear plenty of reflective gear.

- Be sensible about where you ride two abreast.
- Pedestrians stepping into the road, or even walking down the middle of it, are a constant hazard – they will just not hear you coming. Be friendly about it. (You're on holiday!)
- Sunburn can get you even on seemingly dull days – wear sunscreen and consider long sleeves.
- Carry food, water and a basic first aid kit.
- Be prepared for changes in the weather – don't get cold or soaked through.

Security

The following are specific crime points for cyclists.

- Bike theft is a real risk in cities and towns.

The signs on the old Kinsale to Cork road are old enough to be in miles (Route 6, Stage 6)

- Lock your bike every time you leave it – theft is unlikely (apart from in the cities), but bikes occasionally get ridden home from the pub (by someone else) and, in any case, losing your cycle will be a complete holiday disaster.
- If you have quick-release wheels, make sure your lock secures these too.
- Take your valuables in an easily removable bar bag with a shoulder strap and carry it with you. In bigger centres such as Galway, Limerick and Cork, book into your accommodation and secure your bags before exploring around town.

WHAT TO TAKE

Bike

Bikes sold as tourers generally have a relaxed frame geometry, good clearances for mudguards and tyres, mounting points for carriers, and low gear ratios. A set of hand-built touring wheels is a good investment, especially for Ireland where the roads are bumpy. Drop handlebars are not for everyone, but they do give a choice of hand positions and can be a godsend in headwinds. Mountain bikes or mountain–road hybrids are also popular for touring, but since most of this book is on sealed roads, make sure suitable road tyres are fitted.

For Irish conditions, 32–42mm (width) tyres are a good compromise between speed and comfort. A puncture resistant Kevlar band is pretty much essential, because of thorns. Schwalbe Marathons (www.schwalbe.com) work well in Ireland: the basic Marathon is a good choice although you might prefer the faster-rolling Marathon Supreme in wider tyre sizes.

Simple is generally best on tour, and in Ireland, if you have the absolute latest in gear, spares might be hard to get hold of. Sticking to 26-inch or 700c wheel sizes will give you the best choice of spares, if you happen to need them.

If you are already used to clipless pedals, systems with small cleats such as the Shimano SPD are efficient touring platforms, and with the right shoes (see below) the cleats are recessed and you can walk normally. Fit two or three water-bottle holders – if your frame does not have the right fixings, brackets are available.

Take cycle lights just in case you get caught out late or you fancy a ride to the pub. If you don't take lights, pack a torch as rural areas are very dark at night.

Spares and repairs

Get your bike into good condition before you leave: anything tired, worn or loose should be sorted out. After that, be sensible about the tools and spares you take. Being self-sufficient is great in principle but heavy in practice, and more weight means more strain for you and the bike. Match the spares and tools you take to your mechanical ability, and remember that Ireland is not a wilderness, and if the worst comes to the worst, you can get the bus to the nearest big town for repairs. Consider taking a spare chain and a spare folding tyre – just because without these you cannot get anywhere. A spoke spanner is handy for adjusting wheels, but don't tinker unless you know what you are doing. A multi-tool with pliers is handy for small fix-it jobs off and on the bike.

Check round the bike for loose fasteners at least every few days. A liquid chain lubricant suited for wet weather riding is best for Ireland. Dry lubricants are cleaner, but tend to wash off in wet conditions.

Luggage

The traditional full touring set-up is front and rear panniers, bar bag for valuables and day use, and possibly a saddlebag. If you are camping this is a realistic arrangement. For hostelling or B&B tours it is possible to travel light and still be civilised. The only reason, in this case, to have front and rear panniers is to balance out the load on the wheels, or to separate wet and dry gear.

Camping or otherwise, a waterproof bar bag with a quick release and shoulder strap means you can keep valuables with you. Ortlieb (www.ortlieb.com) does one that has an optional map case on top, and also takes a padded insert to convert into

KEY POINTS

- Some luggage must be completely waterproof.
- Take an easily removable bar bag for valuables.
- 'Essential' is negotiable and smaller bags mean lighter loads.
- Think about how you will pack wet and dirty gear.
- Buy good racks.
- Side-to-side balance is important.
- Make sure your lights are visible.

a camera bag. A bar bag is not perfect for cameras because of the vibration, but it is convenient. A small saddle bag can keep tools, spares, sunscreen, and possibly your lunch, away from the rest of the gear – but don't take one if it encourages you to take too much stuff.

A pair of waterproof rear panniers (15–20 litres each) is more than enough for hostelling or B&B. The ones made of a vinyl material with roll-top closures do the job – Ortlieb make these too, although there are alternatives.

For camping, consider putting small waterproof panniers on the front and fitting rear panniers made of cotton canvas. This material is close to waterproof, but still breathes enough so that wet camping gear doesn't sweat inside and soak everything else.

BIKE CHECKLIST

Spares
- front and rear lights
- spare inner tubes
- puncture repair outfit
- cable ties (really useful!)
- PVC insulating tape (ditto)
- inner cables
- chain lubricant
- couple of rags
- handful of spare nuts and fasteners as appropriate to your bike
- few pairs of disposable latex gloves (to keep hands clean)
- brake blocks (on a long tour)
- spare folding tyre (optional)
- spare chain (optional)

Tools
- pump
- tyre levers
- multi-tool including Allen keys to fit your bike
- chain tool – may be part of the multi-tool
- pedal spanner (especially if you are flying), wheel nut spanner (if your bike has nuts), spanners for everything else
- spoke key (optional)
- Leatherman or similar tool with pliers (optional)

Dry clothing, maps, books, notes and so on can be stowed in the front panniers, and the messy stuff in the back. Wherever you carry your sleeping bag, a waterproof stuff sack is a sensible belt-and-braces precaution.

Do not skimp on luggage racks, especially if you are camping. The steel ones made by Tubus (www.tubus.com) are almost indestructible. The ideal load distribution is 60 per cent rear, 40 per cent front, although side-to-side balance is far more important – check this every day to avoid having to wrestle your bike along.

Clothing

General

Ireland's summer climate is warm and at times wet. Atlantic weather systems

43

tend to move through quickly, and it is common for a wet morning to turn into a sunny afternoon (and vice versa), so clothing needs to be adaptable and easily layered. If you are hostelling or using B&Bs, clothing is going to be a significant part of your total load, while on camping trips it is the weight of clothes that can push the load towards being unpleasantly heavy. One set of clothes for the evening and something light to sleep in will always have to be kept dry and quite clean.

As for on-bike gear, the choice is almost limitless. For touring, however, consider not wearing specialist cycling clothes when riding: for example, walking/trekking shorts with zip-off legs, short or long-sleeved T-shirt or base layer and a light jacket or fleece if it's cold. Padded undershorts make ordinary shorts as comfortable as Lycra cycling shorts, and you will feel more human walking around shops and stately homes. Bright colours make sense for safety, but carrying a fluorescent tabard for busy or gloomy conditions means all your gear does not have to be in high-visibility tones. Fingerless cycling gloves stop painful sunburn on the back of the hands and reduce palm soreness.

If all your gear looks presentable off and on the bike, you will need fewer clothes, and they will be easier to organise and keep clean.

Waterproofs

Be prepared for wet weather – keeping your top half dry goes a fair way to avoiding getting too miserable. Whatever coat you have, a peaked cap, preferably waterproof, can be

Author off the beaten track approaching Cleggan (Route 3, Stage 4)

Lissadell House was the childhood home of Irish revolutionary Constance Gore-Booth, later Constance Markievicz (Route 2, Stage 2)

worn under a helmet and stops rain running down your face and into the jacket. The main problems with all waterproofs are controlling temperature and dispersing perspiration. In Ireland it is more likely to be cool and wet than hot and wet, so overheating is not too much of a problem. A lightweight breathable jacket and a long-sleeved base layer will be adequate on most wet days, maybe with a switch to a lighter shirt when it's hot. Another layer might be necessary when you stop, especially if it is windy.

Waterproof trousers are a personal choice, but wet legs are not too uncomfortable, and a pair of Lycra leg warmers will keep out the cold. Waterproof gloves and, depending on footwear, neoprene overshoes complete the wet-weather set-up.

Shoes

Having cycling shoes that are good walking shoes saves carrying extra footwear. Something different to wear in the evenings, however, is important, to give your shoes an airing and your feet a break. One riding option that works well is mountain bike shoes with recessed cleats (if you use clipless pedals). Gore-Tex lined shoes keep the wind and showers off. A pair of light sandals will make a refreshing change in the evening, and you can always wear socks if it's cold.

Cycling sandals (with or without cleats) work well for summer tours. Add socks if it's cold or you want to protect from sunburn; add neoprene overshoes in the wet. It is possible to get away with only taking sandals and no other footwear, as they do not need drying out.

Camping

The four essentials are tent, sleeping bag, mat and stove, and it is worth spending a little money to get these right.

Tent

Sooner or later there is going to be a downpour, so buy a top-quality lightweight hiking tent (some lightweight summer tents are just not up to Irish weather). A double-skin tent works well in Ireland, as ventilation is generally good and there is usually a vestibule area for wet gear. The inner tent should be insect-screened, as biting midges are occasionally a problem.

Sleeping bag and mat

Even in April and September night temperatures rarely drop below 5°C. A reasonable-quality medium-weight bag is sufficient. A silk liner keeps the bag clean, makes it warmer, and doubles up as a hostel sheet bag if you need one. It is worth spending a little extra on a good mat, as tired muscles and an uncomfortable night's sleep are a bad combination.

Stoves

Gas canisters for camping stoves can be hard to come by in rural Ireland. Methylated spirits (alcohol) fuelled stoves are not quite as convenient to use as gas, but they are simple, hot, and you can buy the fuel at hardware stores. Trangia (www.trangia.se/en) are the original brand, but there are alternatives.

Other accessories

You will need plenty more to make a comfortable camp – including

Camping on Inishmore (Route 4, Stage 2)

cooking and eating utensils. If you are new to cycle camping, a test run close to home is a good idea.

MAPS

The directions in the book will get you around, but having access to mapping is sensible for impromptu changes of route, getting 'unlost', exploring further, and generally improving your knowledge of the area you are in.

If you are using a GPS unit, the free OpenStreetMap (www. openstreetmap.org) coverage of Ireland is accurate and up to date. Topographic information is not quite as good as the Ordnance Survey of Ireland (OSI) which you may be able to buy for your GPS unit.

If you want to take paper maps, the best cycling maps for Ireland are the 1:50,000 topographic maps. In the Republic of Ireland these are published as the Discovery Series by the OSI. There is a 10m contour interval throughout.

At this scale you are likely to need a lot of maps, and keeping the current section in view will mean plenty of folding and unfolding. A more compact alternative is the four-map Holiday Series, jointly produced by OSI and Ordnance Survey Northern Ireland (OSNI) at 1:250,000 scale, which covers the whole of Ireland in four sheets (North, South, East and West). You will need the North, West and South sheets to cover the Wild Atlantic Way. They show all roads

According to tradition, St Brendan the Navigator departed on his legendary voyage from Brandon Creek (Route 5, Stage 3)

except the very tiny, and include colour-coded topography above 120m. Some of the tourist information is out of date (hostels, campsites and so on) and there are a few new roads not yet included, but they are generally comprehensive and accurate. If you are relying on GPS, these maps make an excellent addition, especially for planning ahead.

A Wild Atlantic Way road map is available from tourist offices or you can download a copy at www. failteireland.ie but this is best used for general reference rather than detailed navigation.

The Wild Atlantic Way officially starts at the Irish border some 10km north of Derry/Londonderry (Route 1, Stage 1)

USING THIS GUIDE

This guide describes six self-contained tours based on sections of the Wild Atlantic Way, each of which can be comfortably completed in 7–10 days. Three of the routes can be started and finished in the same place: Route 3, Tour of Connacht, returns to Westport, while Route 2 can be ridden as a circular trip beginning in Sligo and Route 5 as a circular trip from Tralee. For those wishing to cycle the full length of Ireland's west coast, the distinct routes link together into a 44-stage, 2400km trip. The route cards provide the route description in detail (see below for information and an example), and some readers may want to follow them to the letter, while for others the route information might be just for inspiration, or a source of general background about what to expect in an area.

Each route begins with an introduction to the area covered by the route, a map, and a route summary table to help you plan your itinerary, especially if you need to speed up or slow down the schedule provided. This is followed by advice on getting to the start and when to go, accommodation choices, maps needed, route options and suggestions for links with other routes.

Each stage within the route begins with distance, terrain and summit of each day's cycling, a description of the landscape and points of interest on that stage, followed by a summary of facilities along the way (shops, ATMs and so on), accommodation choices, and options for alternatives to the route detailed on the route cards.

The Routes vary from 360km to just over 500km. Overall, the stages average out at just over 55km, and should take, again on average, four to five hours of riding. There are a few longer stages in the book which have generally been necessary because of the unavailability of suitable accommodation or, for the sake of completeness, to include some far-flung corners of the island – in which case sensible shortcuts have been suggested in the text.

Experienced tourers will have a fair idea of their capabilities. Newcomers or comparative newcomers should go for a relaxed itinerary rather than trying to cram the longest possible tour into the number of days. A realistic average speed for a loaded tourer on rural Irish roads is in the range of 12–15 km/h.

Do not fall into the trap of underestimating the terrain in Ireland. The highest point in the book, the Connor Pass (Route 5, Stage 2) is only 456m above sea level – this compares to several Alpine passes at over 2700m. But rural Irish roads characteristically have many small rises and falls which sap energy and slow you down.

The high cross at Drumcliff is a remnant of a monastery founded by St Colmcille in the sixth century (Route 2, Stage 2)

The prevailing wind in Ireland is from the southwest – but strong northerlies and easterlies are not unusual, and when the wind swirls around headlands and mountains it can seem to be coming from all directions at once. In some of the exposed coastal areas an unfriendly wind can halve your rate of progress. County Donegal suffers from both poor roads and high winds, making Route 1 by far the most challenging route in the book.

Route cards

To follow the route cards (see example below) you will need a cycle computer set up to read kilometres. Set the trip counter at the start point of the stage indicated. Every attempt was made to ensure accurate and consistent calibration, but in practice there are bound to be some minor discrepancies. For this reason, and because you may well make your own small or large detours to explore around the route, a cycle computer which lets you adjust the trip counter will make things easier. See Appendix E, Calibrating your cycle computer.

The first entry of each route card gives details of the starting point and which direction to head in. 0 in the first column is a reminder to reset your cycle computer. If you are starting mid-way along the route, you should set your cycle computer at the next turn. If it has an adjustable distance counter as above, you can simply then follow the route card. If not, you will have to set the distance to zero

Waterville (Route 5, Stage 6)

and then do some arithmetic to follow the cards. From here on, a solid black arrow indicates a change of direction, or a confirmation to continue in the same direction (included where roads are badly marked or there is likely to be confusion, for example if the traffic priority is changed at a crossroads), and the figure in the LH column is your cumulative distance in kilometres from the start of the stage. (Where the distance column is left blank, this means that features listed are less than 0.1km further on.)

For all directions, a road sign or signed road name is indicated where possible, with the exact wording as it appears on the sign in single quotation marks, for example, 'Belfast' or 'George Street'. If there are no signs, or sometimes just to ensure that

you find the correct road, a further description is included. These descriptions do not have quotation marks. Junctions that have no signs and no distinguishing features are marked as unsigned. At these turns, take special care with distances and keep an eye out for landmarks and other features coming up on the route card to make sure you are on the right road. To help clarify the route, additional information such as 'at T-junction' or 'at crossroads' is included where necessary.

A circle and an arrow together indicates a roundabout. An up and a down arrow side by side mean that you need to turn around.

An outline arrow indicates a turn to a place not directly on the route. This may be a side-trip, a shortcut or a point of interest, accommodation

Sample route card and key

←   change of direction/confirmation of direction

O   roundabout

⇦   direction of side-trip, short-cut or to point of interest, accommodation or shop close to route

WC   public toilet

ATM   cashpoint

▲   accommodation

♦   shop, or, rarely, a café where supplies can be bought

✪   point of interest – a beach, building or architectural interest, or view

△(50)   summits (altitude in metres)

stage no and route name ——
← direction to take ——

←O   direction, roundabout ——
▲ ⇧ accommodation, direction

ATM♦ cashpoint, shop ——

⇦   direction/side trip ——
✪WC point of interest, public toilet

♦   shop ——

✪ point of interest ——

△(50) summit (altitude in metres) ——

Stage 3 Tour of the Dingle Peninsula			
0.0		←	From car park exit on Dingle quay, next to tourist information, turn left
1.0	1.0	←O▲ ⇧	'Slea Head Drive'. Rainbow Hostel, straight on in a few hundred metres
1.3	0.3	ATM ♦	Good shop in service station
7.4	6.1	⇦ ✪ WC	Ventry Strand 100m
10.1	2.7	♦	Small shop
11.2	1.1	✪	Celtic and Prehistoric Museum
12.2	1.0	△ (50)	Steady climb, don't forget to look back

The tiny harbour at Bunbeg (Route 1, Stage 6)

or a shop close to the route. It may be accompanied by another symbol, and the text in the third column will explain further. Some of the side-trips are expanded upon in the main text. If you do take a side-trip, you will need to pause, or reset, you cycle computer as the side-trips are not included in the running total on the route cards. Other symbols indicate a public toilet, cashpoint, accommodation, shops, points of interest and summits (with spot height).

Note that spellings and punctuation of Irish place names vary widely. If a place is quoted in inverted commas on the route card, this is the spelling that you will find on the road sign, which may not match the spelling that this guide has chosen in the route description and elsewhere.

GPX tracks

GPX tracks for all stages of all the routes in this book are available at www.cicerone.co.uk/909/gpx. If you do rely on a GPS, a paper map is still handy as a back-up – who hasn't forgotten to charge the batteries? Maps are also extremely useful for planning short-cuts or variations in itinerary, especially when the unexpected happens – changes in ferry times, punctures, mechanical failure or even illness. After all, no GPS screen is going to be as big as an unfolded map.

THE TOURS

Downpatrick Head has fine views westwards along the Mayo coast (Route 2, Stage 4)

ROUTE 1 TOUR OF DONEGAL

The beach at Narin (Stage 7)

Start	Derry/Londonderry
Finish	Donegal Town
Distance	503.8km
Ascent	6903m

Donegal has the greatest variety of landscape found anywhere along the Wild Atlantic Way. The route described here begins with a tour of the remote Inishowen peninsula, including a visit to Ireland's far north-western tip, Malin Head. The protected inlet of Lough Swilly then provides a more sheltered coastline, backed by lush green fields, before the Atlantic once again hammers into the rocky Fanad Peninsula. All along this coast sandy beaches

nestle in the lee of sharp headlands, and there are popular family seaside resorts at Downies, on the Rosbeg peninsula and elsewhere along the route. Ulster's tallest mountain Errigal is just a few kilometres inland while some of Ireland's highest sea cliffs, plummeting from Slieve League mountain, mark the corner of the coastline as it swings eastwards towards Donegal town.

This is the longest route in the book, and the toughest. The roads will hammer your spokes and spine into submission, accommodation is hard to come by, the road signs are minimal, and if you break down there are precious few bike shops. In short, this is wild Ireland at its very best, but it's not for the faint-hearted.

LOUGH SWILLY

The glacial fjord of Lough Swilly, tucked away in Ireland's far north-west, has witnessed some pivotal events in the island's history. In 1607 the Gaelic aristocracy of Ulster, including Hugh O'Neill, Earl of Tyrone, sailed out of the lough, from Rathmullan (Stage 4), and into exile in Europe. 'The Flight of the Earls' is a historical watershed marking the ascendancy of English power in Ireland. Lough Swilly was also centre-stage in 1798 when Irish nationalist Wolf Tone was captured here with the surrender of a French naval force of some 3000 men backing an uprising. Recognising the sea lough's strategic importance, the British retained a naval base here after Irish independence in 1922. Swilly, along with the County Cork 'Treaty Ports' at Berehaven and Spike Island (Cork Harbour), were relinquished in 1938. The British flag was lowered for the last time in Ireland, at Fort Dunree (Stage 3), overlooking the lough, on 3 October of that year.

Route summary table				
Stage	Distance	Ascent	Accommodation available	Places with shops/other facilities en route
1	Derry/Londonderry to Culdaff	56.1km	949m	Culdaff	Moville, Greencastle
2	Culdaff to Clonmany	55.1km	743m	Malin peninsula, Ballyliffin, Clonmany	McEleney's Cycles (53km)
3	Clonmany to Letterkenny	81.4km	976m	Letterkenny	Fort Dunree, Buncrana
4	Letterkenny to Portsalon	47.9km	756m	Warden Beach (43km)	Rathmelton, Rathmullan
5	Portsalon to Downies	37.7km	593m	Carrickart, Downies	Carrickart
6	Downies to Bunbeg	67.5km	951m	Rosguill, Errigal, Bunbeg	Crolly, Dungloe
7	Bunbeg to Portnoo	52.6km	668m	Narin, Portnoo	Portnoo
8	Portnoo to Carrick	59.9km	1062m	Glencolmcille, Carrick	Ardara, Glencolmcille, Carrick
9	Carrick to Donegal Town	45.6km	798m	Dukineely, Donegal Town	Kilcar, Killybegs
Total		503.8km	6903m		

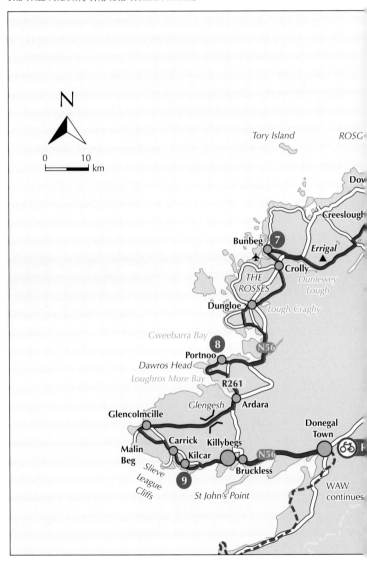

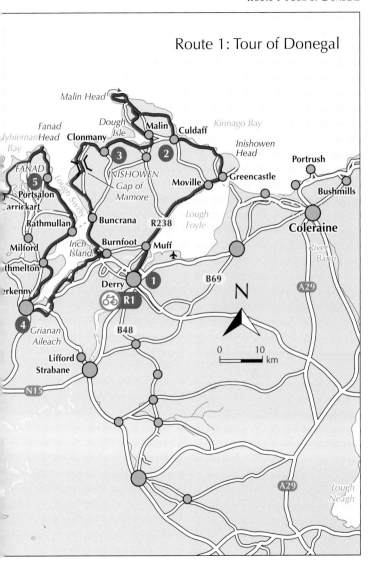

Route 1: Tour of Donegal

In the 19th century ships from the Caribbean docked at the now quiet port of Ramelton (Stage 4)

BETTER BY BIKE

The Wild Atlantic Way driving route from Muff to Donegal Town follows some long sections of main roads, particularly from Downies (Stage 6) southwards. The cycling route described here seeks out quieter roads close to the official route and also takes a couple of opportunities to get away from the coast to ride through some of Donegal's fine mountain scenery. This also helps keep the total distances down as north-west Ireland's deeply indented coast can really rack up the mileage.

GETTING TO THE START

By air

Derry/Londonderry has an airport (www.cityofderryairport.com) about 11km out of the city on the way to Coleraine on the A2. This is a good centre for low-cost flights to and from England and Scotland.

By rail/bus

Derry/Londonderry has regular passenger rail services from Belfast and Coleraine, with connections to Dublin. At the end of the route,

Donegal Town has regular bus services to Dublin.

Tyrone, 10 Donegal, 11 Donegal Fermanagh Tyrone.

WHEN TO GO

It's impossible to pick the weather up here, and there may be many fine spring days as well as awful summer ones. Consider travelling in May and early June, especially if you want to wild camp, as there are fewer people around.

ACCOMMODATION

To get the most out of the trip, consider camping. This far northwest corner of Ireland has some beautiful spots to pitch a tent. Hostels, hotels and B&Bs are also thin on the ground, particularly on the Inishowen peninsula (apart from Malin Head) and Fanad peninsula (Stage 4). Booking ahead for indoor accommodation is advisable and make sure you take some phone numbers with you in case of changes of itinerary or plans. You cannot be certain of being able to get online to make bookings up here.

MAPS

The whole route is covered by the Ordnance Survey Ireland North sheet at 1:250,000. For 1:50,000 coverage, the following sheets are needed: sheet 7 Londonderry, from the OSNI Discoverer Series, and from the OSI Discovery Series sheets: 1 Donegal, 2 Donegal, 3 Derry Donegal, 6 Donegal

OPTIONS

To keep the distance down, consider bypassing Letterkenny by taking the Lough Swilly ferry from Buncrana (Stage 3) to Rathmullan, picking up Stage 4 from the 28km mark, saving 76km in total.

Another shortcut is to miss the Inishowen peninsula and Malin Head altogether, and instead go from Derry/Londonderry, via Grianan Aileach, directly to Lough Swilly, picking up the route from the 46km mark of Stage 3.

ONWARDS

From Donegal Town you can continue along the Wild Atlantic Way with Route 2. Alternatively, you can return to Derry/Londonderry by following the signposted North West Trail cycle route towards Strabane to join the National Cycle Network Route 92 (NCN 92) at Springhill, some 4km west of Lifford, for an approximately 90km route.

Canon on Derry/Londonderry's city walls

STAGE 1
Derry/Londonderry to Culdaff

Start	Derry/Londonderry
Distance	56.1km
Ascent	949m
Terrain	Coastal, stiff climb from Greencastle; hilly along coast.
Summit	275m at 39.3km

This stage follows gentle terrain close to Lough Foyle before hitting some stiff climbs over the hills to Kinnago Bay and on to Culdaff. The opening of the Peace Bridge and associated improvements in cycleways make possible a quick exit from the city.

> The **Peace Bridge** in Derry/Londonderry is a purpose-built cycling and walking bridge which was completed in 2011 at a cost of £14 million.
> The name **Derry** is derived from the Irish 'Doire' – 'the oak grove': the city was previously known as 'Doire Chalgaigh' – 'Calgach's oak grove' – and then 'Doire Cholmcille' – '(St) Columba's oak grove'. It is thought to have acquired the 'London' prefix in 1613, when James I granted the city a royal charter and the London guilds became involved in funding its construction. Unionists call the city 'Londonderry'; Nationalists call it 'Derry'. It's also nick-named the Maiden City because the walls have never been breached – the express bus service from Belfast is called 'The Maiden City Flyer' – and some-times also referred to as 'Stroke City', because the name is so frequently writ-ten with the forward-slash: 'Derry/Londonderry'.

But if you have some free time the city centre is worthy of exploration on foot. If you fancy a leg-stretch on the bike, the ancient fort of **Grianan Aileach**, about 11km north-west of the city on Regional Cycle Route 1 has panoramic views of the route ahead into Inishowen.

Leaving Derry/Londonderry this stage passes the ruins of the Georgian villa of Boom Hall, reputed to be one of the most haunted places in the city.

> The ruins of Boom Hall are close to the site of the **boom across the Foyle** that was used to prevent William of Orange's forces coming to the aid of the

encircled city during the Siege of Derry. The boom was broken on 28 July 1689, effectively ending the siege.

The official Wild Atlantic Way driving route starts when you cross the Northern Ireland/Republic of Ireland border at **Muff**. After **Greencastle** the stage climbs into the coastal mountains before dropping into one of the most beautiful sections of the Irish coast. **Kinnago Bay**, with dark-grey cliffs dropping to a semi-circle of golden sand, is stunning. To the north of here the mountains flatten out to be replaced by a low, rocky, wind-blasted coast all the way to **Culdaff**.

On the road
Take plenty of cash (euros). ATMs are thin on the ground from now on. There are shops at Moville and Greencastle. Moville has the better choice. After Greencastle the roads are slow going. While they are sealed, they are bumpy, and in some places badly potholed.

Accommodation
Derry/Londonderry has no official youth hostel but the independent hostel scene is quite lively. I've stayed at the very friendly Paddy's Palace (028 7130 9051, www.paddyspalace.com). You could also try the Derry City Independent Hostel (028 7128 0542, www.derryhostel.com). Derry has a selection of the major hotel chains plus a wide choice of independents along with a range of B&Bs. It's best to book ahead, particularly at weekends. The nearest camping to Derry/Londonderry is at Elaghvale Camping Park (078 0173 1815) about 8km to the north off the Buncrana road. Culdaff has a limited choice of other accommodation, but McGrory's (074 9379104, www.mcgrorys.ie) is popular. With an early start from Derry/Londonderry, you may choose to push on with Stage 2 where Sandrock Holiday Hostel (086 3256323, www.sandrockhostel.com) is about 18km further on. Wild camping is sometimes possible along the coast but don't wait until you are close to Culdaff, where it is too populated.

STAGE 2
Culdaff to Clonmany

Start	Culdaff
Distance	55.1km
Ascent	743m
Terrain	Low coastal terrain
Summit	120m at 6km

From Culdaff this stage climbs through a pass (180m) in the coastal mountains to enter the central valley in the finger of land leading out to **Malin Head**, mainland Ireland's most northerly point.

In 2016 **Malin Head** was used as a location for the shooting of *Star Wars: Episode VIII.*

The southern side of the peninsula is the better sheltered from the Atlantic, and has a sandy beach at Five Fingers Strand. After **Malin** village the route crosses

Looking east from Malin Head

the low sandy isthmus that now connects **Doagh Isle** to the mainland, before finishing at the neat town of **Clonmany**.

On the road
The area around the Lloyd's signal tower on Malin Head makes a dramatic lunch stop, watching the surging Atlantic. There are a couple of small shops on the way out to the head, but it's best to get your day's supplies at Culdaff. Late in the day there is a rare cycle shop (McEleney's Cycles, 074 9376541).

Accommodation
Clonmany has a few B&Bs, and there is a campsite a couple of kilometres out of town at Bunacrick (Binion Bay Caravan & Camping Park, 074 9376800). To get there continue down Main Road from the Diffley Gardens (where the stage ends). As the road curves left past a parking area look for a small road that continues straight ahead Take this road and after 700m look for a right turn that may be signed 'Caravan Park' to take you there. The 'No Camping' signs haven't appeared on the beaches around here yet, and it may be quiet enough to consider wild camping. Accommodation might be tight during the Clonmany Festival at the beginning of August. Further back on the route there is an independent hostel on the Malin peninsula – the Sandrock Holiday Hostel (at 18km, 086 3256323, www.sandrockhostel.com). For hotel accommodation, consider stopping at Ballyliffin (52km) where holiday accommodation has expanded in recent years.

Options
If pushed for time, consider continuing along the R238 from Culdaff to Buncrana (17km approximately, rejoining route at the 29.1km mark) and skipping the Gap of Mamore and Dunree Head coming up in the next stage.

STAGE 3
Clonmany to Letterkenny

Start	Clonmany
Distance	81.6km
Ascent	976m
Terrain	Steep climb over the Gap of Mamore
Summit	240m at 14km

Tullagh Strand is an early highlight. In fact it's so close you could consider visiting it the day before. The long arc of the dune-backed beach with the rock-strewn Urris Hills towering behind can be breathtaking in the evening light. Soon after the strand the road turns towards the **Gap of Mamore** (summit at 14km) – one of the steepest climbs in the book. The views are back towards Malin Head and on to the long inlet of **Lough Swilly**.

> Lough Swilly's suitability for large ships and its remoteness have made it the
> site of many pivotal scenes in Irish history – notably the Flight of the Earls and

The Mamore Gap is one of the toughest climbs in the book

the capture of **Wolfe Tone**. Dublin-born barrister Wolfe Tone, co-founder of the United Irishmen, took part in two French-backed invasion attempts (1796 and 1798). On the second he was captured at sea, off the mouth of Lough Swilly, and landed near Buncrana. He was sentenced to death by a Dublin court martial, but died in prison before the sentence could be carried out.

The **lough** was one of the three Irish Treaty Ports, and the impressive fortifications at Fort Dunree (turn at 19.8km) were part of the port's defensive cordon. You can often see porpoises here.

South of **Buncrana** the roads get busier, but this stage manages to get off-road, following an old railway embankment across tidal flats in the lee of **Inch Island**. Donegal's largest town, **Letterkenny**, sits at the head of Lough Swilly.

On the road
Buncrana (29km) is a friendly place to stop for a break. There is a decent-sized supermarket as well as ATMs, and a picnic area at the foreshore (30km). A little earlier on Fort Dunree (19km) has picnic tables, toilets and a small café, in season. Letterkenny has a new Halfords with cycle gear in the retail park a few hundred metres down Pearse Street (R250) (074 9113750, www.halfords.ie). Camping supplies are available at Amazonas Outdoors (074 9120649, www.amazonas.town. ie) a short distance further down Pearse Street, also on the left.

Accommodation
For budget accommodation, Letterkenny has the Apple Hostel (074 9113291, www.letterkennyhostel.com), book ahead. The town is also well off for motel/hotel accommodation.

Options
Consider taking the shortcut from Buncrana to Rathmullan on the Lough Swilly ferry (087 2112331, www.swillyferry.com). The turn is at 30.8km (and you rejoin the route at the 27.7km mark of Stage 4). However, be aware that this is a summer service only, and it is not certain whether it will continue to operate. If you are comfortable in traffic, you may consider continuing along the N13 to Letterkenny at 68km. There is one busy roundabout where the N13 joins the N14 on the way in to the town. This saves a couple of km and is a speedy ride.

STAGE 4
Letterkenny to Portsalon

Start	Letterkenny
Distance	47.9km
Ascent	756m
Terrain	Gentle coastal ride, until Knockalla Mountains approaching Portsalon
Summit	150m at 40km

North of Letterkenny the western shore of Lough Swilly, with its lush, gently sloping pasture and small patches of woodland, has a gentler aspect than the eastern shore. The sting in the tail of the ride is the climb over the hard quartzite of the **Knockalla Mountains**, before the descent to Portsalon. These mountains are part of the same structure as the Urris Hills across the inlet, but the ranges have been separated by a glacial breach, now occupied by the sea lough, which is a true fjord.

Earlier in the day comes the faded glory of the port town of **Rathmelton** (also Ramelton), and the strategically important town of **Rathmullan** (27km), where the Flight of the Earls took place. Also worthy of mention is the Franciscan ruin of **Killydonnell Friary** (turn at 12.1km) beautifully positioned on the shores of the lough south of Rathmelton.

During its 19th-century heyday, ships from the Caribbean docked at **Rathmelton**.

The **Flight of the Earls** marked the end of the old Gaelic order in Ulster. On Friday 4 September 1607 the Earls of Tyrconnell and Tyrone and the cream of Ulster's aristocracy sailed out of Lough Swilly into continental exile.

The **Portsalon** area has some sandy, protected beaches. The village does get swamped with visitors on summer weekends.

On the road
Letterkenny is by far the biggest town in County Donegal, so stock up with any hard-to-get supplies before heading north or west. The next decent-sized town on the route is Donegal, in four days' time. ATMs are hard to come by en route, so take cash. Rathmelton and Rathmullan both have reasonable-sized shops to buy lunch and places by the water to eat it. Portsalon has a decent local grocery shop.

Fortifications at the mouth of Lough Swilly with Fort Dunree in the distance

Accommodation

There are no hostels in this part of the Fanad peninsula, but at 43km there is the grandly positioned Knockalla Caravan and Camping Park near Warden Beach (074 9159108, www.knockallacaravanpark.com). Camping is prohibited on all the beaches. Overnight indoor accommodation is currently scarce in and around Portnoo. It is worth checking online at www.discoverireland.ie to see whether anything new has cropped up.

One option is to start Stage 5 where Ballyhiernan Bay has the Fanad Lodge (074 9159057) – carry straight on at the turn at 17.0km and it is 150m on your right. If you are travelling light and staying indoors you might prefer to combine Stages 4 and 5 and travel from Letterkenny to Downies (where accommodation is easier to find) in one 85.6km day.

Options

The Lough Swilly Ferry (087 2112331, www.swillyferry.com) from Buncrana lands at Rathmullan during the summer months (see Stage 3).

STAGE 5

Portsalon to Downies

Start	Portsalon
Distance	37.7km
Ascent	593m
Terrain	Coastal hills
Summit	80m at 2km

The Fanad peninsula north of Portsalon is a world of gorse, heather and Atlantic breakers. In the stretch before the **Fanad Head** lighthouse, Lough Swilly offers some protection, but after 'turning the corner' at the lighthouse, the coastline faces northwest into the full force of the ocean.

Along this shore are the sandy beaches of **Ballyhiernan Bay**. The stage follows the wild coast of the western Fanad before crossing the new Mulroy Bay Bridge and swinging west through the tidy Gaeltacht town of **Carrickart** (or Carraighart). The stage ends by the sandy bay at **Downies**. (The town is also known as Downings.)

Author cycling the quiet roads on the west side of the Fanad peninsula

On the road
There are no shops until near the end of the stage at Carrickart. The prettiest places to stop for a break are early in the day along the north-facing coast. Try either the Fanad Head lighthouse or the beaches from Ballyhiernan Bay onwards (18km). The shop at Carrickart is the best in the area.

Accommodation
There is a youth hostel 7km from Downies. Tra Na Rosann (074 9155374, www. anoige.ie) is signposted on the right just before reaching the town. Apart from that there is the beachfront Casey's Caravan & Camping Park in Downies itself, a few hundred metres past the end of the stage (074 9155000, www.caseyscaravanpark. com). Downies has two decent-sized hotels – the Downings Bay Hotel (074 9155586, www.downingsbayhotel.com) and the Beach Hotel (074 915530, www.beachhotel.ie). Both are in the centre of town on the left as you head in. There is also a handful of B&Bs here and in nearby Carrickart.

Options
You may prefer to push on towards Bunbeg from Carrickart (33km), skipping Downies and the area to the north (and continuing the route from the 22.5km point on the route card).

STAGE 6
Downies to Bunbeg

Start	Downies
Distance	67.5km
Ascent	951m
Terrain	Coastal hills; gentle climb into Derryveagh Mountains.
Summit	280m at 49km

This stage begins with a tour of the beaches and holiday homes of the **Rosguill** peninsula, before heading to the open moorlands and quartzite peaks of the **Derryveagh Mountains**, then turning back to the coast at the quiet fishing village of Bunbeg.

The area around Rinn n Fachla Point (the spur at the top northwest corner) and the beach at **Tra Na Rosann** (5.3km) are the best of the Rosguill peninsula, but some of the coast hereabouts is marred by housing development. So it is refreshing to turn inland for a while and head for the hills. The climb from **Creeslough** is a gentle gem, winding along between meadows flecked white and yellow with wildflowers.

The old church, Dunlewey with Errigal in the background

The route continues to climb across the flanks of **Errigal Mountain**. By now the landscape, with its bare mountains and deep glacial valleys, has a very Scottish feel, which continues along the descent past the Poisoned Glen, **Dunlewey Lough**, Lough Nacung and on to the picturesque harbour at **Bunbeg**.

Errigal (752m) is Donegal's highest mountain. Quartzite summit screes make the top look like a snow-capped cone all year round. It is a three-hour return trip to the summit from the car park at the 51.6km mark.

On the road
Stock up for at least the morning at Downies. A couple of lovely beaches towards Melmore Head are the best swimming spots (turn at 9.7km, and close to the road at 12.2km).

Accommodation
Early in the day you pass Ireland's most northerly hostel, Tra Na Rosann (turn at 10.6km – 074 9155374, www.anoige.ie), off the road to Melmore Head. Also up here is, at 11km, the Rosguill Holiday Park (074 9155766, www. rosguillholidaypark.com). The Errigal Youth Hostel (55km 074 9531180, www. anoige.ie) is the best place to stay later in the route. Bunbeg, at the end of the day, has B&B accommodation.

Options
You could skip the loop around the Rosguill peninsula and rejoin the route at the main road at Carrickart (at the 22.5km mark). This would give you more time to explore around the Poisoned Glen or even climb Errigal. If you are pushing ahead you can skip the trip to Bunbeg by continuing on the N56 at 61.8km and pick up the directions at Crolly (6.7km along Stage 7).

STAGE 7
Bunbeg to Portnoo

Start	Bunbeg
Distance	52.6km
Ascent	668m
Terrain	Some gentle climbs
Summit	150m at 12km

The highlight of the early part of the day is the climb over the low pass from **Crolly** to **Dungloe**.

> The area bounded by the Gweebarra river to the south, the Gweedore to the north and the Derryveagh Mountains to the east is known as **the Rosses**. This is an area of undulating granite with small lakes and windswept heathery moors, where glaciers have dumped thousands of large boulders.
>
> Every year 'Marys' from Ireland and emigrant Irish communities compete to be crowned '**Mary From Dungloe**'. The pageant and international music festival attracts tens of thousands of visitors from late July to early August.

The day finishes at the small fishing and holiday village of **Portnoo**.

A deserted farmhouse in the Rosses

On the road

There are a few shops in Bunbeg, including a pharmacy – just turn left at the R257 crossroads after leaving the pier. Crolly has a big supermarket and Dungloe has a choice of shops, including a big 'Cope' (Co-op). Lough Craghy is a pleasant spot for a break, as is Dungloe, which has some benches in front of the Bank of Ireland, where there is also an ATM. At the end of the day Portnoo has a small shop. Recent improvements to the N56 north of the Gweebarra river include a cycle path.

Accommodation

Narin (50km) has a caravan and campsite, Boyle's Caravans (074 9545131, www.boylescaravans.com). There is the larger Tramore Beach Caravan and Camping Park further round the peninsula on Stage 8, at Tramore Strand – turn at 7.3km (074 9551491, www.tramorebeachrosbeg.com) – but this is a little out of the way. There are no nearby hostels. Narin and Portnoo have B&B accommodation and some small hotels, but they are likely to book up during the summer holidays.

STAGE 8

Portnoo to Carrick

Start	Portnoo
Distance	59.9km
Ascent	1062m
Terrain	Long climb up Glengesh
Summit	280m at 40km

The small peninsula between Gweebarra Bay and Loughros More Bay is a temperamental beast. On a warm sunny day, you might be by the Mediterranean, but when squalls pile in from the west, the wind drains away body heat in an instant.

At the base of the peninsula, **Ardara** is a pleasant settlement town with a central diamond and a choice of supermarkets on the main street. After this, a long climb through Glengesh dominates the remainder of the day. After the pass comes the descent into scenic **Glencolmcille** – a place of spiritual importance because of its links with one of Ireland's most important saints, St Columba.

Slieve League cliffs at Carrick are among the highest in Ireland

St Columba (Old Irish *Colm Cille*) is one of Ireland's three patron saints (along with St Patrick and St Brigid). In the sixth century he founded monasteries at Derry, Durrow and Iona in Scotland.

On the road
Ardara is the best place to stock up on supplies for the day, but they will have to be carted over Glengesh. There is a bike shop (Don Byrne Bikes, 074 9541658 – on the way out of town towards Glengesh). Glencolmcille has a couple of shops, as does Carrick, which is a good base for visiting the Slieve League Cliffs, by some accounts the highest sea cliffs in Ireland.

Accommodation
The Glencolmcille area has a choice of hostels, with, at 44km, the Dooey Hostel (074 9730130) and the Malinbeg Hostel (turn at 48.6km, 074 9730006, www.malinbeghostel.com). Some 3km through Carrick (on Stage 9) is one of Ireland's best hostels, the Derrylahan Independent Hostel (074 9738079, www. derrylahanhostel.ie), which also has good facilities for campers.

Glencolmcille village has the best choice of more upmarket accommodation in the area including a relatively new budget hotel, the Aras Ghleann Cholm Cille (074 9730077, www.arasgcc.com). Carrick has a handful of B&Bs, and the village has a more traditional feel than the more popular Glencolmcille.

Options

To save time, cut across from Ardara to Killybegs (Stage 9) via the N56 and R263 (17km). Continue straight on at the Glencolmcille turn (21km).

To shortcut to Carrick, continue straight on at the Glencolmcille turn (35.6km), Carrick is another 5.6km down this road (at the 41.2km mark). Taking a day to climb Slieve League and see the cliffs is a good way to give cycling legs a rest. The route (7km) is signed from Carrick. The detour to Malin Beg (48.6km) is worth a look, as there is a stunning sheltered beach and bay at Silver Strand.

STAGE 9
Carrick to Donegal Town

Start	Carrick
Distance	45.6km
Ascent	798m
Terrain	Coastal hills
Summit	120m at 40km

After a week or more in the wilds Donegal Town (population about 2500) seems like a big place. Before reaching the town there is some pleasant coastal scenery and the fishing port of **Killybegs** to see.

One of the most interesting features of the route is the slow transition in the **geological landscape** from the metamorphic rocks and bare mountains of Atlantic Ireland to the lower relief produced by glacial deposition. The westward limit of debris from the last glaciation is just to the west of Killybegs, and by the time you reach Donegal, upland Ireland seems far behind.

Donegal Town was home to the O'Donnells from the 15th to the early 17th century. After the Flight of the Earls in 1607 the castle and lands were given to Basil Brooke, an English captain, who added a Jacobean wing to the castle, which had been begun by the O'Donnells in 1505. Earlier still, there was a Viking fort here.

For more recent history there is the Donegal Railway Heritage Centre in the old railway station building, which tells the story of the narrow-gauge railways that were once a vital part of the Irish economy.

Donegal Castle dates from the 15th century

On the road
There are plenty of shops on this stage, including at Kilcar and Killybegs. The latter is a pleasant place to take a break and have a look at the fishing boats.

Accommodation
For budget accommodation, try the Donegal Town Independent Hostel (074 9722805, www.donegaltownhostel.com). There is the An Óige franchised Blue Stacks Hostel about 8km to the northwest of town at Drimarone (074 9735564, www.anoige.ie). On route (27km), is Blue Moon Hostel and Camping at Dukineely (087 2972896). After a sparse few days in the wilds of Donegal, Donegal Town itself has an excellent choice of hotels and B&B accommodation.

Options
At 21.7km the mapped route turns left off the R263 and climbs over a small headland on an unsurfaced track. This track has deteriorated a little since the first edition of *Cycle Touring in Ireland*. If it is wet continue the R263 for a further kilometre before joining the N56 towards Donegal. After that you barely need directions but the mapped route rejoins the N56 at the Spar shop in Bruckless (25.3km into the stage).

ROUTE 1 ROUTE CARDS

Stage 1 Derry/Londonderry to Culdaff			
0			Foyle Embankment at W end of Peace Bridge. Head along cycleway (river on right).
1.4	1.4	♦	Sainsbury's
2	0.6	→	Cycleway crosses road and then turns right (along it)
2.1	0.1	↖	Veer left into side road
2.7	0.6	↑	Straight on into Culmore Road (still on cycleway)
2.9	0.2	←	Now following NCN 1 signs
3.2	0.3	←	NCN 1
3.5	0.3	→	NCN 1
3.6	0.1	✪	Pass ruins of Boom Hall
4.2	0.6	→	Cross at lights and join traffic on A2
6.9	2.7	✪	Shop and pharmacy
7.3	0.4	✪	Shop and ATM
9.5	2.2	✪	Cross border – official start of the Wild Atlantic Way
9.8	0.3	✪	Decent Spar in service station (Muff)
17.9	8.1	♦	Foyleside Caravan & Camping Park
30.9	13.0	♦	Moville has shops and bank (no ATM)
31.2	0.3	♦	Ballynally Cycles on left

Stage 1 Derry/Londonderry to Culdaff			
34.7	3.5	✪	Inishowen Maritime Museum & Planetarium (Greencastle)
35.0	0.3	✪	Lough Foyle Ferry from Magilligan Point on right
35.2	0.2	♦ WC	Views across Lough Foyle
35.5	0.3	⇨	Turn to see castle – but no access
36.0	0.5	↑	'Ballymacarthur Road'
39.3	3.3	△ (277)	Summit – views forward into Inishowen
40.8	1.5	←	'Kinnago Bay'
41.8	1.0	→	'Kinnago Bay'
43.5	1.7	→	Turn to bay – steep
43.8	0.3	↑↓	Kinnago Bay car park
44.1	0.3	→	Back at turn to bay – 'Carrowmenagh 6'
44.9	0.8	→	'Culdaff 10'
47.6	2.7	↗	'Tremone Bay 1'
48.5	0.9	↗	Unsigned
48.8	0.3	⇨	Leads to pretty bay, rocky foreshore
50.8	2.0	→	'Culdaff'
55.4	4.6	→	'Culdaff' R238
56.1	0.7		Arrive Culdaff centre by old pump

Stage 2 Culdaff to Clonmany			
0.0			Culdaff by memorial pump, head towards the shops
0.1	0.1	→	'Bunagee Pier'
1.0	0.9	⇨	Side-trip to Bunagee Pier – 2km return
2.7	1.7	↗	'Malin Head' – road swings right
4.5	1.8	♦	Food shop
4.7	0.2	→	Unsigned
5.1	0.4	↖	'Malin Head'
5.8	0.7	↖	
12.7	6.9	→	At T-junction
15.3	2.6	↑	'Malin Head R242' (at crossroads)
17.2	1.9	▲	Malin Hostel
17.4	0.2	↖	Malin Head
18.4	1.0	→▲⇧	At crossroads continue straight on for Sandrock Holiday Hostel, about 1km
20.3	1.9	✿	Picnic area
22.3	2.0	←	Towards Lloyd's Tower
23.1	0.8	↑↓	Top of car park
23.8	0.7	←	Back at road
25.3	1.5	♦	Curiosity Shop
26.0	0.7	✿	Malin Head meteorological station
26.7	0.7	↑	'R242 Carndonagh'
29.1	2.4	↗	'R242 Carndonagh'

Stage 2 Culdaff to Clonmany			
31.6	2.5	↗ ♦	'Malin R242'. Small shop on corner
33.9	2.3	⇨	Five Fingers Strand turn
39.2	5.3	♦ ▲	Malin village, central diamond. Shop, Malin Hotel across diamond
39.3	0.1	→	'R242 Carndonagh'
42.1	2.8	→	Just after L1211/ Glennagannon river bridge
43.8	1.7	↑	'Ballyliffin 9'
45.1	1.3	→	'Ballyliffin R238'
50.1	5.0	⇨	Doagh Famine Village (8km return)
52.5	2.5	♦	Small shop in Ballyliffin. Take-away next door
		⇨	Pollan Strand 2.5km return
52.6	0.1	♦	Shop at Ballyliffin
53.1	0.5	♦	McEleney's Cycles 074 9376541
54.0	0.9	↖	Road bears left
54.7	0.7	→ ♦	'Mamore Gap', shop on corner
55.1	0.4	♦	Stage ends at Diffley Garden – rest area, benches etc. Tourist information sign. McDonald's Bar is across the road and there is a small shop

Stage 3 Clonmany to Letterkenny			
0.0			Diffley Garden – head left along road
0.1	0.1	↖	Bear left at car parking area
0.4	0.3	↗	'Tullagh Bay'
1.6	1.2	✿	Glenelvin Waterfall
2.3	0.7	⇨	To Tullagh Strand 3km return
4.1	1.8	↑	'Lenan Pier'
6.3	2.2	♦	Dunaff has PO and shop on right
7.4	1.1	↗	Bear right 'WAW (S)'
9.5	2.1	←	At crossroads
10.8	1.3	↑	To beach car park
		↑↓	Turn around at car park
10.9	0.1	→	After leaving car park
12.3	1.4	→	Signed 'Viewpoint'
14.1	1.8	✿	St Eigne's Well shrine
14.3	0.2	△ (238)	Steep climb (Mamore Gap)
15.2	0.9	→	Unsigned turn
19.3	4.1	→	At T-junction
19.8	0.5	↖ ⇨	Bear left, side-trip to Fort Dunree (2km return)
23.5	3.7	♦	Service station and small shop
24.4	0.9	↗	'Buncrana'
27.1	2.7	↗	'Buncrana'
29.1	2.0	→	At T-junction

Stage 3 Clonmany to Letterkenny			
29.4	0.3	♦ WC	Supermarket
29.6	0.2	↖	Road swings round to left through Buncrana centre
29.8	0.2	♦	Large supermarket through alley on right
29.9	0.1	→	'Church Street'
30.1	0.2	↑	At crossroads
30.5	0.4	♦	Picnic area in park on right
30.8	0.3	⇨	To Rathmullan Ferry 0.4km
30.9	0.1	→	At T-junction
31.1	0.2	♦ ATM	At service station, tourist office on right
31.6	0.5	○ ↗	'Derry R238'
37.9	6.3	♦	Service station and shop
39.1	1.2	→	'Inch Island'. If R238 is not too busy you can carry straight on
40.6	1.5	←	Just before Inch Island causeway
43.7	3.1	→	'Burnfoot R238'
44.1	0.4	♦	Shop on right
44.3	0.2	ATM	At service station
45.6	1.3	→	'R239 Letterkenny'
46.7	1.1	→	L75311
47.7	1.0	←	Through gate and onto gravel track

Stage 3 Clonmany to Letterkenny			
50.3	2.6	↑	Straight on through gate (Inch Walkway to your right)
50.9	0.6	→	At T-Junction
51.9	1.0	→	Turn right just past two new houses on right
52.3	0.4	↑	At crossroads signed LCN1
55.9	3.6	→	Signed LCN 1, castle is in front of you
59.3	3.4	→	Onto N13 – be careful of traffic
59.5	0.2	♦	Service station has shop
60.2	0.7	→	L2041 Moyle
62.6	2.4	←	Signed Eurocycle route 1
68.0	5.4	→	N13 Letterkenny – be careful
69.7	1.7	✿	Picnic area on left
70.0	0.3	←	Small road takes you off N13
70.1	0.1	→	At T-junction, post office in front
70.2	0.1	↖	[Straight on would take you to main road.]
71.0	0.8	←	Unsigned
71.8	0.8	→	At N14, turn right
71.9	0.1	←	Turn left after 60m
73.4	1.5	↗	Road bears right by concrete plant
77.5	4.1	↑	At crossroads

Stage 3 Clonmany to Letterkenny			
78.3	0.8	→	At crossroads just before concrete plant
79.2	0.9	←	Onto busy road by tourist information sign
79.5	0.3	O↑	Port roundabout. Turn left for tourist information centre
80.6	0.9	↖O	'Town Centre' – one-way system starts
80.7	0.1	▲⇨	Apple Hostel down street on right
81.0	0.3	↑	At lights
81.4	0.4		Arrive Market Square – benches and picnic area

Stage 4 Letterkenny to Portsalon			
0.0			Letterkenny Market Square. Follow one-way down Main Street
0.1	0.1	←	'Oliver Plunkett Road' – before library
0.3	0.2	←	Following the one-way system
0.4	0.1	↑	At lights
1.0	0.6	O↑	'Ramelton R245'
1.3	0.3	O↑	'Milford'
1.5	0.2	←	'Gortlee'
2.2	0.7	♦	Handy small supermarket
2.5	0.3	←	'Auganinish Abbey'

Stage 4 Letterkenny to Portsalon			
3.5	1.0	⇦	Turn to abbey
4.1	0.6	↑	'Letterkenny Golf Club' (at crossroads)
5.8	1.7	←	Unsigned
7.1	1.3	→	At T-junction
10.6	3.5	↑	'Killydonnell Friary 2'
12.1	1.5	⇨	Killydonnell Friary 500m return
13.2	1.1	✪	Views of Derryveagh Mountains
13.4	0.2	←	'Ramelton 3'
13.5	0.1	→	'Ramelton 3'
13.9	0.4	←	'Ramelton 2'
16.1	2.2	↑	'Milford 9'
		↖	Road swings left
16.4	0.3	↗	Road swings right
16.6	0.2	♦	Shop on left
16.7	0.1	→	'Rathmullan 10' just over bridge
17.2	0.5	⇨	Turn here for good view of town across river
27.2	10.0	↑	'Swilly Ferry'
27.4	0.2	↑	Towards ruined priory
		✪	Rathmullan Priory
27.6	0.2	↑✪	Flight of the Earls of Rathmullan Heritage Centre
27.7	0.1	←	Turn left; ferry and foreshore area to right
28.0	0.3	→	At T-junction

Stage 4 Letterkenny to Portsalon			
28.3	0.3	→	'L5442'
30.1	1.8	→	'At T-junction'
37.7	7.6	✪	An Ghaeltacht
42.9	5.2	WC	Warden Beach
43.3	0.4	⇦▲	Knockalla Camping 1.2km
43.6	0.3	→	'Portsalon R268'
45.3	1.7	→	'R246 Portsalon'
46.5	1.2	→	'R246 Portsalon'
47.9	1.4		Arrive Portsalon Pier, Swells shop on right

Stage 5 Portsalon to Downies			
0.0			Portsalon Pier by Swells shop – head up the hill
0.2	0.2	→	At T-junction
2.2	2.0	→	Unsigned
2.6	0.4	←	Unsigned
3.4	0.8	→	At T-junction
5.6	2.2	↖♦	Road veers left – avoid road to right. Small shop at this junction
6.6	1.0	→	'Pollet Great Arch'
9.1	2.5	→	'Cionn Fhanada'
10.7	1.6	↑↓	Lighthouse car park
11.7	1.0	♦	Lighthouse Tavern does some food
12.3	0.6	↑	'Kerrykeel'
15.4	3.1	⇨	'Beach' (Ballyhiernan Bay) 1.5km return

Stage 5 Portsalon to Downies			
17.0	1.6	→	'Ballyhiernan Bay'
18.7	1.7	♦	Car park for beach (Ballyhiernan Bay)
19.5	0.8	→	'Pier' at T Junction
20.3	0.8	↗	Keep right in Ballyhoorisky
22.2	1.9	→	Unsigned at T-Junction
23.2	1.0	↗	Road swings right
24.6	1.4	→	Unsigned T-junction in front of lake
29.9	5.3	→	At crossroads
30.6	0.7	✿	Cross the Mulroy Bay Bridge [dismount to enjoy the view]
	1.0	⇦	Turn left 30m before right turn for best view of the bridge. 1km return.
31.6	1.0	→	
32.0	0.4	↑	'Carrickart'
33.7	1.7	→	Turn right at T-junction in village
33.8	0.1	♦	Shop
34.1	0.3	→	R248
35.6	1.5	▲ ⇨	Tra Na Rosann Hostel (6km), turn here
37.7	2.1	WC ▲ ♦	Arrive Downies, beach, WC, shops, hotels

Stage 6 Downies to Bunbeg			
0.0			Downies by turn to beach. Head west uphill past caravan park
0.5	0.5	⇦	Side road leads to small park and memorial to lost at sea, and McNutt Tweed factory – 300m return
1.3	0.8	↖	Signed 'Fish Shop'
2.4	1.1	←	Unsigned
3.0	0.6	↑	At crossroads
3.5	0.5	←	'Atlantic Drive'
5.3	1.8	⇦	To beach (Tra Na Rosann)
8.8	3.5	←	'An Meail Mor'
9.7	0.9	⇦	To surf beach 1km return
10.6	0.9	⇦ ▲	Turn to Tra Na Rosann Hostel approx. 150m
11.2	0.6	▲	Parc Rosguill – caravan park and camp site
12.2	1.0	✿	Pleasant beach close to road
12.4	0.2	↑ ↓	Turn around at entrance to caravan park
16.1	3.7	←	Back at road – T-junction
16.2	0.1	✿	Rest area on left – views over Mulroy Bay
17.4	1.2	✿	From small summit views of Mulroy Bay Bridge

Stage 6 Downies to Bunbeg			
20.3	2.9	↑	Back at road to Carrickart
21.1	0.8	↗	'Creeslough'
22.5	1.4	→	At T-junction rejoin main road by church
29.9	7.4	⇨	Side–trip to Doe Castle (2.5km return)
31.4	1.5	→	At crossroads
31.9	0.5	✪	Pass nature reserve
32.1	0.2	↑	Road joins from left
32.5	0.4	→	Join N56 at T-junction
		♦	Creeslough has post office and shop
33.3	0.8	←	Unsigned turn, just past house with columned front porch
40.8	7.5	←	'Kilmacrennan' – at T-junction
42.1	1.3	→	'Gaoth Dobhair'
49.0	6.9	△ (295)	
51.6	2.6	✪	Car park for Errigal Mountain
52.9	1.3	✪	View of deserted village and Poisoned Glen
53.8	0.9	⇦	Side–trip to Poisoned Glen and Dunlewy Lake
55.1	1.3	▲	Errigal Youth Hostel

Stage 6 Downies to Bunbeg			
55.2	0.1	♦	Roarty's Garage (food shop and takeaway – open late
58.5	3.3	←	'N56 An Clochan'
61.8	3.3	→	'R258 Bunbeg'
66.5	4.7	↑	'Pier'
67.5	1.0		Arrive Bunbeg pier

Stage 7 Bunbeg to Portnoo			
0.0			At corner of pier, by stone steps
1.0	1.0	→	'R257' (turn left here for shops)
5.4	4.4	→	'N56 Croithli'
6.7	1.3	♦	Crolly has shop at service station
7.0	0.3	←	'Cro na nCuigeadh' (just before bridge)
11.5	4.5	→	Unsigned road
11.6	0.1	✪	Pass former National School
19.2	7.6	✪	Nice spot for a break by Lough Craghy
20.7	1.5	↑	Cross N56
21.2	0.5	♦	Lidl on right
21.8	0.6	✪	Tourist information
21.9	0.1	→ ♦ ATM	Down Dungloe main street. Shops, bank and ATM
22.1	0.2	←	'An Machair'
23.8	1.7	↗	'An Machair'
24.8	1.0	←	'Min na Croise'

Stage 7 Bunbeg to Portnoo			
28.0	3.2	←	'Glenties' (at crossroads)
31.2	3.2	→	'Glenties'
34.2	3.0	→	Join N56
38.8	4.6	♦	Shop in service station
39.9	1.1	♦	Shop
40.5	0.6	✪	Cross Gweebarra river
45.3	4.8	→	'R261 Narin'
49.9	4.6	→	'Narin, Portnoo'
50.5	0.6	♦	Shop
50.7	0.2	⇨	Access to beach and campsite at Narin
52.4	1.7	♦	Shop
		→	'Harbour' (steep road)
52.6	0.2		Arrive Portnoo harbour

Stage 8 Portnoo to Carrick			
0.0			Portnoo harbour, top of slipway, head uphill
0.2	0.2	↗	'Rossbeg'
0.9	0.7	↖	'Rossbeg'
5.1	4.2	⇨	Turn to pier and small beach. Pier has a tap. (300m return)
7.3	2.2	▲⇨	To Tramore Beach caravan and camp site
7.9	0.6	✪	To left, view of Kiltooris Lough, castle and crannog

Stage 8 Portnoo to Carrick			
8.4	0.5	→	At T-junction
10.4	2.0	→	'Ardara'
12.3	1.9	→	'Ardara R261'
18.3	6.0	♦	Service station and shop
18.4	0.1	→	At T-junction to join N56
18.7	0.3	✪	Tourist information (M–Fr 10am–2pm, Sat 2pm–6pm)
18.8	0.1	✪ ▲ ATM	Benches, car park, ATM at Ardara
19.4	0.6	♦	Shop and service station
21.0	1.6	→	'Glencolmcille'
35.6	14.6	→	'Glean Cholm Cill'
38.9	3.3	△ (187)	Views of glen and ocean
42.0	3.1	←	'Glencolmcille'
43.5	1.5	←	Unsigned road
44.2	0.8	→	'Malainn Mhoir'
44.4	0.2	♦	Shops in Glencolmcille
44.6	0.2	⇦▲	Dooey Hostel
45.4	0.8	✪	Father McDyer's Folk Village Museum (Glencolmcille Folk Village)
48.6	3.2	←	Unsigned. Carry straight on for Malin Beg, Malin Beg Hostel and Silver Strand (9km return)
48.8	0.2	▲	Aras Ghleann Cholm Cille hotel

Stage 8 Portnoo to Carrick			
55.9	7.3	→	'An Charraig R263'
59.9	4.0		Arrive Carrick car park

Stage 9 Carrick to Donegal Town			
0.0			Carrick car park – head downhill towards centre of village
0.1	0.1	⇨	Turn to Teelin
0.2	0.1	→	'Coast Road' – just after bridge
1.8	1.6	→	'Coast Road'
3.1	1.3	▲	Derrylahan Hostel & camping
6.0	2.9	♦	Shop at Kilcar
6.1	0.1	→	(Straight on is R263 – main road)
12.1	6.0	↗	Road veers right
12.6	0.5	→	'R263 Killybegs'
14.1	1.5	✿	Picnic area
15.8	1.7	⇨	Fintra Strand
18.3	2.5	○↑	'Killybegs'
19.5	1.2	→	Road veers right
19.6	0.1	←	R263 Donegal
19.8	0.2	✿	Killybegs, car park and quay
19.9	0.1	⇦	Turn here for town centre
20.8	0.9	♦	Shop in service station
21.2	0.4	♦	Shop in service station
21.7	0.5	→	'Carrick House B&B'

Stage 9 Carrick to Donegal Town			
22.2	0.5	↗	Keep right about 50m past bridge
22.4	0.2	←	'Carrick House'
22.5	0.1	↗	Bear right at junction
22.8	0.3	↗	Bear right at junction. Track becomes stony but very rideable
24.2	1.4	←	T-junction
24.5	0.3	↗	Road veers right
25.0	0.5	↗	Bear right as road swings to the left
25.1	0.1	←	Turn left towards main road
25.3	0.2	→	'N56 Donegal'
		♦	Spar shop opposite
26.5	1.2	⇨	Side-trip to St John's Point (20km return)
27.8	1.3	▲	Blue Moon Hostel and Camping
27.9	0.1	♦	Convenience store
32.2	4.3	♦	Shop and café
32.5	0.3	♦	Shop
43.2	10.7	♦	Shop
43.4	0.2	⇨	Beach
44.3	0.9	▲	Donegal Town Independent Hostel
44.7	0.4	○↗	'Donegal'
45.6	0.9		Arrive Donegal Town central diamond

ROUTE 2 INTO THE ATLANTIC

Achill's wild southwestern shore (Stage 7)

Start	Donegal Town
Finish	Sligo
Distance	559.9km
Ascent	6142m

Continuing southwards along the Wild Atlantic Way from Donegal Town, the coastline and hinterland begin to soften with the wide beaches of Rossnowlagh and Streedagh Point ahead. The scenery around Sligo is particularly fine with grand limestone escarpments abutting a fertile coastal strip. The respite is, however, temporary as the Wild Atlantic Way turns westwards towards the ancient rocks and pounding seas of Achill Island.

BETTER BY BIKE

The Wild Atlantic Way driving route from Donegal Town to Westport is mostly also fine cycling. The chief exceptions are the main roads around Sligo, which are seriously fast and busy. The good news is that main N15 sucks in nearly all the coastal traffic, leaving many quiet coastal roads asking to be cycled. Between Achill Island, Newport and Westport, this guide follows the Great Western Greenway cycle route – a much more peaceful option not available to the motorist!

GETTING TO THE START

By rail/bus
Sligo has a regular rail service to Dublin which carries cycles. Donegal Town has Bus Éireann services to and from Dublin.

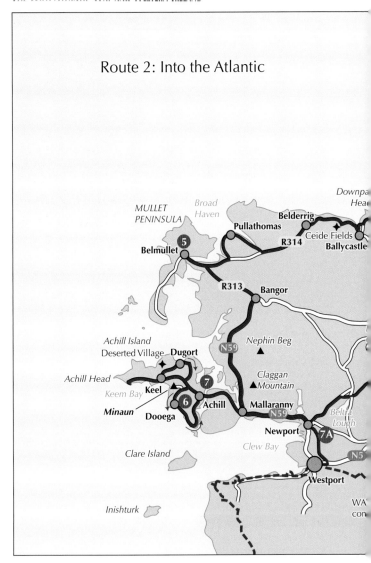

Route 2: Into the Atlantic

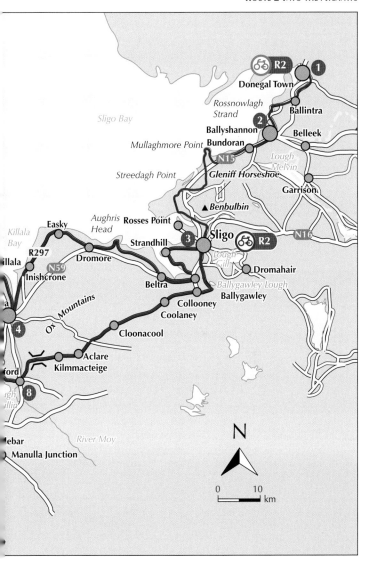

COASTAL LANDSCAPES

This section of the Irish coast is peerless in its variety of landscape. The tumbling sea cliffs and sweeping strands of **Achill Island** present some of Ireland's most dramatic coastal scenery. On the way there, the Sligo coast, with its backdrop of flat-topped limestone peaks, is gentler, but equally beautiful. Out towards the windswept tombolo of **Belmullet**, the landscape adopts an openly desolate air of hardscrabble farms and peat bog which continues until Achill comes into view. If you are continuing along the Wild Atlantic Way through Newport and Westport, the islands that you will see studding the tranquil waters of **Clew Bay** are drumlins, left by retreating glaciers at the end of the last Ice Age.

WHEN TO GO

Travel any time from Easter to September.

ACCOMMODATION

This is an excellent route for cycle campers with fine sites in Ballyshannon, Sligo, Ballina, and on Achill Island. Budget accommodation is also good too with Donegal and Sligo and Achill Island having an active hostel scene. There is also an excellent hostel, which allows camping, at Pullathomas (Stage 4). The quality of B&B and hotel accommodation has picked up all along this route in recent years and you should have no problem finding suitable places to stay. Booking ahead is advisable.

The beach at Rosses Point, Sligo has camping nearby (Stage 8)

MAPS

At 1:250,000, the Ireland North and Ireland West sheets from the Ordnance Survey series will be needed. If you start from Sligo, rather than Donegal, you will only need the West sheet. In 1:50,000 the OSI Discovery Series, sheets 11 Donegal Fermanagh Tyrone, 16 Donegal Fermanagh Leitrim Sligo, 22 Mayo, 23 Mayo, 24 Mayo, 30 Mayo and 31 Mayo.

OPTIONS

At Newport, on Stage 7, you have the choice of returning to Sligo via Foxford or continuing southwards along the Wild Atlantic Way to Westport. For a circular route from Sligo, simply begin with Stage 3.

ONWARDS

Take Stage 7A to continue along the Wild Atlantic Way from Westport (Route 3).

Route summary table					
Stage		Distance	Ascent	Accommodation available	Places with shops/other facilities en route
1	Donegal Town to Ballyshannon	28.7km	366m	Bundoran (5km beyond Ballyshannon)	
2	Ballyshannon to Sligo	61.9km	622m	Strandhill (8km beyond Sligo)	Bundoran, Mullaghmore
3	Sligo to Ballina	88.2km	877m	Belleek Park (3km beyond Ballina)	Strandhill, Ballysadare, Enniscrone
4	Ballina to Belmullet	99.9km	946m	Pullathomas	Killala, Ballycastle, Belderrig
5	Belmullet to Achill	65.0km	564m	Keel (15km beyond Achill Sound)	Bangor
6	Tour of Achill Island	75.1km	1241m	Keel, Dugort	
7	Achill to Foxford	71.2km	765m		Newport
7A	WAW Link from Newport to Westport (Route 3)	(12.8km)	(182m)		
8	Foxford to Sligo	69.9km	761m		Aclare, Coolaney
Total		559.9km	6142m		

STAGE 1
Donegal Town to Ballyshannon

Start	Donegal Town
Distance	28.7km
Ascent	366m
Terrain	Low coastal route
Summit	110m at 25km

This is an endearing section of coastline. The terrain is generally easy and the roads smooth and fast. At **Rossnowlagh** the stage crosses one of Ireland's most popular beaches. At the end of the day, **Ballyshannon** is an attractive hillside town overlooking the river Erne.

> During the second world war, Ireland was neutral. But **flying boats** taking off from Lough Erne, in Northern Ireland, were permitted to fly along the 'Donegal Corridor' over Ballyshannon to protect Allied convoys out in the North Atlantic thanks to a secret deal between the UK and Irish governments.

Rossnowlagh Strand draws a crowd on holiday weekends

On the road

Get what you need for the day in Donegal Town. If you don't fancy town-centre shopping the route passes a good-sized supermarket on the way out of town (6.5km). Rossnowlagh Strand is patrolled during the holiday season if you fancy a dip.

Accommodation

For budget accommodation in Donegal Town, try the Independent Hostel (074 9722805, www.donegaltownhostel.com). There is the An Óige franchised Blue Stacks Hostel about 8km to the northwest of town at Drimarone (074 9735564, www.anoige.ie). On route (27km), is Blue Moon Hostel and Camping at Dukineely (087 2972896). After a sparse few days in the wilds of Donegal, Donegal Town itself has an excellent choice of hotels and B&B accommodation.

Ballyshannon has a well-run campsite at the Lakeside Centre (071 9852822, www.lakesidecaravanandcamping.com). Cross the river on the town-centre bridge and immediately turn left (eastwards) at the roundabout and you will find the site 1km on the left. Take some midge repellent in summer. Ballyshannon has a choice of B&Bs and a few hotels, including Dorrians Imperial Hotel (071 9851147, www.dorriansimperialhotel.com) right in the heart of town.

If you push on a further 5km on the next stage, Bundoran has a lively hostel scene with a friendly surfer vibe. You could try Rougey Lodge on the way into town (087 1199622, www.rougeylodge.com).

Options

The Kingfisher Trail – a 230km cycle route on minor roads taking in Sligo, Enniskillen and Carrick-on-Shannon – can be joined at Beleek, 8km inland from Ballyshannon. A map of is available from Sustrans (www.sustrans.org.uk). Rossnowlagh beach should be firm enough for cycling but there is an alternative road signposted just behind the beach.

STAGE 2
Ballyshannon to Sligo

Start	Ballyshannon
Distance	61.9km
Ascent	622m
Terrain	Low coastal route
Summit	80m at 55km

Much of this stage follows a section of the long-distance cycle route the 'North West Trail' (NWT on the signs). The coastal scenery of low-slung hills and wide beaches continues south of **Ballyshannon** before the sharp-edged limestone hills of the Dartry Mountains build into a fine backdrop later in the day. The trip around **Mullaghmore Point** (from 20km) provides expansive coast and mountain views. The approach to **Sligo** is through a rolling landscape of limestone walls and buttercup-strewn meadows.

> Drumcliffe churchyard (50km) is the final resting place of poet **WB Yeats**. Another Yeats connection comes through Lissadell House where the poet was a frequent guest (071 9163150, www.lissadellhouse.com, side-trip 47km). The distinctive flat-top shape of Benbulbin (spellings vary!) mountain gives the title to the WB Yeats' final poem, 'Under Ben Bulben', and true to the poem he is buried in view of the mountain at Drumcliffe church.
>
> The current **Classiebawn Castle** was commissioned by 19th century British Prime Minister Lord Palmerston who inherited the lands in these parts.

On the road
Ballyshannon or Bundoran are the best places to pick up supplies. There are a few small shops on route, notably at Mullaghmore, which is also a scenic area for a break.

The Bike Stop cycle shop is in Bundoran (085 2488317, www.thebikestop. ie). Sligo has a handful of cycle shops, ask for details at the tourist office (071 9161201, www.sligotourism.ie).

Accommodation
The Strandhill Caravan and Camping Park (071 9168111, www.sligocaravanand camping.ie) is on the coast some 8km west of Sligo. From the end of the stage

Benbulbin is a limestone outcrop of the Dartry Mountains which extend inland into County Leitrim

continue along the road past the station and take the Strandhill turn at the roundabout at 7.5km, then look for the signs. Greenlands Caravan and Camping Park (071 9177113, also www.sligocaravanandcamping.ie) is at Rosses Point to the northwest. The R291 will take you there. Sligo hostels include the Railway Hostel (087 6905539, www.therailway.ie). Sligo has a wide choice of modern hotels and a good number of B&Bs. It is a popular centre for tourists so book ahead, particularly in high summer.

Options
A 6km diversion to Streedagh Strand just after the 40km mark offers some windswept tranquillity.

STAGE 3
Sligo to Ballina

Start	Sligo
Distance	88.2km
Ascent	877m
Terrain	Low and coastal; can be windy.
Summit	50m at 55km

The stub of land to the west of Sligo is dominated by the 327m limestone mountain **Knocknarea**.

> On top of Knocknarea is the tomb of **Queen Maeve** – a warrior queen of Connacht in Celtic mythology.

Some of Sligo's prettiest coastal scenery follows, hiding along the strip of land between the Ox Mountains and the coast. Along a 3–4km wide fertile plain, cattle graze languidly in neat fields marked by blackthorn-smothered stone walls. Protected by Aughris Head is the kilometre-long **Dunmoran Strand**. The fine coastline continues southwestwards, towards and along Killala Bay past the seaside resort of **Inishcrone/Enniscrone**.

Ballina sits on the River Moy – Ireland's premier salmon-fishing river

On the road
There is a short section (200m or so) of rough track behind the beach to the east of Aughris Head. It can be a bumpy to ride. There are shops at Strandhill, Ballysadare and Enniscrone, along with a handful of smaller stores. Ballina has Hopkins Cycles (096 21609) on Pearse Street in the middle of town.

Accommodation
At the time of writing there were no hostels in Ballina, but check www.ballina.ie for the latest information. Just north of town is the excellent Belleek Park Caravan and Camping (096 71533, www.belleekpark.com). The next stage goes past the site (3km), or head out of town on the R314 towards Killala and look for the signed turn on the right a couple of kilometres out of town. Ballina is well supplied with hotels and B&Bs.

Options
From Ballina you can travel onwards to Westport by train, with a change at Manulla Junction, near Castlebar, if you want to skip a couple of stages and start again with Route 3.

STAGE 4
Ballina to Belmullet

Start	Ballina
Distance	99.9km
Ascent	946m
Terrain	Low coastal hills
Summit	120m at 50km

On the way out of **Ballina** are the fine Gothic gates of the **Belleek Demesne** and house, built in 1831 and now the Belleek Castle Hotel. Further along, **Moyne Abbey** (13km) has a grand tower and almost intact Franciscan cloister. **Killala** has a well preserved round tower.

> French forces under General Jean Joseph Amable Humbert landed near **Killala** on 22 August 1798 to support the United Irishmen. Humbert beat the British at Castlebar, but was later defeated at Ballinamuck.

Moyne Abbey is one of the finest Franciscan buildings in Ireland

As this stage leaves Killala Bay the country begins to open up and the landscape foreshadows the windswept rocky Atlantic coastline of the far west. In this transition zone, to the west of beautiful Downpatrick Head, is **Ceide Fields** – Europe's most extensive Iron Age monument.

> Archaeologists have mapped the Neolithic sub-peat walls at **Ceide Fields** to reveal regular fields similar to the surrounding above-ground field systems in the area today. This field system, buried in bog, has been mapped to over 1000 hectares.

By the time you reach **Pullathomas**, mountains, moor and sea dominate the scenery, and this is clearly Atlantic Ireland. Belmullet, with about 1200 inhabitants, is the most significant settlement hereabouts. It lies at the neck of a tombolo (narrow spit of land) joining the **Mullet Peninsula** to the coast.

On the road
There are shops at Killala, Ballycastle and Belderrig, but after that not much until close to Belmullet. Pullathomas has a small shop, but if staying in this area it is better to stock up at Ballycastle or earlier.

Accommodation
Pullathomas has the Kilcommon Lodge Holiday Hostel (097 84621, www.kilcommonlodge.ie). Belmullet has B&B accommodation and the area has seen

an upsurge in hotel developments in recent years, including the Broadhaven Bay Hotel (097 20600, www.broadhavenbay.com) which is on the main road on the way into town.

Options
Rather than turning off for Pullathomas at 71.4km, continuing via the R314 and R313 to Belmullet saves about 9km. If heading straight to Achill Island, Belmullet can be skipped by turning left at 95.5km and taking up Stage 5 from the 4.3km mark.

STAGE 5
Belmullet to Achill

Start	Belmullet
Distance	65.0km
Ascent	564m
Terrain	Low coast; gentle climbs
Summit	60m at 52km

South to Achill Island is a potentially fast run through lonely boglands. **Bangor** is the only town of note along the way. Even here a frontier atmosphere prevails, as the grey slash of a gravel quarry hangs over the town and the rounded green summits of the **Nephin Beg** range swell up to the south.

Approaching **Achill Island** the stage swings north and west onto the Great Western Greenway – a former railway line – to the foot of the bridge across Achill Sound.

The **Great Western Greenway** follows the route of the Westport to Achill railway line which reached Achill in 1895 and closed in 1937. The Greenway opened in 2011.

Clutching a return rail ticket to London, Belfast-born artist **Paul Henry** arrived at Achill Sound station in 1910. He stayed for nine years on the island, producing famous works such as 'Launching the Currach' (1910–11) and 'The Potato Diggers' (1912).

On the road
Bangor has a picnic area by the river and a supermarket on the way into town. There is a big supermarket at Achill Sound, just across the bridge, along with an ATM.

Accommodation
The modern Achill Island Hotel (098 45138, www.achillislandhotel.com), the last building on the left before reaching the island bridge, is in a good location if you prefer to explore the island with little or no luggage. For an up-to-date list of B&Bs see www.achilltourism.com. If you wish to camp you can push on to one of the island's campsites including the centrally positioned Keel Sandybanks (098 43211, www.achillcamping.com), 15km along the next stage.

Options
If the Great Western Greenway does not appeal, ignore the turn at 51.4km then turn right onto the R319 300m further on. This takes you all the way to the island (14km) and is marginally faster. Achill Island is mountainous so consider exploring the island with a lightened load.

The mountains build to the west as you head towards Achill Island

STAGE 6
Tour of Achill Island

Start	Achill Sound
Distance	75.1km
Ascent	1241m
Terrain	Hilly
Summit	160m at 22km

From Achill Sound this stage follows a lazy figure-of-eight, by heading straight out to the far west of the island, where the best beaches on the island are to be found – the dune-backed strand at **Keel** on the south shore and **Keem Bay** at the far west, a sandy cove protected by the knife-edged ridge of **Achill Head**.

From there the route backtracks a little way and heads to the north shore, where the beaches are also sandy and attractive, and passing the **Deserted Village**, a popular and photogenic destination.

> The **Deserted Village** consists of the ruins of between 80 and 90 mainly one-room cottages along a mile-long section of an ancient trackway crossing the back of Slievemore. Archaeological evidence suggests that the buildings were lived in permanently for little more than a century, from the mid-1700s until the 1850s, but the cottages were used as a 'booley' settlement into living memory, being occupied for the part of the year when livestock were moved to summer grazing.
>
> The ridges and furrows of the 'lazy-beds' where potatoes were once grown are visible around the settlement, and a wander through the un-roofed cottages on this lonely hillside give some insight into life in 19th-century rural Ireland.

From here you cross the outward leg to tour anticlockwise along the southern part of the island soon taking in the 300m climb of **Minaun**. This is the best view you can ride to in Ireland. The road to the top is well surfaced but steep.

Heading to the far west first means a probable tail wind back to Achill Sound, but on a fine morning consider heading straight to Minaun to be sure not to miss the view. The turn is 4.7km along the R319 from Achill Sound and signed 'Atlantic Drive'.

Keel Beach, Achill Island

On the road
The best shop on the island is the supermarket at Achill Sound. Across the car park is the island's only ATM. Most signs around the island are in Irish, and spellings vary considerably, so take care.

Accommodation
There are campsites at Keel (Keel Sandybanks Caravan and Camping Park, 098 43211, www.achillcamping.com) and Dugort (Achill Seal Caves Caravan and Camping 087 3536379, www.achillsealcaves.com). Also on the north side of the island is the Valley House hostel and bar (098 47204, www.valley-house.com), where tents can be pitched. For the quick way there, turn on to the L1406 at the 8.1km mark and follow the signs for about 3km. The Keel area has the best choice of B&Bs. Hotels on the island have improved of late and you could try the Achill Cliff House Hotel (098 43400, www.achillcliff.com) in the heart of Keel.

Options
If you have time to explore, there are many signed cycle routes on the island. You can download a map at www.achilltourism.com under the activities link.

STAGE 7
Achill to Foxford

Start	Achill
Distance	71.2km
Ascent	765m
Terrain	Low hills
Summit	80m at 50km

From **Achill** it is a pleasant two-day run back to Sligo. The route follows the railway bed of the Great Western Greenway as far as Newport. From here, if you are following the Wild Atlantic Way, you turn south towards along Stage 7A to Westport to join the next route. But if you are heading back to Sligo, the quiet roads and the wide, lake-filled glacial valleys make Stages 7 and 8 ones to savour.

This stage misses the centre of **Newport**, but it's worth a slight detour to visit the town. The back-to-back glens of Glen Hest and Glen Nephin then provide an escape route through the mountains to the bridge over the narrow confluence of loughs **Conn** and **Cullin**. Nearby **Foxford** is a hospitable and interesting town.

Foxford sits on Ireland's most famous salmon river, the Moy.

  William Brown, born in Foxford in 1779, is a hero in Argentina for his role in the war of independence,

Foxford's William Brown is a hero in Argentina for his role in their war of independence

103

Newport is a quiet picturesque port on Clew Bay

including defeating the Spanish in the Battle of the River Plate (1814). Find out more about the 'father of the Argentine navy' at the Admiral Brown Centre.

On the road
There are no ATMs until the end of the stage at Foxford. Newport is the best place to have a break. To reach the town, carry straight on at the R317 turn (33.8km) and the town centre is a few hundred metres further on. Expect some minor rerouting of the Great Western Greenway.

Accommodation
Gannon's Hostel (086 2659066) at Foxford also has camping. It is by the post office on the left as you leave town on the N26 towards Swinford. Foxford's popularity as a fly-fishing centre maintains a healthy number of B&Bs and hotels. The Mayfly Hotel (094 9256518, www.mayflyhotel.com) is a traditional Irish hotel right in the centre of town.

Options
Ballina is only 20km to the north, for an alternative route back to Sligo via the coast.

STAGE 7A

WAW link from Newport (Stage 7) to Westport

Start	Newport
Distance	12.8km
Ascent	182m
Terrain	Well-graded former railway line
Summit	40m at 10km

The short stage follows the signed Great Western Greenway all the way to **Westport** where you can continue on the Wild Atlantic Way.

On the road
If you need bike repairs, JP Breheny (098 25020) in Westport at 46km is the best bet in the area.

Accommodation
Westport has the Old Mill Holiday Hostel (098 27045 www.oldmillhostel.com) on James Street in the centre of town. Westport House has camping (098 27766, www. westporthouse.ie) on the south shore of the river close to town. The town is well-supplied with small and medium hotels and B&Bs and you should be able to find somewhere to suit your budget. For a touch of luxury you might try the four-star Hotel Westport (098 25122, www.hotelwestport.ie). Look for the right turn immediately after Holy Trinity Church as you come into town, before you reach the river.

STAGE 8

Foxford to Sligo

Start	Foxford
Distance	69.9km
Ascent	761m
Terrain	Stiff climb over the Ox Mountains
Summit	200m at 14km

Author crossing the Ox Mountains above Foxford

After an initial climb into the **Ox Mountains**, the stage follows a gently sloping plateau through fertile farmland in the lee of the hills. The ridge thins out towards the west, but the mountains remain a barrier all the way to Lough Gill, making the wide col filled by Ballygawley Lough a welcome route into Sligo. Keep an eye out for the old handball court at Kilmacteige (18km).

> Outdoor **handball courts** are a distinctive feature of the west of Ireland. Irish handball is traditionally played in a 60ft by 30ft 'big alley', such as the one at Kilmacteige. The sport has similar principles to squash. Points are scored by hitting shots into the wall that the opponent cannot return – but no racquet is involved – the ball is struck with the hand.

On the road
Aclare and Coolaney both have shops.

Accommodation
See Stage 2.

ROUTE 2 ROUTE CARDS

Stage 1 Donegal to Ballyshannon			
0.0			Donegal central diamond start outside Magee's and set off towards Letterkenny
0.7	0.7	→	Signposted 'NWT'
5.9	5.2	←	'NWT' (signed left but actually straight on)
6.3	0.4	→	'NWT'
6.5	0.2	♦	Large supermarket on right
		←	'N15 Sligo'
6.9	0.4	→	'NWT'
9.7	2.8	←	'NWT The Strand'
9.9	0.2	↗	Bear right 'NWT'
11.2	1.3	←	'NWT' at crossroads
12.1	0.9	↗	'NWT'
12.7	0.6	→	'NWT'
13.5	0.8	←	'NWT' Turn up hill
15.3	1.8	→	'NWT' sharp right turn
16.6	1.3	→	'Rossnowlagh R231'
17.2	0.6	→	'Rossnowlagh NWT'

Stage 1 Donegal to Ballyshannon			
19.0	1.8	⇦	This is the alternative route if the beach is impassable
19.3	0.3	←	Turn left along beach and find a firm section to ride
20.8	1.5	→	Leave beach via slipway
20.9	0.1	→	'NWT'
21.8	0.9	←	'Rossnowlagh'
22.2	0.4	♦	Small shop
		→	'NWT'
26.3	4.1	→	'NWT'
26.5	0.2	←	'R231 Ballyshannon NWT'
26.7	0.2	→	'NWT L2415'
27.1	0.4	←	'NWT'
27.7	0.6	→	'NWT'
28.1	0.4	←	at T-junction
28.2	0.1	→	'Town Centre'
28.3	0.1	→	'Town Centre'
28.7	0.4		Arrive Ballyshannon bridge

Stage 2 Ballyshannon to Sligo			
0.0			Start on town (N) side of Ballyshannon Bridge, just outside bus station, head across river
0.1	0.1	○ →	'Bundoran R267' straight after bridge
5.1	5.0	↑	'Bundoran R267'
5.6	0.5	✿ ⇨	Beach access
6.0	0.4	♦	Supermarket
6.1	0.1	♦	The Bike Shop
6.2	0.1	✿ ⇨	Beach access
6.4	0.2	♦	Bank of Ireland ATM
6.7	0.3	♦	Tourist Information
8.5	1.8	↗	'NWT'
10.1	1.6	→	'NWT'
13.6	3.5	→	'NWT N15 Sligo'
14.4	0.8	→	'L71041 NWT'
14.7	0.3	←	'NWT'
16.1	1.4	→	'NWT'
17.2	1.1	⇦	If you are following NWT turn here
18.8	1.6	→	at T-junction
19.9	1.1	↗	Bear right by gate lodge to Classiebawn Castle
20.5	0.6	✿	Beach access and cycle rack
21.0	0.5	♦	Small shop

Stage 2 Ballyshannon to Sligo			
21.1	0.1	←	'L7101'
25.6	4.5	↑	Cross your outward road (rejoin R279)
27.1	1.5	↑	Cross N15
30.0	2.9	→	'NWT' at T-junction
31.5	1.5	↑	'NWT'
33.2	1.7	←	'NWT' at T-junction
35.6	2.4	→	'NWT' first turn after bridge
38.9	3.3	→	'NWT' at T-junction
39.1	0.2	←	N15 NWT'
39.4	0.3	→	'Streedagh'
40.5	1.1	✿ ⇨	Side trip to Streedagh Strand – 6km return
42.9	2.4	←	'NWT'
44.2	1.3	↑	'NWT'
45.5	1.3	↑	'NWT'
47.3	1.8	← ⇨	'NWT' Turn right here for Lissadell House (4km return)
50.7	3.4	→	'Yeats' Grave' (N15)
51.4	0.7	✿	Entrance to Drumcliff Church (Yeats' grave)
52.7	1.3	♦	Shop
52.9	0.2	←	'L3405'
53.1	0.2	←	'L3405'
54.9	1.8	→	'NWT'

Stage 2 Ballyshannon to Sligo			
56.5	1.6	↑	'NWT'
57.4	0.9	↑	Unsigned
58.9	1.5	O ←	'NWT'
59.7	0.8	→	Turn up hill
60.3	0.6	→	Follow Connaghton Road as it swings to right
60.7	0.4	←	Into Lake Isle Road signed 'City Loop'
60.8	0.1	↑	Continue straight on into Bridge Street
61.0	0.2	↑	Continue straight ahead over bridge
		→	At crossroads, signed 'City Core'
61.3	0.2	↑	Continue straight on into John Street. Turn right here down O'Connell Street for the tourist office, 200m away
61.5	0.2	→	Into Adelaide Street, signed 'City Loop'
61.7	0.2	←	At crossroads 'R292 Strandhill'
61.8	0.1	↑	Across junction
61.9	0.1		Arrive Sligo station

Stage 3 Sligo to Ballina			
0.0			Sligo, Knappagh Road opposite bus station outside the Railway Bar
1.0	1.0	↑	At traffic lights
7.6	6.6	↖ O ♦ ▲	'R292 Ballysadare' (bear right here for shop (600m) and Strandhill Caravan Park)
10.6	3.0	⇦	To Knocknarea
14.1	3.5	O →	'R292 Ballysadare'
17.9	3.8	→	'N59 Ballysadare'
18.1	0.2	→	'N59 Ballysadare'
19.6	1.5	O ↗ ♦	'N59 Ballina', shop on corner, more in Ballysadare
19.9	0.3	→	'N59 Ballina'
27.2	7.3	♦	Service station has small shop
29.3	2.1	→	'Aughris Head'
37.3	8.0	→	'Dunmoran Strand' (could skip this)
38.3	1.0	↑↓ WC	Car park at strand
39.3	1.0	→	Rejoin road
39.6	0.3	→	'Aughris Head', just over bridge

Stage 3 Sligo to Ballina			
42.3	2.7	→	'Corcagh church and burial ground'
44.1	1.8	↑	Road ends, follow track behind shingle
44.3	0.2	↑ ▲	Cross footbridge next to small campsite
44.4	0.1	↑	At Maggie Maye's Beach Bar join road
44.6	0.2	↑ ⇨	At crossroads, side-trip 500m return to small harbour and walk to headland
47.4	2.8	→	At T-junction
54.5	7.1	→	'Easkey'
60.8	6.3	↗	Road swings right after bridge
61.0	0.2	♦	Easkey has a few shops
65.6	4.6	♦	Rathlee has small shop
71.6	6.0	✪	Irish Free State letter box
74.3	2.7	♦ ATM	Food store. Service station has shop and ATM
74.5	0.2	✪	Tourist information at Inishcrone/Enniscrone
74.9	0.4	⇨	To sweeping, dune-backed beach

Stage 3 Sligo to Ballina			
75.2	0.3	▲	Atlantic Caravan Park
76.9	1.7	→	'Coast Road'
85.9	9.0	←	(Straight on is no entry)
86.5	0.6	→	'Town centre'
87.7	1.2	→	Swing to right across river
87.8	0.1	↑	Continue straight on after bridge
88.0	0.2	←	Follow one-way into O'Rahilly St
88.2	0.2		Arrive Ballina PO

Stage 4 Ballina to Belmullet			
0.0			Ballina post office – head down Casement Street (with back to PO, head to your right)
0.1	0.1	←	At T-junction
		→	At T-junction
0.6	0.5	→	'Nally Street' – just before Ballina civic offices
1.1	0.5	←	Through stone gates – Belleek Forest Park
2.1	1.0	✪	Belleek Wood
2.2	0.1	⇨	Belleek Castle Hotel
2.9	0.7	←	Road turns left

Stage 4 Ballina to Belmullet

3.6	0.7	▲	Ballina Caravan and Camping Park
4.1	0.5	→	Follow cyclepath at main road
4.4	0.3	→	'Tour d'Humbert'
9.4	5.0	⇨	Side-trip to Rosserk Friary (3km return)
11.0	1.6	↑	At crossroads. Have right of way but be careful – visibility poor
13.0	2.0	✿	Moyne Abbey – 300m walk down track to right
14.9	1.9	→	On to R314
15.6	0.7	✿	Killala tourist office in centre on left
15.9	0.3	✿	Humbert statues
16.0	0.1	⇨	Killala Round Tower, 150m return
16.1	0.1	→ ♦	'Ballycastle', shop opposite
16.2	0.1	←	'Ceide Fields'
16.3	0.1	♦	Service station and shop
20.5	4.2	→	'Tour d'Humbert', immediately over bridge
23.1	2.6	←	At crossroads

Stage 4 Ballina to Belmullet

24.6	1.5	↑ ⇨	Road joins from right. For Humbert's Landing (5.1km), turn right.
24.8	0.2	→	'Ballycastle via coast road', at T-junction
26.5	1.7	↑	Ignore fork to right
29.7	3.2	⇨	To Lackan Bay
37.1	7.4	⇨	To Downpatrick Head (4km return)
39.0	1.9	→	At unsigned crossroads
40.3	1.3	✿	Pass sandy beach backed by dunes
42.0	1.7	→ ♦	At T-junction (turn left for Ballycastle, which has a shop)
49.9	7.9	✿	Ceide Fields
57.2	7.3	♦	Belderrig has small shop
57.5	0.3	⇨	For the alternative, mountain route along coast
71.4	13.9	→	'Poll a tSomais'
77.8	6.4	⇦	Turn past shrine for small shop and post office at Pullathomas
77.9	0.1	▲	Kilcommon Lodge Holiday Hostel, Pulathomas

Stage 4 Ballina to Belmullet

78.6	0.7	▲	McGrath's has accommodation
86.0	7.4	⇨	To small beach and pier, 2.3km return
89.2	3.2	→ ♦	At main road – R314. Supermarket about 50m on left
95.5	6.3	→	'Beal an Mhuirthead R313'
99.9	4.4		Arrive Belmullet central roundabout

Stage 5 Belmullet to Achill

0.0			Belmullet central roundabout, outside Shevlins shop, head towards Bangor
16.4	16.4	✪	Picnic table on old bridge
19.6	3.2	♦ →	'N59 Mallaranny', supermarket on corner
19.7	0.1	✪	Bangor tourist information
19.9	0.2	✪	Picnic area by river
30.2	10.3	✪	Picnic area and access to river

Stage 5 Belmullet to Achill

34.5	4.3	✪	From low summit, views towards Achill Island
47.8	13.3	✪	Pass Claggan Mountain
51.3	3.5	✪	Old Achill Island railway bridge
51.4	0.1	←	Turn left up hill to join Great Western Greenway
51.5	0.1	←	Turn along Greenway and follow to Achill
63.0	11.5	←	At end of Greenway, turn left onto road
63.5	0.5	→	Join main road
65.0	1.5		Arrive Achill Island bridge

Stage 6 Tour of Achill Island

0.0		→	Exit shop car park on island side of Achill bridge and turn right
5.2	5.2	✪	Lavelle's Garage and shop and Achill Tourism
8.1	2.9	▲ ⇨	Turn for Valley House Bar & Restaurant (5.5km)
10.8	2.7	⇦	Rough track has view of crannog (approx 200m)

ROUTE 2 ROUTE CARDS

Stage 6 Tour of Achill Island			
12.4	1.6	⇨	Dugort turn
14.7	2.3	←▲⇧	'Beach'; Carry straight on here for Achill Cliff House Hotel, 150m.
14.9	0.2	▲	Keel Sandybanks Caravan Park
15.0	0.1	→	Follow road along back of beach
15.3	0.3	WC	On left
15.4	0.1	←♦	Shop across road
18.5	3.1	⇦	Small stony beach with picnic table
24.1	5.6	↑↓ WC	Arrive Keem Bay
32.9	8.8	←	'L1407 Dugort'
34.9	2.0	⇦	To deserted village, 1km return
39.3	4.4	✿WC ♦ ▲	Access to Dugort Strand, small shop across road. Achill Seal Caves Caravan and Camping on right.
41.4	2.1	✿	Nice beach
42.9	1.5	→	At crossroads
		⇦▲	For Valley House (300m)

Stage 6 Tour of Achill Island			
47.4	4.5	←	Atlantic Drive, at T-junction
50.6	3.2	→	'Dumha Eige' (Dooega)
52.2	1.6	⇨	To 'Baran Mhionnain' – turn here for climb to Minann
56.5	4.3	↖	'Cycle Route 1'
56.9	0.4	←	At T-junction
57.2	0.3	→	At T-junction
57.3	0.1	↑	'Gob an Choire'
57.5	0.2	✿WC	Pretty Blue Flag beach
59.9	2.4	→	'Cursana Farraige'
61.5	1.6	✿	Picnic table – fine views
65.1	3.6	✿	Best view on stage
66.3	1.2	←	'Atlantic Drive'
66.9	0.6	✿	Caislean Ghrainne
72.8	5.9	♦	Small shop
74.0	1.2	→	'Gob an Choire'
75.1	1.1		Arrive shop car park (on left)

Stage 7 Achill to Foxford

0.0		←	At entrance to small car park on mainland side of the bridge turn left onto main road
1.5	1.5	←	Follow Greenway signs
2.0	0.5	→	Turn onto Greenway and follow all the way to Newport
14.5	12.5	♦	Café and local shops in Mulranny
33.8	31.8	←♦	Leave Greenway onto R317 signed 'Crossmolina' (if continuing south on the Wild Atlantic Way, carry straight on here and continue with the directions from 33.8km on Stage 7A); shop in service station at this junction, further shops in Newport town centre (300m straight ahead).
39.3	5.5	✪	IRA memorial
43.8	4.5	→	'Beltra'
46.6	2.8	←	At T-junction
		→	After 20m
53.2	6.6	←	Castlebar signed to right
54.1	0.9	♦	Shop Bofeenaun
54.4	0.3	♦	Shop
54.7	0.3	→	'Pontoon'
57.9	3.2	→	'Pontoon'
63.2	5.3	←	'R310 Foxford'
65.0	1.8	✪	Pontoon bridge
66.6	1.6	→	'R318 Foxford'
67.2	0.6	✪	Access to lake beach
67.9	0.7	✪	Access to lake beach
68.0	0.1	✪	Access to lake beach
69.7	1.7	⇐	To Foxford Station
71.0	1.3	→	'Swinford'
71.2	0.2	♦	Arrive Foxford town centre; the Mayfly Hotel is 50m down the street to your right

Stage 7A WAW link from Newport to Westport (Route 3)

33.8		↑	Follow the Greenway into Newport and on to Westport
34.1	0.3	♦	Supermarket and other shops in Newport
44.7	10.9	→	Leave cycleway and turn onto road

Stage 7A WAW link from Newport to Westport (Route 3)			
45.2	0.5	←	Join N59 into Westport
46.1	0.9	←	'N5 Dublin' just before river
46.2	0.1	♦ →	'Town Centre' Turn left here for JP Breheny Cycle Shop (100m)
46.5	0.3	→	Turn right at clock tower
46.6	0.1		Arrive Glendenning Monument of St Patrick in the Square

Stage 8 Foxford to Sligo			
0.0			Foxford cross-roads, corner N26 and Lower Main Street, head down Lower Main Street
0.1	0.1	↑	Past Admiral Brown Centre
		✪	Foxford Woollen Mills
2.0	1.9	←	'Foxford Way (FFW)', at T-junction
2.5	0.5	←	'FFW', at T-junction
2.7	0.2	→	'FFW', at crossroads
3.1	0.4	←	'FFW', at T-junction

Stage 8 Foxford to Sligo			
4.4	1.3	←	'FFW', at T-junction
4.5	0.1	→	Down grassy lane, bit stony but very rideable
5.4	0.9	↑	Meet better road
5.7	0.3	→	On to sealed road
6.9	1.2	→	'FFW', at T-junction
8.1	1.2	△ (134)	Bench if you need a rest
9.5	1.4	✪	Monastic site, 5th/6th century (not much to see)
9.9	0.4	↖	'Aclare'
11.6	1.7	✪	Bridge is Sligo county border
14.0	2.4	△ (199)	
17.6	3.6	←	Turn left as road joins from the right
18.0	0.4	✪	On right is hand-ball court, left is Kilmacteige fam-ine cemetery
19.8	1.8	← ♦	'Tobercurry'; Aclare has shop
23.7	3.9	←	'R294 Ballina'
23.9	0.2	→	'Cloonacool'
31.7	7.8	↑	'Coolaney'
33.3	1.6	✪	Pass Knocknashee Common – dis-tinctive hillfort

Stage 8 Foxford to Sligo			
39.4	6.1	⬉	Take left fork
45.2	5.8	✿	Rockfield... has a rock in a field
46.2	1.0	←	At T-junction by IRA memorial in Coolaney
46.5	0.3	♦	Shop
47.6	1.1	→	'Collooney'
54.6	7.0	→	At T-junction, continue on main road through Collooney
55.4	0.8	←	'Sligo'
55.5	0.1	O ↑ ♦	'R290 Dromhair' – careful, busy roundabout – shop at service station
56.1	0.6	✿	Markree Castle
58.8	2.7	←	'R284 Sligo'
58.9	0.1	♦	Shop in service station at Ballygawley
62.8	3.9	✿	Views of Benbulben and Knocknarea
65.6	2.8	←	'N4 Sligo'
65.7	0.1	→	After 50m
		O →	'R287 Sligo'
66.5	0.8	✿	Cycleway starts
		O ↑	'R287 Sligo' (cycleway ends after roundabout)

Stage 8 Foxford to Sligo			
68.1	1.6	↑	'Town centre' – need to be in right-hand lane at lights
68.3	0.2	⇨	Alternate route to Hyde Bridge
68.9	0.6	✿	Pass court house
69.0	0.1	←	'All routes', at lights
69.5	0.5	→	'Town centre', at lights
69.7	0.2	←	'All other routes', at lights
69.8	0.1	↑	'Station', at lights
69.9	0.1		Arrive at bus station

ROUTE 3 TOUR OF CONNACHT

Aasleagh Falls (Stage 3)

Start/Finish	Westport
Distance	407.6km
Ascent	4354m

Connacht is one of the four provinces of Ireland. It consists of the counties of Galway, Leitrim, Mayo, Roscommon and Sligo.

Westport is a rare Irish example of an architect-planned town, and nearby Croagh Patrick has one of the grandest views in the country. This route includes trips to two fine islands; if you only have time for one, visit Inishbofin with its pristine

beaches and dramatic cliffs and sea stacks. It's a real treasure.

The way into the heart of Connemara is through melancholic Doo Lough Glen. The coast from here south to Clifden is idyllic. To the south and east of Clifden the miles of bog-land and lakes take over. The final stretch of road into Galway from Casla is the only disappointing part of the route – see Options for alternatives.

The prettiest scenery immediately around Galway is along the shores of Lough Corrib and, further on, Lough Mask and Lough Carra. Another highlight of this northwards stage of your tour is the old village of Cong.

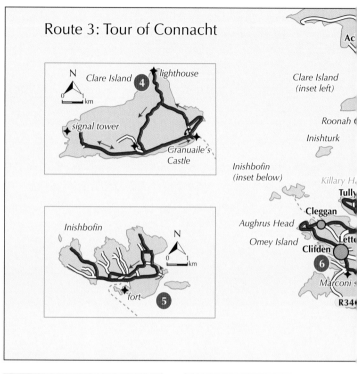

Route 3: Tour of Connacht

Ac

Clare Island   lighthouse   **4**

N

Clare Island
(inset left)

0   km

Roonah

signal tower

Inishturk

Granuaile's
Castle

Inishbofin
(inset below)   Killary H.

Tull

Cleggan

Aughrus Head

Inishbofin

Omey Island   **Lette**

N   **Clifden**

0   km   **6**

fort   **5**   Marconi s

R34

Clare Island (inset left)
Inishbofin (inset below)

BETTER BY BIKE

From Westport to Galway this route largely follows the Wild Atlantic Way driving route. But it also includes explorations of Clare Island and Inishbofin that are not on the official route. Sticking exclusively to the coast does, however, mean missing out on some of the distinctive Connemara moorland landscape of the interior. Taking at least one inland shortcut also helps keep the distance down into Galway.

GETTING TO THE START

By rail/bus

There are seven rail services a day to and from Dublin Heuston, with the journey to Galway taking under three hours. Buses and trains depart from the same central location – just off Eyre Square.

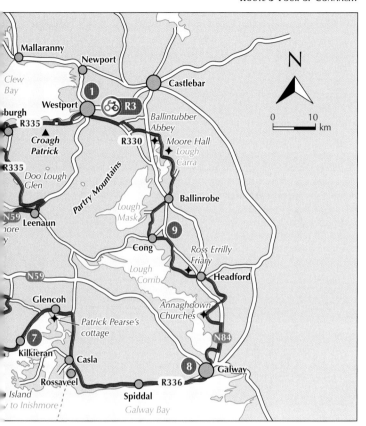

The roads to the west of Galway are busy during holiday weekends. Galway itself is hectic for the two weeks of the Galway Arts Festival, from mid-July, and the following week of the Galway Races.

There is ample accommodation most of the way along the route and in Galway city. The options on Clare Island have improved in recent years. The other island on the route, Inishbofin, also has a range of choices for overnight stays. Accommodation is scarce in the section between

CROAGH PATRICK AND THE PATRICIAN PILGRIMAGE

On the last Sunday of each July, more than 20,000 pilgrims climb Croagh Patrick (Stage 1), near Westport, to honour St Patrick, who fasted on the mountain for 40 days in the year 441. According to tradition it was from here that the saint banished all snakes from Ireland. If you can spare the time and energy for a stiff four-hour return walk, there are fine views into the mountainous heart of Connacht, across the drumlin-strewn Clew Bay to the north, and out to the island jewels of **Clare Island** (Stage 2) and **Inishbofin** (Stage 5) in the open Atlantic.

Pick a quieter time for the climb, however, unless Reek Sunday has special meaning for you. Taking in the mountain and ocean panorama from Ireland's holy mountain is a grand way to start this tour of the western part of Connacht with its picturesque coast and rich ecclesiastical history.

Clifden and Galway (Stages 6 and 7). Consider taking a couple of shortcuts and combine the stages into a single day. If you are staying overnight in the Kilkieran area, make sure you have a booking before leaving Clifden.

Route summary table					
Stage		Distance	Ascent	Accommodation available	Places with shops/other facilities en route
1	Westport to Roonah Quay	31.5km	365m	Croagh Patrick	Louisburgh
2	Tour of Clare Island	21.9km	433m		Clare harbour
3	Roonah Quay to Tully	59.1km	825m	Delphi Resort, Leenaun, Rossroe	Leenaun
4	Tully to Clifden	49.7km	604m	Letterfrack	Letterfrack, Cleggan
5	Tour of Inishbofin	15.7km	219m	Various hotels and hostel/ campsite	Inishbofin harbour
6	Clifden to Kilkieran	45.0km	419m	Carna	Carna
7	Kilkieran to Galway	68.1km	515m		Spiddal, Casla, Kilronan
8	Galway to Cong	63.6km	521m		Cloonboo
9	Cong to Westport	53.0km	453m		Ballinrobe
Total		**407.6km**	**4354m**		

Renvyle Beach, Tully marks the start of some fine coastal scenery (Stage 4)

MAPS

The Ordnance Survey Ireland West sheet covers the route at 1:250,000. At 1:50,000 the following OSI Discovery sheets are required: 45 Galway, 46 Galway, 38 Galway Mayo, 31 Mayo, 30 Mayo (for Clare Island and the strip of coast Westport to Louisburgh), 37 Mayo Galway and 44 Galway. Galway city is positioned right on the edge of sheet 45, which makes navigation to the north more awkward than it might be.

OPTIONS

The full tour is detailed as nine stages, and is just over 400km. The tours of Clare Island (Stage 2) and Inishbofin (Stage 5) can be omitted if time is short, and Stages 1 and 3 combined into a Westport to Tully stage (approximately 77km) giving a 356km six-day tour. A further shortcut is possible from Clifden to Galway, via Oughterard (78km), which knocks another 35km off the total.

The Galway Greenway project, which would create a cycle route from Galway to Clifden using sections of a disused railway line, was stalled at the time of writing.

On Stage 7, as an alternative to the fast road from Casla back to Galway, consider taking the ferry to the Aran Islands from Rossaveel. From the islands you could return to Galway via Doolin and the Burren or continue south to Limerick or County Kerry bypassing Galway altogether.

STAGE 1

Westport to Roonah Quay

Start	Westport
Distance	31.5km
Ascent	365m
Terrain	Flat coastal
Summit	50m at 23km

The spin along the shores of drumlin-filled **Clew Bay** to the ferry at **Roonah Quay** follows a well-protected coast. The conical shape of **Croagh Patrick** dominates the scenery for most of the route.

> St Patrick's association with **Croagh Patrick** dates from AD441, when he fasted on the summit for Lent, and banished all the snakes from Ireland. Allow three to four hours for a return trip to the summit.

On the road
Stock up at Louisburgh before going to Clare Island.

Murrisk Abbey nestles beneath Croagh Patrick

Accommodation

Westport has the Old Mill Holiday Hostel (098 27045, www.oldmillhostel.com) on James Street in the centre of town. Westport House has camping (098 27766, www.westporthouse.ie) on the south shore of the river close to town. The town is well-supplied with small and medium hotels and B&Bs and you should be able to find somewhere to suit your budget. For a touch of luxury you might try the four-star Hotel Westport (098 25122, www.hotelwestport.ie). Look for the right turn immediately after Holy Trinity Church as you come into town from the north, before you reach the river.

The route passes the Croagh Patrick Caravan Park (098 64860) at the foot of the mountain. Roonagh Quay is just a quay so if you are not heading to Clare Island, push on. The next accommodation is at the Delphi Resort (095 42208, www.delphiadventureresort.com) 24.3km along stage 3. Here you will also find budget accommodation at the Wild Atlantic Hostel (same contact details).

Options

Ferries leave Roonah Quay for Clare Island at 10.45 and 11am (O'Malley Ferries, 098 25045, www.omalleyferries.com and the Clare Island Ferry Company 098 23737, www.clareislandferry.com) and the crossing takes less than half an hour. There are extra sailings in summer. With an early start, it is easy to make a morning ferry and spend the afternoon exploring the island, returning to the mainland the next morning. Check departure times when you arrive.

If you are not going to the island and heading on into Connemara, taking the R335 direct to Leenaun, at the same junction, saves about 4km and, again, this is a faster route. You can pick up the directions again after 6km, where Stage 5 rejoins the R335 at the 11.1km mark. If combining Stages 1 and 3 in this way, the total distance, Westport to Tully, is just over 77km.

STAGE 2
Tour of Clare Island

Start/Finish	Clare harbour
Distance	21.9km
Ascent	433m
Terrain	Small hills
Summit	110m at 10km

Clare Island has only a handful of roads. These directions take in the **lighthouse** at the northern point of the island and the **signal tower** at the west end. The best beach is the one in front of the campsite near the harbour. The medieval wall paintings at the island's **abbey**, with their depictions of warriors, herdsmen, animals and dragons, are some of the finest in Europe. The abbey is locked, so ask around in the village for current access arrangements.

The Pirate Queen, **Grace O'Malley** (Granuaile or *Gráinne Mhaol* in Irish), controlled the seafaring traffic on much of the west coast from her Clare Island fortress during the 16th century.

Pirate queen Grace O'Malley used Clare Island as a base in the 16th century

On the road
Pick up supplies at Louisburgh before sailing for the island, as the shop there is small. The community centre near the port offers food 9am to 9pm at the time of writing. Check at www.clareisland.ie.

Accommodation
The campsite is little more than a paddock with a tap at the rear of the beach, but the position is fantastic and there are showers and toilets at the nearby community centre. For other accommodation check www.clareisland.info. A hostel has now opened a few hundred metres north along the coast from the quay (098 26307, www.goexplorehostel.ie).

STAGE 3
Roonah Quay to Tully

Start	Roonah Quay
Distance	59.1km
Ascent	825m
Terrain	Hilly
Summit	80m at 43km

The gateway into Connemara from the north is through **Doo Lough Glen**, one of the most scenic passes in Ireland. The pass ends at one of Ireland's few fjords, Killary Glen. A steady climb to the west of the crossroads town of **Leenaun** (sometimes Leenane) leads into the heart of the mountains, before another glacial pass leads to the sand dunes and beaches of northwest Connemara at **Tully**.

> In 1849, at the height of the **famine**, hundreds of men, women and children marched up Doo Lough Glen to plead with the Famine Commissioners meeting at Delphi Lodge. Help was refused, and many died in the snow on the return march.

On the road
There are no shops until Leenaun and no ATMs at all on this stage.

Killary Harbour is a true fjord

Accommodation
Delphi Resort has budget accommodation in its Wild Atlantic Hostel (24km, 095 42208, www.delphiadventureresort.com) or you can stay in the more luxurious resort itself (same contact details). There is a hostel near Leenaun – Sleepzone Connemara (091 566999, www.sleepzone.ie) at 41km. Further on, the turn to Killary Harbour Hostel at Rossroe pier is at the 48.2km mark, and it's about 4km to Rossroe from the turn (095 43933, www.killaryharbourhostel.com). Other camping options are at 52km, the Connemara Caravan and Camping Park (095 43406, www.connemaracamping.com), and just at the start of the next stage is Renvyle Beach Caravan and Camping Park (095 43462, www.renvylebeachcaravanpark. com). Tully and Renvyle have a smattering of B&Bs and a couple of hotel offerings, including the Maol Reidh Hotel at Tully Cross (095 43844, www.maolreidhhotel. com).

Options
If you really need to cut short your Tour of Connacht, you can skip Stages 4 to 8 by taking the R336/R345 to Cong from Leenaun (approximately 35km).

STAGE 4
Tully to Clifden

Start	Tully
Distance	49.7km
Ascent	604m
Terrain	Low hills
Summit	80m at 8km

This far western part of Connemara is a disquieting mixture of the serene and the severe, with sandy beaches a few hundred metres from bog and rock-filled glens and glowering brown hills. The towns here are particularly well kept. **Letterfrack** was founded by Quakers in the 19th century. A little further up the valley is one of Ireland's top tourist attractions, **Kylemore Abbey** (turn at 13.8km, open daily from 9am in spring and summer, closing time is generally around 5pm 095 52001, www.kylemoreabbey.com).

> **Kylemore Abbey** was originally built as a family home for one the wealthiest men in Victorian Britain, Manchester politician and financier Henry Mitchell,

Benedictine nuns forced to flee Ypres during the First World War founded Kylemore Abbey in a former stately home

with the foundation stone laid in 1867. In the 20th century, it was sold to the Duke of Manchester, who left in 1914 for financial reasons. Benedictine nuns founded an abbey here in 1920. They were looking for a new home after their abbey in Ypres (Belgium) was destroyed early in the Great War. Their Belgian foundation had long enjoyed the patronage of influential Irish families, some living in exile due to anti-Catholic measures in Ireland.

Ferries to Inishbofin (Stage 7) leave from the small harbour at **Cleggan** (26km). From here the route skirts the low peninsula of **Aughrus Head**. The road towards Clifden then follows the shore of a narrow inlet before a short climb over the neck of another peninsula drops you into **Clifden**.

On the road
The best shop on route is in Letterfrack, where there is an ATM. If you are heading to Inishbofin, stock up at Letterfrack or Cleggan. Clifden has a bike shop – John Mannion's – on Bridge Street (095 21160). The tourist information office is on Galway Road (095 21163).

Accommodation
Letterfrack has two hostels – Connemara National Park Hostel (095 41222, www.connemaranationalpark.com) and Old Monastery Hostel (087 2349543, www.oldmonasteryhostel.com). For camping try, at 39km Clifden Eco Beach Camping & Caravanning Park (095 44036, www.actonsbeachsidecamping.com), while at 47km Clifden Campsite & Caravan Park (095 22150, www.clifdencamping.com) is on a hillside close to town. Clifden Town Hostel (095 21076, www.clifdentownhostel.com) is on your left a 100m or so before the end of the stage. Clifden has a choice of B&B accommodation and hotels, including Foyles (095 21801, www.foyleshotel.com) which you will find in a white-painted Victorian building in the central square at the end of the stage.

Options
At Cleggan you can take the ferry to Inishbofin for Stage 7, leaving the remaining 23km of Stage 6 for the following day. Check for the latest timetable (095 45819, www.inishbofinislanddiscovery.com). In June July and August sailings are usually 11.30am, 2pm and 6.45pm or 7.30pm. You can buy a ticket in town or on the boat, and they do take bicycles. It makes sense to sort out your accommodation before you depart for the island – see Stage 7.

If you fancy getting even further off the beaten track, access to Omey Island is across a sandy beach uncovered at low tide.

STAGE 5
Tour of Inishbofin

Start	Inishbofin quay
Distance	15.7km
Ascent	219m
Terrain	Low hills
Summit	50m at 8km

Inishbofin, measuring barely 6km by 3km, manages to capture the best of the Connemara landscape in a package easily toured in an afternoon. The protected beaches on the eastern side of the island are pristine, while on the north and western shores the Atlantic has pounded the shoreline into cliffs and sea stacks.

> The star-shaped **fort** guarding the harbour was built around 1656. It also was used to house captured Catholic clergy, declared guilty of high treason by statute in 1655, ready for transportation.

Wild bogland on Inishbofin

The island is a stronghold for traditional music, and hosts an arts and music festival in late April/early May. Traditional farming practices held out longer here than in many places in Ireland, making this one of the few sites where the distinctive call of the ground-nesting corncrake can be heard.

On the road
There is a shop which has the basics and some fresh food right by Inishbofin harbour, just turn left at the landward end of the quay. Opening hours vary and it's best to have at least some supplies when you arrive. There are three hotels on the island that serve meals.

Check for the latest ferry timetable (095 45819, www.inishbofinislanddiscovery. com). There is a 5pm departure from the island daily (4pm in winter), as well as a morning sailings at 8.15am, 9am or 10am, depending on the day of the week. You can buy a ticket in Cleggan or on the boat, and they do take bicycles.

Accommodation
The Doonmore Hotel (9.5km 095 45814, www.doonmorehotel.com) and the Dolphin Hotel, 1km away (095 45991, www.dolphinhotel.ie), are both on the route card, while for the Inishbofin House Hotel (095 45809, www. inishbofinhouse.com) take the right fork at the junction at 0.3km.

Inishbofin Island Hostel (095 45855, www.inishbofin-hostel.ie) also allows camping, and is in a beautiful high position on the island. For other accommodation options www.inishbofin.com has up-to-date lists. Sort out accommodation before departing the mainland.

STAGE 6
Clifden to Kilkieran

Start	Clifden
Distance	45km
Ascent	419m
Terrain	Low and coastal
Summit	30m at 30km

South of Clifden the mountain spine of Connemara recedes and bog, lake and rock take over. Before heading out across the wilds, there is a chance to visit the

The beaches in the lee of Finish Island are often deserted

site of the old Marconi wireless station at Derrigimlagh Bog. To reach the Marconi station, carry straight on at 3.5km and look for a left turn at 4km, and follow the track to the site by a lake. When the facility opened in 1907 it was the first permanent transatlantic radio station.

> Captain John Alcock and Lieutenant Arthur Whitten Brown landed at Derrigimlagh Bog in 1919, completing **the first non-stop transatlantic flight**.

At **Carna** there is a discernible change in the landscape, as small optimistic fields replace the miles of unimproved bog. Down the unsigned lanes are some of Ireland's best beaches. In the lee of **Finish Island**, bright white sands hold out against the suck of the Atlantic tides in **Galway Bay**.

On the road
Stock up on supplies in Clifden. There are no shops until Carna (36km).

Accommodation

Consider wild camping along the coast. Alternatively, there are B&Bs in the Kilkieran area. Stage 6 passes Hillside House (095 33420) at 4.2km. Book accommodation before leaving Clifden. The Carna area (36km) has some of the best options including the Carna Bay Hotel (095 32255, www.carnabay.com).

Options

If the Galway-to-Clifden Connemara Greenway route gets off the ground, this would be an attractive quick-return route to Galway. A less drastic shortcut is to cross the peninsula separating Bertraghboy Bay and Kilkieran Bay. For this option turn left at 23.6km (and rejoin the route cards at the 9.6km mark of Stage 7). This shortcut is 10km long and gives a total Clifden-to-Galway distance of about 93km, but unless you plan to ride this in a day, accommodation options are limited.

STAGE 7

Kilkieran to Galway

Start	Kilkieran
Distance	68.1km
Ascent	515m
Terrain	Flat coastal
Summit	30m at 40km

The early part of this route back to Galway is the best riding. On the west side of Kilkieran Bay the road hugs a narrow strip of land between the razorback of the encroaching Cnoc Mordain mountain and the calm island-studded water. This coastal area and the offshore islands are a Gaelic-speaking stronghold, and this was one of the reasons Patrick Pearse built a cottage here (turn at 12.5km).

> **Patrick (or Pádraig) Pearse** was one of the leaders of the 1916 Easter Rising and famously read the Proclamation of the Irish Republic on the steps of the Dublin General Post Office on Easter Monday, 24 April 1916. He was also chosen as President of the Republic. Pearse and 13 other leaders of the uprising, including his brother Willie, were court-martialled and shot by the British. Many of the key figures in the rising visited the cottage Pearse built in Rosmuc. It is open 9.30am–6pm daily (4pm in winter) (091 574292, www.heritageireland.ie/en).

Patrick Pearse's cottage in Ros Muc

After the turn to the Aran ferries (30.8km) the road (R336) becomes too busy, fast and narrow for enjoyable cycling but there is no alternative if you're continuing on to Galway.

On the road
Spiddal has ATMs, takeaways shops and public toilets. If heading directly to the Aran Islands via Rossaveel, there is a large supermarket at Casla – turn at 29.1km – but there is also a good shop at Kilronan on Inishmore (see Route 4, Stage 1) if you are bypassing Galway via the islands.

Accommodation
Coming into Galway there are three campsites close together at Salthill (63km). These are Bayview Caravan & Camping Park (091 523316, www.bayviewcaravanpark.com), O'Halloran's Caravan & Camping Park (086 8747422, www.ohalloranscaravanpark.com) and Salthill Caravan Park (091 523972, www.salthillcaravanpark.com).
Galway itself has a youth hostel (091 566999, www.anoige.ie) close to the town centre, as well as a choice of independents. The city has a bewildering range of hotels including some of the major chains. Alongside the large number of guesthouses and B&Bs, you should be able to find something to suit your budget.

Just be wary of the three-week period from mid-July when the town fills up for the Galway Arts Festival followed by the Galway Races.

Options
Avoid the busy R336 back to Galway by heading to the Aran Island ferries at Rossaveel (the turn is at 30.8km). From the islands you could return to Galway via Doolin and the Burren, or continue south along the Wild Atlantic Way to Limerick or County Kerry.

STAGE 8
Galway to Cong

Start	Galway
Distance	63.6km
Ascent	521m
Terrain	Flat
Summit	30m at 42km

After clearing Galway, this stage follows the picturesque farmland on the eastern shore of Ireland's second largest lake, **Lough Corrib**, as the mountain barrier of Connemara looms to the west. This area is littered with castles and ecclesiastical sites. **Annaghdown** has a fine collection of religious buildings, and is well known for its connections with St Brendan, who built a nunnery here for his sister Briga. Further on, **Ross Errilly Friary** (turn at 43.3km) is one of the best-preserved monastic sites in the country. It was a Franciscan foundation in the 14th century.

The 1952 John Ford film **The Quiet Man**, starring John Wayne and Maureen O'Hara, was filmed in Cong.

Cong guards the neck of land separating Lough Corrib from its northern neighbour, Lough Mask. There is plenty to see around here, including Ashford Castle, the ruined abbey and the Dry Canal.

The Dry Canal was built to carry steamer traffic between Lough Mask and Lough Corrib. Construction began in 1848, but the massive locks and the neat rock-cut channel remain empty to this day, as the porous limestone of the canal route swallowed up all the water.

In the Middle Ages Galway was a thriving port trading with Spain and France

On the road

Getting out of Galway to the north is simple and, barring a rather unattractive 7km stretch through the industrial estates lining the N84, pleasant riding. There are a couple of shops and an ATM in the Cloonboo area (19km, just before Annaghdown). ATMs are scarce, although Connolly's service station in Cong has one. The best access to Lough Corrib is early in the day (9km).

Accommodation

Cong Hostel and Cong Caravan and Camping Park (61.1km, 094 9546089, www.quietman-cong.com) are on the same site – not far from the lake and adjacent to the Ashford Demesne a kilometre or so from the village. The steady flow of tourists supports a number of B&Bs and smaller guesthouses and hotels in the area, but prices tend to be on the high side. Ryan's Hotel (094 9546243, www. ryanshotelcong.ie) is in the heart of the village.

STAGE 9
Cong to Westport

Start	Cong
Distance	53km
Ascent	453m
Terrain	A few gentle hills
Summit	60m at 45km

North of **Cong** the route loops around the north side of **Lough Carra**. The mountains retreat from view until Ireland's holy mountain, **Croagh Patrick**, appears near Westport. Most of the through-roads in the area run 2–3km from the loughs, and there are no panoramic views until the vicinity of **Moore Hall**.

> **John Moore** of Moore Hall was made president of the short-lived Republic of Connacht during the 1798 uprising. In 1961 he was officially recognised as Ireland's first president.

Georgian Moore Hall – the ancestral home of John Moore

Ballintubber Abbey marks the start of the ancient pilgrimage route to Croagh Patrick mountain

North of the hall is **Ballintubber Abbey**, the oldest royal abbey in Ireland that has been in constant use (established 1216). It is on an ancient pilgrim path heading towards Croagh Patrick.

At the end of the stage, **Westport** is a bright and lively town with wide streets and a tree-lined mall along the river.

On the road
Ballinrobe is the only significant town on the route. Moore Hall, or the foreshore thereabouts, is the most pleasant place for a break.

Accommodation
See Stage 1.

Options
At the 7.2km mark there is a 5km side-trip to Inishmaine Abbey – the ruins are not spectacular, but it is finely positioned on a low peninsula on Lough Mask.

ROUTE 3 ROUTE CARDS

Stage 1 Westport to Roonagh Quay			
0.0			Westport opposite monument, take Louisburgh (R335) direction
0.4	0.4	→	'Westport House'
0.7	0.3	△	From low summit, views of Croagh Patrick and Clew Bay
1.4	0.7	♦	Small supermarket
1.6	0.2	⇨	To Westport House (2.5km return)
	2.5		
4.9	3.3 0.8	→	'Murrisk'
5.4	0.5	♦	Service station and shop
8.7	3.3	→ ⇧	'L5878 Murrisk Pier' (straight on for more direct route)
8.9	0.2	✿	Murrisk Fisherman's Monument
9.5	0.6	↑ ✿	Murrisk pier has picnic tables, views. Keep following road
9.8	0.3	↑	Road joins from left
10.0	0.2	←	At T-junction
10.4	0.4	✿	View of priory
10.7	0.3	→	'R335 Louisburgh'

Stage 1 Westport to Roonagh Quay			
10.9	0.2	✿	Croagh Patrick car park – bike racks
12.9	2.0	⇨	Bertra Strand
14.8	1.9	▲	Croagh Patrick Caravan Park
19.7	4.9	▲ ⇨	L1827 Old Head – to Old Head Forest camping about 0.5km
22.9	3.2	♦	Louisburgh has shops – open early
23.2	0.3	→ ⇦	'L5885 Carrowmore' (or left 'R335 Leenaun' to miss Clare Island)
23.9	0.7	→ ⇧	'Carrowmore' (or, if rushing for ferry, continue straight on R378)
24.7	0.8	✿	Beach and sand cliffs
24.9	0.2	↑	At crossroads
25.4	0.5	→	At T-junction
27.9	2.5	↖	Ignore right fork
29.2	1.3	↑	
30.0	0.8	→ ⇧	At crossroads (straight on if not going to island and continue from 1.4km mark, Stage 5)
31.4	1.4	✿	Ticket office
31.5	0.1		Roonagh Quay

Stage 2 Tour of Clare Island			
0.0			Clare Island, by gates of Granuaile's Castle, head towards village
0.2	0.2	→	Follow road along back of beach
0.3	0.1	▲ →	Head right at camping area
0.4	0.1	♦ WC	Community centre on left serves food 9am–9pm and has toilets
2.3	1.9	→	At T-junction
4.3	2.0	↑	'Lighthouse'
6.2	1.9	↑↓	Arrive lighthouse
8.1	1.9	↗	'Ballytoughey Bay'
11.1	3.0	✿	Clare Abbey
11.2	0.1	♦	Small shop and PO
11.3	0.1	→	'Napoleonic tower'
14.4	3.1	↗	At fork
15.3	0.9	↑↓	At 'Site 19' sign
19.1	3.8	⇦	Road leads to rocky shore 0.5km return
19.3	0.2		Road from Clare Abbey joins from left
21.7	2.4	↑	Unsigned
21.9	0.2		Arrive back at Granuaile's Castle

Stage 3 Roonah Quay to Tully			
0.0			From the ticket office head inland
1.4	1.4	→	At crossroads
1.8	0.4	←	Unsigned
2.9	1.1	←	At T-junction
3.0	0.1	→	At T-junction
4.4	1.4	←	At T-junction
5.0	0.6	→	At crossroads
6.1	1.1	←	At crossroads
11.1	5.0	→	'R335 Leenaun 25'
12.7	1.6	✿	National School – 1945
18.0	5.3	✿	Doo Lough Memorial
21.7	3.7	⇦	Turn to Drummin
23.1	1.4	✿	Delphi Lodge (private, behind trees)
24.3	1.2	▲	Delphi Mountain Resort
27.0	2.7	✿	Views across water as road skirts Killary Harbour
32.2	5.2	✿	Gate to Aasleagh Falls – few hundred metres to falls
32.8	0.6	→	'N59 Clifden'
33.5	0.7	✿	Coyne's 'First Pub in Connemara'

Stage 3 Roonah Quay to Tully			
36.1	2.6	♦	Leenaun (Leenane) has shops – note road layout may change, follow N59 Clifden
38.9	2.8	✿	Quay for Killary Cruises
41.5	2.6	▲ ⇨	To Sleepzone Connemara hostel (1km)
41.6	0.1	▲	K2 Killary Adventure Centre
42.7	1.1	△ (77)	Surrounded by mountains
43.4	0.7	→	'Tully Cross'
48.2	4.8	▲ ⇨	To Harbour House Hostel at Rosroe Pier
51.1	2.9	⇨	Side-trip to nice beach (2km return), signed Scuba Dive West
51.8	0.7	♦	Shops
52.6	0.8	▲	Connemara Caravan and Camping Park
57.8	5.2	→	'Tully' – need to give way at second part of junction
58.9	1.1	♦	Service station at Tully
59.1	0.2		End at Teach Ceoil ('house of music'), Renvyle – has picnic tables

Stage 4 Tully to Clifden			
0.0			From main road in front of Teach Ceoil – head uphill
0.9	0.9	▲	Renvyle Beach Caravan and Camping Park
1.3	0.4	⇨	Beach access
1.7	0.4	↖	At Renvyle House Hotel
4.1	2.4	←	Renvyle Casle (tower house) in front
4.3	0.2	←	'Connemara loop'
7.6	3.3	→	At T-junction
9.8	2.2	↑	Continue on road, right leads to Ballynakill quay
11.1	1.3	→	At T-junction
13.8	2.7	→ ⇦ ▲ ⇧	'N59 Clifden', at Letterfrack crossroads. Side-trip to Kylemore Abbey (9km return). Old Monastery Hostel is 200m through crossroads
		♦ ATM	Fresh food shop
14.1	0.3	⇦	Connemara National Park visitor centre
17.8	3.7	♦	Small shop in service station
18.2	0.4	→	'Cleggan' (second of two turns close together)

Stage 4 Tully to Clifden			
20.4	2.2	→	At T-junction
20.8	0.4	↖	Road bears left
23.4	2.6	⇨	Road leads to idyllic beach (3km return)
26.1	2.7	→	'Cleggan'
26.7	0.6	♦ ⇨	Shop in Cleggan. Side trip to Cleggan pier for Inishboffin ferry
27.4	0.7	⇨	Beach access
29.3	1.9	⇦	Shortcut – saves about 8km
30.3	1.0	→	Unsigned
32.3	2.0	⇨	Beach access
33.8	1.5	← ⇨	At T-junction (right goes to Aughrus Head, which you can walk to)
34.3	0.5	→	At T-junction
36.4	2.1	♦	Small shop and bar
36.5	0.1	♦	Service station and shop – short-cut rejoins from left
37.0	0.5	↗	Road bears right
37.7	0.7	⇨	Side trip to Omey Island and beach (1km return to beach)
39.3	1.6	▲	Clifden Ecobeach Caravan and Camping Park
45.6	6.0	→	'N59 Clifden'

Stage 4 Tully to Clifden			
47.4	1.8	⇦ ▲	Clifden Camping and Caravan Park
49.1	1.7	→	At T-junction
49.2	0.1	←	Follow one-way
49.4	0.2	→	'Sky Road'
49.7	0.3		Arrive Clifden central square

Stage 5 Tour of Inishbofin			
0.0			Landward end of Inishbofin quay facing inland, head right
0.3	0.3	↖	Bear left at fork
1.0	0.7	⇦ ▲	Hostel and Dolphin Hotel 100m
2.1	1.1	⇨	To beautiful sandy beach – about 400m
2.4	0.3	←	At T-junction
2.8	0.4	→	Turn onto track at rear of beach
3.3	0.5	←	At end of beach turn onto road up hill
3.5	0.2	→	Through gate onto grass track
4.6	1.1	↑↓	Small bridge here is about as far as you can go
5.7	1.1	→	Back at gate turn right
6.6	0.9	→	'To pier'
7.2	0.6	⇦	Takes you back to hostel

Stage 5 Tour of Inishbofin			
7.7	0.5	⇦	Takes you back to quay
7.9	0.2	↗	'Doonmore Hotel'
9.1	1.2	→	'Doonmore Hotel'
9.5	0.4	▲	Doonmore Hotel
9.6	0.1	→	Unsigned
10.4	0.8	✪	Fine shingle spit
10.9	0.5	↑	Through gate
12.0	1.1	↑↓	Track peters out near small cove
15.0	3.0	↑	At Emerald Cottage B&B
15.6	0.6	⇦ ♦	Road to community centre. Shop on corner.
15.7	0.1		Back at pier

Stage 6 Clifden to Kilkieran			
0.0			Clifden, from the bike racks outside Foyles Hotel head down Main Street (one-way)
0.1	0.1	→	One-way
0.3	0.2	↑	'Roundstone'
0.5	0.2	→	'Roundstone'
3.5	3.0	← ⇧	Just before a bridge – easy to miss, straight on for Alcock and Brown memorial and Marconi station
13.3	9.8	←	'Cashel'

Stage 6 Clifden to Kilkieran			
15.0	1.7	→ ⇧	'Cashel', straight on for Ballynahinch Castle 8km return
23.0	8.0	→	'Glinsk'
23.6	0.6	⇦	Alternative route/shortcut to Kilkieran Bay (c10km)
30.9	7.3	⇨	Alternative by coast road
36.3	5.4	♦ ⇨	Turn right for shop at Carna (1.2km
36.7	0.4	♦ ATM	Service station has shop
39.1	2.4	⇨	To beach 600m
39.6	0.5	⇨	To pier
40.5	0.9	♦	Shop
45.0	4.5		Arrive Kilkieran 'Quikpick' shop

Stage 7 Kilkieran to Galway			
0.0			Kilkieran 'Quikpick' shop
1.0	1.0	♦	Shop
4.2	3.2	▲	Hillside House B&B
9.6	5.4		Short-cut from 23.6km on Stage 6 arrives via road on left
12.4	2.8	⇨	Side-trip to Pearse's Cottage 0.5km return

Stage 7 Kilkieran to Galway			
12.9	0.5	✿	At Glenoch Village
17.5	4.6	→	'Casla'
29.1	11.6	←⇨♦ ATM	'Gallimh'.400m to shops at Casla.
30.8	1.7	⇨	Turn here for Aran ferries from Rossaveel (c2km)
35.4	4.6	♦	Small shop
45.1	9.7	♦	Shop
49.3	4.2	WC	At Spiddal
49.4	0.1	♦	Shop at service station
49.8	0.4	✿	Beach, Burren views
54.9	5.1	✿	Beach
55.8	0.9	♦	Medium-sized shop at service station
59.6	2.8	♦	Barna has range of shops
63.2	3.6	→	'Salthill'
63.6	0.4	▲	Bayview Holiday Park
		▲	Salthill Caravan Park
63.7	0.1	▲	O'Hallorans Caravan Park
63.9	0.2	♦	Shop in service station
64.9	1.0	✿ WC	Beach – can be busy!
65.6	0.7	○↗	'R336 via Claddagh'
66.3	0.7	→	'Grattan Road'

Stage 7 Kilkieran to Galway			
68.0	1.7	→	Turn right and cross bridge into Galway city
68.1	0.1		Pull over safely to pedestrian area

Stage 8 Galway to Cong			
0.0			Galway, Eyre Square, by Liam O Maoiliosa statue in northern corner, head uphill, away from square
1.1	1.1	○↑	'Sligo, Roscommon'
1.6	0.5	↑	At traffic lights
2.7	1.1	○←	'(N48) Castlebar' – cycle lane
4.6	1.9	○↑	'Menlo' – third exit
5.0	0.4	✿	An Ghaeltacht
5.3	0.3	→	At T-junction
7.4	2.1	←	'Monlach'
		→	After about 40m
7.9	0.5	→	At T-junction
8.8	0.8	✿	Lough Corrib appears to left
9.5	0.7	✿	Access to lake
10.3	0.8	←	Unsigned
11.3	1.0	←	At T-junction
12.6	1.3	←	On to N84 – care in traffic
12.7	0.1	♦	Shop

Stage 8 Galway to Cong			
19.6	6.9	♦ ATM	Service station, shop, ATM at Clonboo
19.8	0.2	←♦	Just past a bigger shop
20.2	0.4	←	T-junction
20.5	0.3	→	'Clonboo Riding School'
22.6	2.1	↖	Road veers left
23.7	1.1	→	'Annaghdown'
24.6	0.9	←	'Annaghdown Pier'
25.1	0.5	⇦	Annaghdown Pier (also Annaghdown Priory) (1km return)
		✪	Annaghdown Cathedral
30.3	5.2	→	On to N84
30.5	0.2	←	'Caherlistrane'
32.3	1.8	♦	Small shop Bunatober
32.7	0.4	←	At T-junction
39.9	7.2	←	At crossroads
41.7	1.8	←	'N84' in Headford
		♦ ATM	
42.1	0.4	♦ ↑	'Ross Errilly Friary', shop on corner
43.3	1.2	⇨	Ross Errilly Friary 1.5km return
45.2	1.9	→	'Ballycurrin Lighthouse' (first turn past ruined church)

Stage 8 Galway to Cong			
46.9	1.7	↑	At crossroads
47.2	0.3	✪	Cross Black River
52.5	5.3	↑	At crossroads
55.1	2.6	←	'R334 Ballinrobe'
57.5	2.4	♦	Cross has supermarket
		←	'R346 Cong'
61.1	3.6	⇦ ▲	Cong hostel, campsite and caravan park (400m)
61.5	0.4	← ⇧	Gates of Ashford Castle, alternative route to Cong straight on
62.8	1.3	→	Turn right before bridge to castle
62.9	0.1	→	After 20m
63.5	0.6	✪	Pass Cong Abbey
63.6	0.1		Arrive – tourist information across road

Stage 9 Cong to Westport			
0.0			Cong visitor information centre, head downhill (one-way)
0.1	0.1	WC	
0.3	0.2	←♦ ATM	'An Fhar', shop opposite
0.4	0.1	→	After river bridge
0.9	0.5	←	Just past Dry Canal bridge
4.6	3.7	→	At T-junction

Stage 9 Cong to Westport

5.0	0.4	←	'Caherrobert' on wall
6.6	1.6	→	At T-junction
7.2	0.6	⇦	Inishmaine Abbey (5km return, track rough near end). Turn right through gate at 9.4km then right again
11.6	4.4	←	'R334 Ballinrobe'
12.0	0.4	←⇨♦ ATM	'Castlebar/ Westport'. Turn right then left at bottom of Ballinrobe market place for supermarket and ATM
		♦ ATM	In service station
12.5	0.5	↑	'Claremorris Knock', at crossroads
12.6	0.1	↰	'Connaught Signs'
12.8	0.2	✪	Ballinrobe Abbey
15.0	2.2	←	Unsigned road
15.4	0.4	→	At T-junction
18.2	2.8	←	'Brownstown'
21.0	2.8	←	At T-junction
24.6	3.6	←	'Burriscarra Abbey'
25.4	0.8	✪ WC	Car park for Moore Hall (about 1km return walk)

Stage 9 Cong to Westport

26.0	0.6	→	'Burriscarra Abbey'
28.8	2.8	✪	Burriscarra Abbey and Church
29.3	0.5	←	'Castlebar'
30.8	1.5	←	Unsigned road opposite iron gates
33.6	2.8	↑	Care – give way to right
33.8	0.2	✪ WC	Ballintubber Abbey
35.3	1.5	↑ ATM	'Killavalley' (cross N84), shop across road
38.5	3.2	→	Information point about mill on corner
42.0	3.5	←	At T-junction
43.5	1.5	→	'Westport'
51.9	8.4	✪	Westport railway station
52.1	0.2	♦	Tesco supermarket
52.5	0.4	↑ ○	Unsigned
52.9	0.4	↗	Follow one-way system at clocktower
53.0	0.1		Arrive Westport, Glendenning Monument. Turn right for tourist information and hostel

ROUTE 4 THE ARAN ISLANDS AND THE BURREN

The Cliffs of Mohr are one of Ireland's leading tourist attractions (Stage 5)

Start	Galway
Finish	Limerick
Distance	381.2km
Ascent	4053m

This tour takes you from the granite lands around Galway, through the limestone karst of the Aran Islands and the Burren, and on to the sandstone plains of County Clare, before a sweep up the Shannon estuary to Limerick.

The Wild Atlantic Way skips the Aran Islands (it is a driving route and there are no car ferries) but they are a popular cycling destination. There are three islands – Inishmore to the west, Inishmaan in the middle and Inisheer towards the Clare coast. The big island, Inishmore, often just called Aran, is the best set up for visitors, with regular ferries and plenty of accommodation. The smaller islands are, however, exceptionally beautiful.

The tour outlined here stays two nights on Inishmore and one on Inisheer before heading to Doolin on the Clare coast to rejoin the Wild Atlantic Way.

The cultural importance of this corner of County Clare belies the outwardly barren landscape. The ring-fort at Cahermacnaghten (Stage 4) was a base for the O'Davorens, a clan of hereditary Irish law scholars, or Brehons, who ran an important law school nearby well into the 17th century.

Doolin is both a hotspot for traditional music and a good base for exploring the Burren and the nearby Cliffs of Mohr. The wildflower-encrusted limestone pavements of the Burren are one of the great landscapes of Europe, and the dark cliffs of the Clare coast are one of Ireland's top tourist draws.

Further on, the north shore of the Shannon estuary is off the main tourist routes and has a pleasant, backcountry feel and it is an attractive run to Limerick via the historic town of Ennis.

BETTER BY BIKE

Route 4 includes a tour of the Aran Islands and the Burren. The islands are not on the Wild Atlantic Way driving route. Neither is the inland part of the Burren. It does seem a shame, however, to come this far and not work two of Ireland's great cycling experiences somehow into your itinerary.

Route summary table

Stage		Distance	Ascent	Accommodation available	Places with shops/other facilities en route
1	Galway to Inishmore	39.0km	284m		Spiddal
2	Tour of Inishmore	37.6km	464m	Various sites on the island	Dun Aengus
3	Tour of Inisheer	10.4km	167m	Doolin	
4	Round the Burren	63.7km	774m	Kilfernora, Lisdoonvarna	Ballyvaughan
5	Doolin to Kilrush	130.6km	1317m	Lahinch, Kilkee, Kilrush, Doonabeg, Doonaha, Querrin	Quilty, Kilkee
6	Kilrush to Ennis	60.1km	697m	Corofin (15km beyond Ennis)	Killadysert, Ballynacally
7	Ennis to Limerick	39.8km	350m		Quin, Sixmilebridge
7A	WAW Link from Limerick to Tarbert	(59.4km)	(530m)	Curraghchase	Kildimo, Askeaton
Total		**381.2km**	**4053m**		

Route 4: The Aran Islands and the Burren

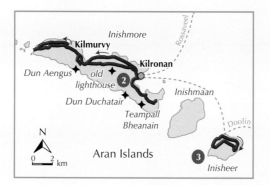

THE BURREN

The shining white slopes of the Burren (Stage 4) gleaming against the waters of Galway Bay are one of the great views of Ireland. The name Burren comes from the Irish *Boireann* – a rocky place. But a close inspection shows this boulder-strewn landscape is far from barren. Stone dominates, but between the slabs of limestone pavement the fissures are a haven for wildflowers and

grasses. For geologists this is one of the finest glacio-karst landscapes in the world. The retreat of the glaciers some 10,000 years ago left a limestone plateau with little or no soil cover. Then rainfall got to work opening small fissures and weaknesses in the rock to produce the limestone pavement pattern seen across the Burren and the neighbouring Aran Islands.

IRISH TRADITIONAL MUSIC

Irish music continues to flourish in the shadow of the Burren. The village of Doolin (Stage 4) has blossomed as a haven of traditional Irish music since the 1960s, when recordings and broadcasts brought a strong local tradition to wider attention. Local pubs host a nightly mixture of spontaneous and planned sessions that manage to maintain a traditional feel despite the growing cascade of visitors.

If you choose to stick to the Wild Atlantic Way route all the way from Galway to the Shannon, you can take the N6 and N67 to Ballyvaughan and then pick up Stage 4 in reverse, afterwards following the rest of the route described here from Doolin.

GETTING TO THE START

By rail/bus
There are seven rail services a day to and from Dublin Heuston and the journey from there to Galway takes under three hours.

WHEN TO GO

The wildflowers of the Burren are impressive through spring and summer. Galway itself is very busy for the two weeks of the Galway Arts Festival from mid-July and the following week of the Galway Races.

ACCOMMODATION

Limerick itself is the problem area for budget accommodation on this route and this might be another factor pushing you towards the Shannon ferry to Tarbert and the next route.

There are plenty of camping/hostel options around Doolin, but only two camp sites (Green Acres and Pure Camping, both near Doonaha) between Loop Head and Limerick.

MAPS

The Ordnance Survey Ireland West sheet covers the route at 1:250,000. At 1:50,000 the following Discovery series sheets are required: 45 Galway, 51 Clare Galway (covers Aran Islands), 57 Clare, 63 Clare Kerry, 64 Clare Kerry Limerick, 65 Clare Limerick Tipperary and 58 Clare Limerick Tipperary. If heading south via the Shannon ferry, sheets 58 and 65 are not required. The best maps of the Burren and the Aran Islands are the hand-drawn Tim Robinson folding landscapes series – although they can be hard to find. They have more detail than the 1:50,000 maps, and should be considered if otherwise relying on the 1:250,000 maps. The Aran map is at 1:28160 scale and the Burren at 1:31680 scale.

Author enjoying Inishmore's quiet roads (Stage 2) (photo by Charlotte Cooper)

OPTIONS

If skipping the Aran islands, the Wild Atlantic Way route from Galway to Ballyvaughan is a scenic ride (46km), although it can be busy as far as Kilcolgan. From Ballyvaughan there is the choice of climbing over the Burren (second part of Stage 4) or continuing along the coast (first part of Stage 4 in reverse) where a further 32km of riding will take you to Doolin.

If heading further south into Kerry, taking the official Wild Atlantic Way route via the Shannon ferry from Killimer (Stage 6), 9km east of Kilrush, allows you to join the next route at Tarbert (the start of Route 5, Stage 1) saving a whopping 150km or more of cycling via Ennis and Limerick.

ONWARDS

Route 5 connects at Tarbert. Limerick has rail services to Dublin and Galway.

STAGE 1
Galway to Inishmore

Start	Galway
Distance	39km
Ascent	284m
Terrain	Flat, busy road
Summit	30m at 29km

The coast between **Galway** and the **Rossaveel** ferry port is pretty, with sandy beaches and views across Galway Bay to the Burren and the Aran Islands. **Spiddal** was once a refined seaside resort where the Connemara gentry would escape from the summer heat. At the start of the route keep an eye out for the Claddagh Piscatory School, which is a reminder that the west bank of the River Corrib was once home to a fishing village distinct from the city across the river. The school was established by Dominican brothers to educate the children of fishermen.

The ferry lands at the Kilronan quay on **Inishmore**. The next stage starts from the Ridgeway and Blyth commemoration by the quay, opposite the tourist information centre.

On the road
Try and book your ferries before you travel to the islands and check for the latest on taking cycles. At the time of writing cycles must be booked on the Rossaveel to Inishmore services. The Doolin ferries are quite small boats and are the most likely to be cancelled due to weather. Inishmaan has fewer ferries and some careful juggling of the schedules is required if you want to extend your tour to get there.

You can buy tickets for Rossaveel to Inishmore services at the Galway offices of Aran Island Ferries (091 568903, www.aranislandferries.com) in the city centre on Forester Street. You can also buy tickets at Rossaveel although the risk is that bike places may have been booked.

To follow the suggested itinerary in this book, take an early afternoon ferry from Rossaveel to Inishmore, stay two nights, then take the late morning Doolin Ferries (065 7074 455, www.doolinferries.com) service, which stops at Inisheer, stay a night and pick up the midday ferry to Doolin. Check the ferry timetables for other inter-island services.

Bike hire rush hour on Inishmore

Kilronan on Inishmore has an excellent shop with plenty of fresh food and an ATM, so there is no need to haul a huge amount on the road.

This stage is Route 3, Stage 9 in reverse as far as the turn at 33.3km. The R336 can be fast and busy so wear bright colours and take care.

Accommodation

To the south west of Galway there are three campsites close together at Salthill (63km). These are Bayview Caravan & Camping Park (091 523316, www.bayviewcaravanpark.com), O'Halloran's Caravan & Camping Park (086 8747422, www.ohalloranscaravanpark.com) and Salthill Caravan Park (091 523972, www.salthillcaravanpark.com). Galway itself has a youth hostel (091 566999, www.anoige.ie) close to the town centre, as well as a choice of independents. The city has a broad range of hotels including some of the major chains. Alongside the large number of guesthouses and B&Bs, you should be able to find something to suit your budget. Just be wary of the three-week period from mid-July when the town fills up for the Galway Arts Festival followed by the Galway Races.

Inishmore has a selection of independent hostels. The biggest is the lively Kilronan Hostel in the heart of the village (099 61255, www.kilronanhostel.com). The camping options include a small site to the west of Kilronan, which has no showers but it is in a quiet spot looking across Galway Bay. Alternatively there is Aran Islands Camping & Glamping (086 1895823, www.irelandglamping.ie) at Frenchman's Beach about half a kilometre along the coast north of the harbour.

Turn right at the foot of the pier. Inishmore has a modern hotel, the Aran Islands Hotel (099 61104, www.aranislandshotel.com), close to Kilronan. There is also a good selection of B&Bs, again mainly clustered around Kilronan, where the ferries come in.

STAGE 2
Tour of Inishmore

Start	Inishmore
Distance	37.6km
Ascent	464m
Terrain	A few very short steep sections
Summit	80m at 25km

The **geological structure** of the three main Aran Islands is the same. They are the remnants of a limestone escarpment, with the strata dipping gently to the southwest. The southwestern shore is generally the steep, cliff-bound one, while the northeast shore is gentler. The layers of limestone are interleaved

Dun Aengus fort sits in a dramatic coastal spot

with narrow bands of clays and shales, and as a result the islands have weathered into a series of terraces separated by short sharp rises.

Writer **JM Synge**'s one-act Aran play 'Riders to the Sea' is perhaps his best work, while 'The Aran Islands' (1907) portrays an island life very different to that seen today.

A good general plan for Inishmore is to head out to the west on the coast road and come back on the more exposed road along the spine of the island. The highlight of the day is the Bronze Age ring fort of **Dun Aengus**. The vertiginous cliff-top location is spectacular and there are views down the island. One of the most tranquil spots on the islands is the diminutive **Teampall Bheanain**. Set on a bare limestone pavement high above Killeany, it is particularly beautiful around sunset (turn at 30.5km). **Dun Duchatair** (or the Black Fort) doesn't have the intriguing geometry of Dun Aengus, and the cliffs aren't quite so high, but the promontory location, massively undercut shoreline and the lack of visitors make it the equal of its more famous sibling (turn at 29.2km).

Transatlantic rowers John Ridgway and Chay Blyth landed on Inishmore on 3 September 1966 after 91 days at sea. They accepted help from the Aran lifeboat, which was called out when the emptying of a toilet bucket was mistaken for emergency bailing.

The very steep climb to the **old lighthouse** and nearby Dun Eochla (turn at 25.2km) leads to the island's highest point. The ride out to the western end of the island takes you to an exposed storm beach, while at the eastern point, grey water surges down the channel separating Inishmore and Inishmaan. **Kilmurvy** is the most popular choice for a swimming beach.

On the road
There are a few spots to get snacks around the island, mostly around Dun Aengus, but the best option is to stock up at the Kilronan supermarket.

Accommodation
Listed in Stage 1.

Options
If you need to arrange onward ferry connections or bookings on the other islands the tourist office is by the quay at Kilronan (099 61263).

STAGE 3
Tour of Inisheer

Start	Inisheer
Distance	10.4km
Ascent	167m
Terrain	Gentle and coastal
Summit	50m at 5km

At under 3km² and with fewer than 250 inhabitants, Inisheer is tiny. There are a few concessions to tourism – a hostel, campsite, bike rental and the odd pony trap for hire – but this is far removed from the tourist-processing facilities of Inishmore.

Inisheer, and the Plassy Wreck, shot to fame by featuring as Craggy Island in the opening sequence of the comedy TV show **Father Ted**.

On 8 March 1960, while sailing through Galway Bay carrying a cargo of whiskey, stained glass and yarn, the **MV Plassy** was caught in a severe storm. She ran onto Finnis Rock. A group of islanders managed to rescue the entire crew of 11 before she was caught in another storm and blown ashore.

This route takes you to the Plassy Wreck on the rocky pavement of the east shore and out to the eerie west shore. Along the way there is a ride along a grassy lane, a castle, and a fine beach near the pier.

On the road
There is a shop on the island. From the pier turn left, then when you see the track to the beach on your left, follow a road up the hill to your right for about 200m. There are three pubs that serve food, and a café too.

Accommodation
The campsite (099 75008) behind the beach (600m) has basic facilities, but the shower/toilet block was locked quite early when we stayed. The hostel (Bru Radharc Na Mara, 099 75024, www.bruhostelaran.com) is close to the pier – just turn right. The Hotel Inis Oirr (099 75020, www.hotelinisoirr.com) is the island's only hotel. For other accommodation, see the island cooperative website (www.discoverinisoirr.com).

The iconic Plassy Wreck

Back on the mainland, Doolin supports a number of independent hostels including the Aille River Hostel, where you can also camp (065 7074260, www.ailleriverhosteldoolin.ie) and Doolin Hostel (065 7074421, www.doolinhostel.ie). The Hotel Doolin (065 7074111, www.hoteldoolin.ie) is a modern hotel right in the heart of the village. There are also a number of B&Bs nearby. But be wary of festival weekends when the village fills up, particularly the Folk Festival in mid-June. See www.doolin.ie/events for a list of events.

For campers there is a large site, Nagles Camping & Caravan Park (065 7074458, www.doolincamping.com) close to the ferry pier or O'Connor's Riverside Camping & Caravan Park (085 2819888, www.campingdoolin.com) across the road from the Aille River Hostel.

Connections

Confirm your departure time with the boat's crew when you arrive. Sailings are subject to change. The ferry from Inisheer to the Clare coast lands at Doolin pier, the start of the next stage.

STAGE 4
Round the Burren

Start	Doolin Pier
Distance	63.7km
Ascent	774m
Terrain	Hilly
Summit	190m at 49km

The limestone slab of the Burren is similar geologically to the Aran Islands, but the extra altitude adds a dramatic perspective. There are dozens of different ways through the Burren, and many more on a mountain bike following the traditional 'green roads'. But it is the climb from the small town of **Ballyvaughan** that makes the route described here the pick of the bunch. Before reaching Ballyvaughan, however, there is some coastal scenery to enjoy along the Wild Atlantic Way. Ballinalacken Castle (6.8km) guards the southern approaches to the Burren. The bare escarpments stack up to the north, but before riding away from the coast, it is worth taking a short walk either along one of the pavements, or straight up **Black Head** from behind the lighthouse.

Back on the road, Ballyvaughan's woodlands and lush coastal vegetation feel removed from the Burren itself, but this creates a wonderful change in the landscape climbing out of the town. The trees and hedges slowly fade away, then the soil and pasture become thinner, and within a few kilometres you are in a land of

BREHON LAW

Before the imposition of English rule, Ireland had an indigenous system of law dating from Celtic times. The law was administrated by Brehons, and is hence known as Brehon Law. The Brehons' task was to preserve and interpret the laws that had been handed down through the generations and were only written down for the first time in the seventh century. English common law slowly encroached on Brehon Law from the Norman invasion of 1169. Away from the areas of strongest English influence Irish law survived well into the 17th century. Cahermacnaghten was the core of the estate of the Uí Dhabhoireann (O'Davoren) hereditary legal family from about 1300 to 1700, and the law school here was probably at its peak in the mid-16th century.

wind and rock. Adding prehistoric interest to this landscape is the **Poulnabrone Dolmen** – a Neolithic portal tomb dating from about 4200BC to 2900BC. Nearby Caherconnell stone ring fort is similar to those on the Aran Islands. In the same area is **Cahermacnaghten** (turn at 48.1km).

The way back to Doolin follows the southern edge of the Burren through **Lisdoonvarna**, site of a famous wedding fair in September.

> Doolin's development as a hot spot for **Irish music** began in the 1960s, pretty much on the back of flute player and tin whistler extraordinaire the late Micho Russell.

On the road
Ballyvaughan has the best choice of food for lunch, either to eat there or take into the high Burren. There is a farmers' market at the village hall on Saturday mornings from May to October. There are no ATMs in this area. The nearest to Doolin is at the Cliffs of Mohr visitor centre, 6km into Stage 5.

Accommodation
For accommodation in Doolin, see Stage 3. Kilfenora has a hostel a few kilometres off-route – Kilfenora Hostel (065 7088908, www.kilfenorahostel.com). If you are staying somewhere along the route, Lisdoonvarna has the best choice of accommodation with a handful of hotels and a decent number of B&Bs as well as an An Óige hostel – the Burren Hostel (01 8304555 for bookings, www.anoige.ie).

Limestone dominates the Burren's landscape

STAGE 5

Doolin to Kilrush

Start	Doolin
Distance	130.6km
Ascent	1317m
Terrain	A few coastal hills
Summit	180m at 6km

This is a monster stage if you want to get all the way to Loop Head at the mouth of the Shannon but there are shortcuts. The cliff scenery to the west of Kilkee is very fine, but realistically it is better to either split this stage in two, or skip the trip out to the head.

The first point of interest of the day is the **Cliffs of Mohr**. At 200m high and 8km long this is one of the leading attractions of the Wild Atlantic Way. A low coast of fine beaches and sand dunes then follows to the resort town of **Kilkee**.

The **Cliffs of Mohr** are one of the great coastal sights in Ireland. The underground visitor centre here cost €31.5 million to build.

Lahinch is one of the prettiest spots on the Clare coast

West of here the cliff scenery returns. **Loop Head** itself an be a little disappointing, especially if you are tired. But the views across the mouth of the Shannon to the Kerry coast are filled with the promise of mountains unclimbed.

Kilrush is a heritage estate town and port that was developed extensively in the 18th century by the Vandeleur family. Boat trips to the early Christian sites on **Scattery Island** depart from here.

On the road
Any of the small towns along this stage are pleasant places for a break. Quilty (35km) has a fine open aspect and benches near the shore. The resort town of Kilkee (60km) has the pick of the beaches.

Accommodation
There are hostels at Lahinch – Lahinch Surf Hostel (065 7081040, www. lahinchhostel.ie), Kilkee – Kilkee Hostel (085 8293040) and Kilrush – Katie O'Connor's Hostel (065 9051133, www.katieshostel.com). Kilrush and Kilkee also have the pick of hotel and B&B accommodation, including the Kilkee Stella Maris Hotel (065 9056455, www.stellamarishotel.com) and the Crotty's Pub (065 9052470, www.crottyspubkilrush.com) in Kilrush market square.

For camping in Lahinch there is Ocean View Park (065 7081626) some 400m south of town on the N67. Doonbeg has Strand Camping (065 9055345, www. strandcampingdoonbeg.com), Doonaha has Green Acres (065 9057011, www. greenacrescamping.ie) and, just a few kms further on, Querrin has Pure Camping (065 9057953, www.purecamping.ie) both overlooking the Shannon.

Options
There are several shortcuts to Kilrush. Continuing straight on at 60.3km in Kilkee and following the N67 to Kilrush gives a total distance of approximately 73km. A quieter option is to turn at 49.2km at Doonbeg. From here it is 12km to Kilrush, giving a total distance from Doolin to Kilrush of 61km.

STAGE 6
Kilrush to Ennis

Start	Kilrush
Distance	60.1km
Ascent	697m
Terrain	Short sharp hills
Summit	60m at 30km

The strip of land along the Shannon between **Kilrush** and Ennis features picturesque rolling farmland, with hedge-lined hay meadows and small pockets of woodland.

There is a statue of the Colleen Bawn at **Killimer**.

The Colleen Bawn is a 19th century melodrama by Dion Boucicault based on the shocking murder of a beautiful Irish farmer's daughter. Ellen Hanley was shot and her body was dumped in the Shannon by her husband John Scanlan.

The road here alternates between high sections with fine views over the shining Shannon, and low crossings of inlets alongside small fishing harbours. The roads and small towns are peaceful and this is an enjoyable day's cycling.

Ennis is a historic market town that grew up around the site of a Franciscan friary.

On the road
Killadysert and Ballynacally have shops and are pleasant places to take a break.

Statue to 'The Colleen Bawn' at Killimer

Accommodation
Ennis now has the Rowan Tree Hostel (065 6868687, www.rowantreehostel.ie) in the centre of town just across the river from the Ennis Friary via the Abbey Street Bridge. The town has a number of good quality town-centre hotels – although they do tend to be at the upper-end of the price scale – and a selection of B&Bs. The closest camping is 15km (northwards), at the Corofin Camping & Hostel (065 6837683, www.corofincamping.com).

Options
The main choice on this stage, if heading further on into Kerry on the Wild Atlantic Way, is whether to take the ferry across the Shannon to Tarbert (9km) to cut out about 150km of cycling via Limerick. This is the official Wild Atlantic Way Route. Shannon Ferry (065 9053124, www.shannonferries.com) operates the service from Killimer (on the north bank), every hour, on the hour, and in the reverse direction every hour, on the half hour. The first service is at 7am, 9am on Sundays, and the last one at 9.30pm in summer and 7.30pm in winter. From May to September the service is upgraded to half hourly. The fare is €5 one way. Alternatively the next stage is short and you may choose to push on to Limerick for a total combined distance of 100km.

STAGE 7
Ennis to Limerick

Start	Ennis
Distance	39.8km
Ascent	350m
Terrain	A few gentle hills
Summit	50m at 19km

The run into Limerick from Ennis is short and sweet, with no major climbs and sur-prisingly little traffic. To the east of Ennis, at **Quin**, is the 15th-century Franciscan foundation of Quin Abbey.

The countryside is pleasant and, judging by the number of castles, was at one time of strategic importance. Some of the fortifications, such as **Knappogue**, have been developed, while others lie as rather romantic roadside ruins.

King John's Castle in Limerick is one of Europe's best-preserved Norman fortifications

The approach to **Limerick** from the west continues through woods and farms until 4 to 5km from the heart of the city.

Limerick was founded by the Vikings at the lowest crossing point of the Shannon. The Normans built a walled town and castle here that remains largely intact.

On the road
On this short stage, the best places to stop are at Quin and Sixmilebridge, both of which have shops. There is an ATM on the way into Limerick, which saves you hunting around the town centre.

Accommodation
Courtbrack Accommodation (061 302500) is student accommodation, available on a hostel basis from late May to mid-August, about 2km south of the city centre. If you are pushing on southwards into Kerry, the next hostel is the Ferry House Hostel (068 36555) 60km away at Tarbert. For camping, Curraghchase Caravan and Camp Site (061 396349, www.curraghchase.info) is 20km away along the next stage. Limerick as a dozen or so city-centre hotels, so you should be able to find something to suit.

STAGE 7A
WAW link from Limerick to Tarbert

Start	Limerick
Distance	59.4km
Ascent	530m
Terrain	Main roads, mostly flat
Summit	50m at 41km

This stage takes you from **Limerick** to rejoin the Wild Atlantic Way at Tarbert and link with Route 5.

As you cycle west, the castellated Gothic towers of Dromore Castle are an impressive sight from the road. A little further on you pass **Curraghchase Forest Park** which hides the shell of a fine neoclassical house.

For a brief few years Foynes was the most important commercial **airport** in the world. The first direct commercial transatlantic passenger flight landed on the Shannon here in July 1939. During the Second World War, Ireland's neutrality meant the airlines kept operating here. The last flight was in 1945. The Foynes

The Foynes flying boat museum

Flying Boat & Maritime Museum, open daily March to November, 9.30am–6pm (5pm from October), last admission one hour before closing (069 65416, www.flyingboatmuseum.com) remembers this period.

The east-facing **escarpment** at Foynes marks the end of the Carboniferous Limestone of the central lowlands and the start of the hillier Namurian Sandstones.

Tarbert is a small, quiet town, best known as the jumping-off point for the Shannon ferry. There are a couple of things to see around town, including the 19th-century gaol, the Tarbert Bridewell (068 36500, www.tarbertbridewell.com).

On the road
This stage has long sections on the N29 that can't be avoided. The road is mostly wide, with broad hard shoulders.

Get any bike-related or camping supplies in Limerick before you leave. The local shops at 4.7km are a good place to re-supply with food. Kildimo also has a shop and ATM. Medieval Askeaton village has shops and is interesting to look around. At the end of the day, Tarbert has shops and an ATM.

Accommodation
Tarbert has the Ferry House Hostel (068 36555). There are a couple of hotel and B&B options in the area, including the centrally-located Keldun House B&B (068 36405, www.keldunhouse.com). There is camping at Curraghchase Caravan and Camp Site (at 20km, 061 396349, www.curraghchase.info), open from mid-March to the end of October.

Options
Route 5 starts where the road from the Tarbert ferry meets the N69 (about 2.5km from the ferry). If you're pushing on south, pick up the route card for Route 5 at the beginning.

ROUTE 4 ROUTE CARDS

Stage 1 Galway to Inishmore			
0.0			Galway, west end of Wolfe Tone Bridge, join traffic when safe!
0.1	0.1	←	'Salthill via coast road'
0.2	0.1	✪	Claddagh Piscatory School
1.7	1.5	←	At T-junction, can join shared cycleway here but road is easier
2.2	0.5	✪	National Aquarium
2.4	0.2	← ○	'R336 an Spiddal'
3.2	0.8	WC	Beach as well
3.5	0.3	↑ ○	'an Spiddal'
3.8	0.3	WC	
4.4	0.6	▲	O'Halloran's Caravan Park
4.5	0.1	▲	Salthill Caravan Park
		▲	Bayview Caravan Park
4.9	0.4	←	'an Spiddal'
6.4	1.5	♦	Shop at service station
8.3	1.9	↑ ♦	At lights, Barna has shops and pharmacy
13.3	5.0	✪	Beach

Stage 1 Galway to Inishmore			
18.9	5.6	♦ ✪ WC	Shop in garage, picnic area opposite and beach close by
19.2	0.3	♦ ATM	An Spiddal Spar shop has ATM
23.2	4.0	♦	Supermarket in service station
24.3	1.1	♦	Small shop
27.0	2.7	▲	Seaview Lodge Holiday Hostel
33.1	6.1	♦	Small shop
33.3	0.2	↑	Straight ahead (R336 turns right)
35.7	2.4		Road swings right
38.5	2.8	←	'R372 ferries'
39.0	0.5		Arrive ticket office at quay

Stage 2 Tour of Inishmore			
0.0			Kilronan, Inishmore, by Ridgway and Blyth memorial, head away from ferries
0.1	0.1	WC	
0.2	0.1	↘	Road swings round to right
0.3	0.1	♦ ATM	Supermarket and ATM down lane to right

Stage 2 Tour of Inishmore			
0.5	0.2	✪	Ionad Árann (heritage centre) – currently closed
		✪	Bank
0.8	0.3	→	At Joe Watty's Pub
1.9	1.1	▲	Campsite in field on left
2.4	0.5	⇦ ✪	Teampall Chiarain (260m return)
3.1	0.7	⇦ ✪	Teampall Asurnai (900m return)
4.5	1.4	✪	Seal colony on right, telescope
7.1	2.6	←	Beach at Kilmurvy on right
		→	After 50m
7.5	0.4	WC	
		↖	'Dún Aengus'
7.9	0.5	♦	Souvenir shop
8.1	0.2	↑↓	Dun Aengus car park – bike racks
8.2	0.1	←	At shops
9.2	1.0	←	At T-junction
10.0	0.8	⇦ ✪	'Dún Eoghanachta'
10.9	0.9	✪ →	Na Seacht dTeampaill – on the corner
11.3	0.4	←	Along shore
14.8	3.5	→	At T-junction
15.2	0.4	↑↓	End of the island
21.9	6.7	↗	Veer right

Stage 2 Tour of Inishmore			
25.2	3.3	✪ ⇨	To lighthouse and Dun Eochla – views (800m return)
26.7	1.5	▲	Mainstir House Hostel
28.1	1.4	→	Just before Aran Sweater Market
29.2	1.1	✪ ⇨	Turn here for the Black Fort, turn right after 300m (2.5km ride then 1km return walk)
30.5	1.3	✪ ⇨	Turn to Teampall Bheanain
30.6	0.1	⇦	Turn to small harbour
31.0	0.4	✪	Monument to lost at sea
31.1	0.1	⇦	Turn to airfield and access to beach
31.8	0.7	↖	Bear left at fork
32.8	1.0	↑↓	Beach – views to Inishmaan
37.4	4.6	→	Back towards quay
37.6	0.2		Arrive back at memorial

Stage 3 Tour of Inisheer			
0.0			From head of pier, go left
0.2	0.2	✪	Beach on the left
0.4	0.2	←	Just past Bronze Age tumulus Cnoc Raithni

Stage 3 Tour of Inisheer			
0.6	0.2	▲	Camp site on left
1.4	0.8	←	Unsigned
2.4	1.0	⇦ ✪	To Plassy Wreck
2.8	0.4	→	Straight on is rough track along foreshore
3.8	1.0	←	At T-junction
3.9	0.1	←	At T-junction
4.2	0.3	→	Turn down gravel track, turns to firm grass
4.6	0.4	←	At T-junction (go right for castle)
4.7	0.1	✪	Pass signal tower
5.0	0.3	→	Down grassy track
5.2	0.2	→	At T-junction
5.5	0.3	→	At T-junction
		←	At T-junction
5.6	0.1	→	At T-junction
5.7	0.1	←	At T-junction past church
5.9	0.2	←	At T-junction
6.1	0.2	←	Road swings left
7.3	1.2	→	'Burren Way', grassy lane
7.5	0.2	←	Join tarmac
7.6	0.1	✪	St Enda's Well
7.8	0.1	→	Onto rocky track
8.9	1.1	↗	Bear right at fork
9.6	0.7	←	At T-junction
9.8	0.2	→	At T-junction
10.1	0.3	←	At T-junction

Stage 3 Tour of Inisheer			
10.2	0.1	←	Unsigned
10.4	0.2		Arrive back at quay

Stage 4 Round the Burren			
0.0			Doolin Pier
0.2	0.2	WC ▲	Toilets in car park and access to Nagles Camping and Caravan Park
1.5	1.3	♦	Small shop
1.6	0.1	←	Just over bridge
		▲	Doolin Hostel
2.2	0.6	⇦ ▲	turning to Aille River Hostel and O'Connor's Riverside Camping & Caravan Park (c200m)
2.9	0.7	▲	Rainbow Hostel
3.2	0.3	▲	Flannagan's Hostel
6.7	3.5	←	'Fanore'; Ballinalacken Castle across road
9.6	2.9	✪	Great rock terraces
14.5	4.9	♦	Small café
16.3	1.8	♦	Small shop
18.5	2.2	⇦ ✪ WC	Fanore beach, 150m
21.2	2.7	✪	Rock pavements

Stage 4 Round the Burren			
22.9	1.7	✪	Pass Black Head lighthouse; can stop here and walk up into the Burren
27.9	5	⇦ ✪	Gleninagh Castle (c400m)
31.6	3.7	✪	Picnic area on way into Ballyvaughan followed by small harbour
32.4	0.8	↑	'N67 Lisdoonvarna', at centre of Ballyvaughan, shops to left
34.1	1.7	←	'R480 Ennis'
35.5	1.4	✪	Aillwee Caves
36.5	1.0	✪	Limestone pavements start to appear
39.8	3.3	△ (187)	Now surrounded by limestone pavements
41.7	1.9	✪	Limestone depression
41.9	0.2	✪	Car park for Poulnabrone Dolmen
42.5	0.6	✪ ⇨	Caherconnell – stone fort
43.3	0.8	→	'L5094'
47.4	4.1	→	At T-junction
48.1	0.7	← ⇨ ✪	Turn right for Cahermacnaghten (1.2km return)

Stage 4 Round the Burren			
49.1	1.0	→	Unsigned
51.2	2.1	←	Unsigned
53.3	2.1	←	At T-junction
54.0	0.7	→	Just at end of pine wood
55.8	1.8	← ♦ ▲ ⇧	At Lisdoonvarna, shops to left, Sleepzone The Burren hostel (300m straight ahead)
56.2	0.4	→	'R478 Enystmon', at T-junction
56.5	0.3	♦	Small shop
57.6	1.1	↑	'Doolin', (slightly staggered) at crossroads
61.2	3.6	♦ →	'R479 Doolin', service station shop
63.1	1.9	←	Doolin crossroads
63.7	0.6	▲	Arrive, Doolin Hostel

Stage 5 Doolin to Kilrush			
0.0			Head south (hostel on your left)
0.1	0.1	↖	Swing left away from bridge to head uphill
1.1	1.0	↗	Road joins from left; view of Doonagore Castle (private) ahead.

Stage 5 Doolin to Kilrush			
1.2	0.1	→	Signed 'Clare Jam Shop'
3.4	2.2	→	At T-junction
6.2	2.8	✪ ATM	Cliffs of Mohr
8.5	2.3	✪	O'Brien's Pillar (memorial to Cornelius O'Brien)
9.6	1.1	✪	The Story of Liscannor Stone (shop and visitor centre)
11.5	1.9	♦	Liscannor, service station and shop
15.1	3.6	✪	O'Brien's Bridge and ruined castle
16.8	1.7	→	At T-junction
16.9	0.1	✪	Tourist information at Lahinch
		♦	Shop
17.1	0.2	♦ ▲	Shop on left, centre of Lahinch, hostel across road
18.1	1.0	▲	Ocean View Caravan Park
27.3	9.2	→	'R482 Spanish Point'
29.1	1.8	♦	Convenience store
30.7	1.6	✪	Cliff-top car park
30.9	0.2	→	'R285 Quilty'
31.0	0.1	✪	Beach
31.2	0.2	♦	Small shop
31.9	0.7	→	'Kilrush'
35.0	3.1	✪	Quilty – *Leon* wreck information
36.0	1.0	♦	Shop in service station
38.8	2.8	→	'Kilkee'
46.2	7.4	↗	Road joins from left
49.0	2.8	♦ ✪	Doonbeg has shop and beaches
49.2	0.2	⇦	'Kilrush 12'
49.5	0.3	♦	Bigger shop
49.6	0.1	▲	Strand Camping
60.2	10.6	↖ ⇨	Entering Kilkee, road veers left. Turn right for 'Waterworld' and beach
60.3	0.1	♦ →	Just in front of Neville's and past shop on the left – carry straight on for direct route to Kilrush (13.5km)
60.5	0.2	→	At main road, tourist information is behind you before the turn
60.7	0.2	ATM	Bank of Ireland
		▲	Kilkee Hostel
60.9	0.2	○ ↗	'Coast road'
61.1	0.2	WC ♦	Mace store on corner

Stage 5 Doolin to Kilrush			
61.4	0.3	←	'Loop Head Drive'
67.4	6.0	⇨	Viewing area and car park for Kilkee Cliffs
69.5	2.1	→	At T-junction
71.8	2.3	→	'Loop Head'
74.6	2.8	→	'R487 Loop Head'
76.8	2.2	♦	Cross has small shop
80.2	3.4	→	'L2000 Ross'
83.3	3.1	⇨	Bridges of Ross (0.5km return plus 1km return walk)
84.2	0.9	→	'Loop Head Lighthouse'
87.5	3.3	→	'Loop Head'
89.2	1.7	↑↓	Arrive lighthouse
94.2	5.0	✿ ♦	Kilbaha memorial garden. Keatings Bar on the corner.
94.9	0.7	↗	'Coast Road'
106.5	11.6	♦	Small shop/post office and a couple of bars at Carrigaholt
106.9	0.4	↑	'L2006 Doonaha'
107.0	0.1	✿	Beach (after bridge)
112.0	5.0	▲ ⇨	Green Acres Caravan & Camping Park (0.9km)

Stage 5 Doolin to Kilrush			
115.6	3.6	▲	Purecamping
116.0	0.4	←	'Kilrush', at crossroads
118.9	2.9	↗	Road joins from left
121.1	2.2	→	At T-junction
125.1	4.0	⇦ ✿	West Clare Railway Yard
130.1	5.0	O ↑	Unsigned
130.3	0.2	✿ ♦	Clancy Cycle Centre
130.4	0.1	O →	'R473'
130.6	0.2	▲	Hostel and tourist information, Kilrush

Stage 6 Kilrush to Ennis			
0.0			Hostel and tourist information, Kilrush, head towards the market square
0.1	0.1	O ↗	'N67 Killimer'
0.4	0.3	→	'N67 Killimer'
1.2	0.8	✿	Vandeleur Walled Garden & Centre
9.1	7.9	✿ ♦ ⇨	Turn to Shannon ferry (300m) if you are heading straight over to Tarbert; shop in service station and memorial to the Colleen Bawn (Ellen Hanley)

Stage 6 Kilrush to Ennis

12.8	3.7	✪	Track to small beach
		✪	Steep hills in this section
15.7	2.9	→	'R473 Killadysert'
16.9	1.2	♦	Small shop
23.4	6.5	←	'R473'
30.3	6.9	✪	View across Shannon to Namurian sandstone escarpment near Foynes
36.4	6.1	↗ ♦ATM	'R473 Ennis'; Killadysert has shop, ATM
43.1	6.7	✪	Ballynacally has benches and grass area
43.3	0.2	♦	Shop
49.7	6.4	♦	Medium-sized supermarket
57.1	7.4	←	At T-junction
57.3	0.2	O↑	'Ennis'
57.4	0.1	O↑♦	'Ennis', Evolution Bikes on the left
58.3	0.9	O↑	'Town centre'
58.7	0.4	→	'Town centre', at lights
59.3	0.6	O↑	Unsigned
59.7	0.4	←	'Tourist centre'
59.8	0.1	O↑	'Tourist centre'
60.1	0.3	✪	Ennis tourist office and Clare Museum straight ahead through car park; bike racks

Stage 7 Ennis to Limerick

0.0			From bike racks at Ennis tourist office, head through car park
0.3	0.3	O↑	Unsigned
0.4	0.1	→	At T-junction
0.8	0.4	←O	'Quin R469'
		✪	Pass bus and train station
1.7	0.9	♦	Medium-sized shop in service station
9.7	8.0	⇐	Turn for view of Quin Abbey and picnic area
9.8	0.1	♦	Medium-sized shop
		♦	Shops in Quin town centre
		←	'Quin Abbey, Limerick'
10.1	0.3	✪	Quin Abbey
13.9	3.8	✪	Entrance to Knappogue Castle on right (800m return)
17.9	4.0	→	'Shannon Airport'
23.1	5.2	↑	Sixmilebridge crossroads at centre of village
28.3	5.2	⇐	To Cratloe Forest Recreation Area (1km)
28.6	0.3	←	Opposite Woodcross restaurant

Stage 7 Ennis to Limerick			
28.7	0.1	◆	Shop
31.2	2.5	↗	Cross level crossing
34.9	3.7	✪	Limerick city limits
36.2	1.3	◆ ATM	At shop
37.0	0.8	◆	Supermarket
37.3	0.3	O ↑	'City centre'
37.8	0.5	✪	Pass GAA stadium
37.9	0.1	↑	At lights
38.8	0.9	✪ →	Just past square-towered church, before river, Treaty Stone on this corner
39.4	0.6	←	Turn left over bridge
39.6	0.2	←	'Liddy Street'
39.7	0.1	→	At lights
39.8	0.1		Arrive Limerick tourist information

Stage 7A WAW link from Limerick to Tarbert			
0.0			Corner of O'Connell Street and Cruises' Street, outside McDonald's, head down street (one way)
0.7	0.7	✪	O'Connell Monument
0.9	0.2	◆	The Bike Shop

Stage 7A WAW link from Limerick to Tarbert			
1.8	0.9	↑	At lights (need to be in RH lane)
2.0	0.2	↑	'N69 Foynes'
3.1	1.1	O ↗	'R526 (N69) Patrickswell'; cycleway starts
3.6	0.5	O →	Unsigned
3.9	0.3	◆	Medium-sized shop
4.8	0.9	◆	Local shopping centre, pharmacy, convenience store
4.9	0.1	O ↑	'Mungret College Office Park'
5.3	0.4	✪	Pass former Jesuit college
6.6	1.3	←	'N69 Tralee', now at Mungret
9.3	2.7	O ↑	At Clarina
15.2	5.9	ATM ◆	At service station – Kildimo
17.1	1.9	✪	Gothic towers of Dromore Castle on right (1.2km away)
20.6	3.5	⇦ ▲	Curraghchase Forest Park (c3.5km, closest camping to Limerick)
26.1	5.5	←	'Askeaton'
27.3	1.2	ATM ◆	Service station has large shop and ATM

Stage 7A WAW link from Limerick to Tarbert			
27.6	0.3	✪	Askeaton East Square has tourist information; view of castle through square
28.7	1.1	←	'N69 Tralee'
33.3	4.6	✪	Entry to Aughinish Alumina, be wary of large trucks in this area.
36.6	3.3	⇦	Knockpatrick Gardens (c2km)
38.1	1.5	♦	Service station has large shop
38.8	0.7	♦	Supermarket
38.9	0.1	✪	Foynes Flying Boat & Maritime Museum

Stage 7A WAW link from Limerick to Tarbert			
46.4	7.5	✪	Rest area has views of Shannon
52.7	6.3	ATM ♦	Service station has shop
52.9	0.2	✪	Picnic area
53.5	0.6	✪	Pass Glin Castle
58.2	4.7	✪	Enter Kerry
58.6	0.4	✪	Picnic area, power stations ahead
59.3	0.7	▲ ♦	At Tarbert crossroads, hostel on left
59.4	0.1	ATM ♦	Shops and ATM
			Finish at turn to ferry (to right)

ROUTE 5 THE DINGLE AND KERRY PENINSULAS

Skellig Michael monastery is a testament to the power of faith (Stage 5)

Start	Tarbert
Finish	Tralee
Distance	468.4km
Ascent	6323m

Dingle and Kerry represent quintessential coastal Ireland. This is the Ireland of film and fable – if you have seen the Emerald Isle on the big screen, a calendar or in a coffee table book, the chances are you will recognise some of the scenery on Route 5. Highlights of the route include the early Christian monastery on Skellig Michael, the lakes and forests around Killarney, and the tetrapod trackway on Valentia Island. The finest piece of coastal road is the section around Slea Head on the Dingle peninsula.

Of the towns, Kenmare and Tralee are the most relaxed places to stay, while Killarney is surrounded by beautiful scenery.

BETTER BY BIKE

From Tarbert to Kenmare the route described here closely follows the Wild Atlantic Way as it takes a fairly predictable path along national and regional roads by the coast. On a bike, seeking out the occasional

Route 5: The Dingle and Kerry Peninsulas

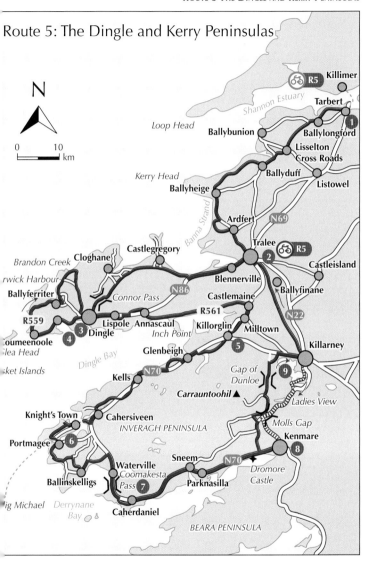

N

0   10
└────┘ km

Killimer

R5

Tarbert

Shannon Estuary

Loop Head

Ballybunion

Ballylongford

1

Lisselton
Cross Roads

Kerry Head

Ballyduff

Listowel

Ballyheige

Banna Strand

N69

Ardfert

Castlegregory

Tralee

R5

2

Castleisland

Brandon Creek

Cloghane

Blennerville

rwick Harbour

N86

Connor Pass

Castlemaine

Ballyfinane

Ballyferriter

R559

Lispole   Annascaul

R561

Killorglin

Milltown

N22

3   Dingle

Inch Point

oumeenoole
lea Head

4

Glenbeigh

5

Killarney

ket Islands

Dingle Bay

N70

Kells

Gap of
Dunloe

9

Carrauntoohil ▲

Ladies View

Knight's Town

Cahersiveen

INVERAGH PENINSULA

Molls Gap

Portmagee

6

Kenmare

8

Waterville
Coomakesta
Pass   7

Sneem

N70

Parknasilla

Dromore
Castle

Ballinskelligs

ig Michael   Derrynane
Bay

Caherdaniel

BEARA PENINSULA

DINGLE AND INVERAGH

The southwest of Ireland reaches out into the Atlantic like the fingers of an outstretched hand. The northeast to southwest alignment of the finger peninsulas follows the direction of tectonic folding from around 250 million years ago. Millions of years of erosion laid low mountains once as high as the Alps, and when sea levels rose at the end of the Ice Age, water flooded into coastal valleys to form the southwest's characteristic furrowed shoreline. The result for the visitor is an almost endless variety of landscape with protected sandy shores giving way to wave-beaten rocky cliffs with just a turn in the road. The **Inveragh peninsula** (Stages 5, 6 and 7) – marketed as the 'Ring of Kerry route' – draws much of the attention, but the beautiful and compact **Dingle peninsula** (Stages 2, 3 and 4) offers some of the finest cycle touring in Ireland. This more northerly peninsula has a heady mix of bucolic countryside, sweeping beaches and razor-edged cliffs, much of which can be seen in a day or so. Much of the 1970 David Lean film *Ryan's Daughter* was filmed on the Dingle peninsula, including a memorable storm scene on Coumeenoole Beach (Stage 3).

quieter country road and including the occasional climb away from the shore is worthwhile – both for the views and to add a little variety.

GETTING TO THE START

The route starts at the T-junction where the road from the Tarbert ferry meets the main road. Getting to Limerick is also included below, as many riders will want to start the route in Limerick, taking Stage 7A of Route 4 as the first day.

By air

The closest airport is Shannon (www. shannonairport.com), about 30km out of Limerick on the other side of the estuary. Shannon has the best international connections of any of the Irish airports outside Dublin. There are flights to the US, Europe, including eastern Europe, and the UK.

By rail/bus

Limerick has half-a-dozen or so trains to Dublin per day, often with a change at Limerick Junction in County Tipperary. Trains also run direct to Galway. There are Bus Éireann services to Tralee, Killarney and Kenmare, but you are unlikely to get your bike on a bus during peak times.

WHEN TO GO

April and September are quiet, but Kerry seems to cope with visitor numbers well, so mid-summer travel is

Blennerville Windmill marks the entry to the Dingle peninsula (Stage 2)

Route summary table

Stage		Distance	Ascent	Accommodation available	Places with shops/other facilities en route
1	Tarbert to Tralee	69.7km	575m	Banna Strand	Lissleton Cross Roads
2	Tralee to Dingle	48.5km	668m		Blennerville
3	Tour of the Dingle Peninsula	57.1km	783m	Gallus Oratory, Ballyferriter, Dunquin	Ventry, Ballyferriter
4	Dingle to Killorglin	54.9km	649m	Glenbeigh (13km beyond Killorglin)	Castlemaine
5	Killorglin to Portmagee	65.8km	1019m	Glenbeigh, Cahersiveen	Cahersiveen
6	Portmagee to Caherdaniel	45.5km	816m	Ballinskelligs	Waterville
7	Caherdaniel to Kenmare	48.2km	559m		Sneem
8	Kenmare to Killarney	47.7km	840m		Gap of Dunloe
9	Killarney to Tralee	31.0km	414m		
Total		**468.4km**	**6323m**		

fine. The Rose of Tralee festival (late August) and the Puck Fair at Killorglin in the second week of August can make things busy in those towns.

ACCOMMODATION

Camping, hostel, B&B and hotel accommodation is plentiful and mostly of a very high standard, making this county one of the easiest places to organise a tour in Ireland.

MAPS

The OSI Ireland South 1: 250,000 sheet covers the whole route. At 1:50,000 you will need the following sheets from the Discovery series: 64 Clare Kerry Limerick, 63 Clare Kerry (these first two only if doing Tarbert to Tralee), 70 Kerry, 71 Kerry, 78 Kerry, 83 Kerry, 84 Cork Kerry (only for a 19km stretch to the west of Kenmare) and 85 Cork Kerry (only for a 1km stretch between Templenoe and Kenmare).

OPTIONS

Killarney is not on the Wild Atlantic Way but there are two excellent cycling routes from Kenmare to Killarney – either via the Gap of Dunloe (Stage 8), or along the main N71 and through Killarney National Park, taking in Ladies View. If the plan is to continue southwards, but you would like to see Killarney, these two routes combined make a pleasant, lightly loaded, return day trip from Kenmare.

Either route can be done in either direction, the only hitch being the one-way system operating for bikes in the national park from Muckross House (5.6km from Killarney on the Ladies View route) to the Meeting of the Waters (11.9km). This makes the national park/N71 route work better in the Killarney to Kenmare direction, so route cards are included for Kenmare to Killarney via the Gap of Dunloe (Stage 8) and Killarney to Kenmare via Ladies View.

ONWARDS

The Wild Atlantic Way continues at Kenmare.

STAGE 1
Tarbert to Tralee

Start	Tarbert
Distance	69.7km
Ascent	575m
Terrain	A few climbs
Summit	120m at 17km

This stage leaves the lowlands of the Shannon far behind. And from the low summit just north of **Ballyheige** the view suddenly opens up along the wide sweep of **Banna Strand** and out to the mountain wall of the Dingle peninsula.

> **Roger Casement** landed on Banna Strand on Good Friday 1916 from a German U-boat as part of an ill-fated expedition to provide arms for the Nationalist cause. He was caught, tried and hanged by the British.

During the 19th century many of those convicted by the court at Tarbert Bridewell were transported to Australia

This northwest corner of Kerry is probably the only part of the county passed over by tourism. **Lisselton Cross Roads** is little more than a shop and a few scattered houses.

The world's first motorised passenger **monorail service** ran through Lisselton Cross Roads for 36 years. A small plaque gives a few details of the remarkably successful line, which opened in 1888.

The Rose of Tralee festival, which draws thousands of visitors at the end of August, is inspired by a song. 'Roses' from around the world compete for the title.

On the road

The section out towards Kerry Head, from the turn onto the coast road at 27.4km, is remote, so pick up supplies by Lisselton Cross Roads at the latest. The junction here is rather odd, but it usually is signed. Take the Ballyduff road. The beaches at Banna and Ballyheige are patrolled in season.

Accommodation

Tarbert has the Ferry House Hostel (068 36555). There are a couple of hotel and B&B options in the area, including the centrally-located Keldun House B&B (068 36405, www.keldunhouse.com).

Tralee has a choice of hostels. Try the Castle Hostel (066 7125167, www. castlehostel.ie) on Upper Castle Street or Finnegans Hostel (066 7127610) on the street leading to the Kerry Museum. Woodlands Touring Caravan & Camping Park (066 7121235, www.kingdomcamping.com) is within walking distance of town. From the town centre follow signs for the Aquadome. When you hit the Aquadome roundabout on the ring road, turn left and the site is signed a few hundred metres on the right. The alternative for camping is before you reach Tralee at 62km, Sir Roger's Caravan and Camping Park at Banna Strand (066 7134730, www.sirrogers.com).

The town has number of both modern and traditional hotels and the prices are reasonable, compared to some of the more 'tourist' towns further on. The same applies to B&Bs. So if you feel like splashing out on a bit of luxury, you should get good value here.

STAGE 2
Tralee to Dingle

Start	Tralee
Distance	48.5km
Ascent	668m
Terrain	Long climb
Summit	410m at 41km

Just outside **Tralee**, Blennerville Windmill (2km) – the largest working mill in Ireland – marks the northern entry to the Dingle Peninsula. From here the road continues level along the north side of the peninsula as the mountains slowly close in from the left.

The highlight of the day is the ascent of Ireland's second highest road pass, the 400m **Connor Pass**. The early stages of the 10km climb are not too steep but the final kilometre to the summit is via a single-lane road cut into overhanging cliffs. The descent towards Dingle is not as steep as the climb, and, while it makes sense to control your speed, the road is excellent.

Looking north from the Connor Pass, the highest point in the book

Dingle town has grown from being a small fishing and farming town into the tourist hotspot of the peninsula. There is plenty of accommodation and good shops, but it can be crowded.

On the road

The N86 between Blennerville (2.8km) and the Anascaul turn (152.km) is busy in the morning and evening commute periods. It is cheaper to stock up in one of Tralee's supermarkets than on the Dingle Peninsula if you don't mind carrying the weight over the Connor Pass. At least, buy some snacks in Tralee, or Blennerville. Dingle has shops and ATMs.

Accommodation

In Dingle try the Rainbow Hostel & Camping (1km along Stage 2, 066 915 1044, www.rainbowhosteldingle.com) which has the advantage of being a couple of kilometres out of town, so it's quiet. The Grapevine Hostel (066 915 1434, www.grapevinedingle.com) is on Dykegate in the heart of town.

Dingle has had a splurge in new visitor accommodation in recent years and you should be able to find a hotel or B&B to suit. The Dingle Skellig Hotel (066 9150200, www.dingleskellig.com) has a cycle storage room and other cycle-friendly facilities. Head out of town on the N86 (Tralee) and look for the signs on the right a few hundred metres out from the town centre.

Options

This is a short stage, so it is possible to push on after Dingle into Stage 3 but be warned that the road ahead around Slea Head is hilly and also spectacular – so don't rush in.

STAGE 3
Tour of the Dingle Peninsula

Start	Dingle quay
Distance	57.1km
Ascent	783m
Terrain	Hilly
Summit	120m at 50km

Dingle

West of Dingle is one of Ireland's most spectacular coastal roads. A steady climb leads to a rock ledge about 50m above the Atlantic. Around **Slea Head** itself (16km), seabirds wheel in the updrafts from Atlantic winds hitting the grey cliffs, and the air is heavy with salt. After the head, the coast flattens out, though it remains just as attractive. The **Blasket Islands** stand proudly to the west, and there is a cliff-foot sandy cove at **Coumeenoole Bay**, which was used as a location for the film *Ryan's Daughter*.

For David Lean's 1970 film **Ryan's Daughter**, a village was built, and later dismantled, on Cruach Mharthain above Clogher.

The fine scenery continues with the lovely mountain-encircled **Smerwick Harbour**. The Gallarus Oratory is an interesting example of mortarless building. A short side-trip takes in **Brandon Creek** – the site from which St Brendan set off on his epic voyage to the promised land – possibly the Americas. The stage returns to Dingle with a climb along the side of Mount Brandon.

St Brendan's voyages were of Homeric proportions, and included a close encounter with a giant sea-cat, riding on the back of a whale, and meeting Judas Escariot on a temporary release from Hell.

On the road
Ventry has a small shop as does Ballyferriter. Carry some cash, as there are no ATMs.

Accommodation
There is a campsite right next to the Gallarus Oratory (34km) – Oratory House Camping (066 9155143) – while Ballyferriter has the Black Cat Hostel (066 9156286). The Dunquin (Dun Chaoin) An Óige hostel (22km) is the westernmost hostel in Europe (066 9156121, www.anoige.ie). There is a narrower choice of accommodation away from Dingle itself but there are an increasing number of guesthouses and B&Bs coming into operation. www.dingle-peninsula.ie lists a decent selection.

STAGE 4
Dingle to Killorglin

Start	Dingle
Distance	54.3km
Ascent	649m
Terrain	Fast stage
Summit	110m at 13km

Across the bay from Dingle the wall of mountains of the Iveragh Peninisula and the Ring of Kerry are calling.

In Annascaul (17km) a bronze statue commemorates **Tom Crean**, a veteran of three epic Antarctic trips, including Robert Falcon Scott's ill-fated 1910–13 expedition.

Before the mountains, **Inch Point** has a popular bathing beach on a low peninsula that almost touches the Iveragh Peninsula near Glenbeigh. Continuing east, Dingle Bay becomes a protected lowland estuary with broad tidal flats. A 4km section of the N70 follows **Castlemaine**, but at **Milltown** a scenic road leads over the hilltops with stunning views of the shining Laune river at **Killorglin**, and beyond to the mountains of Dingle and Iveragh.

Killorglin is best known for its **Puck Fair**. Held on 10, 11 and 12 August, this is one of Ireland's oldest and oddest fairs. A wild goat is captured, crowned

The Kerry mountains come into view approaching Killorglin

King Puck (*poc* = billy-goat), and kept in a cage on a high stand in the middle of town to look down on three days of revelry.

On the road
The N72 can be followed all the way to Annascaul, but the route described here takes a couple of deviations from the main road where this is practical. When the R561 takes over at Annascaul the traffic quietens down.

This is a quick stage, with the flat section from Inch to Castlemaine particularly fast. It is possible to follow main roads all the way to Killorglin, but best to get off the N72 at Lispole and out of the traffic, despite the steep climb.

Inch, with its long beach, makes a good stop. Castlemaine has a shop and a stone bench close by. At the end of this stage, Killorglin has a decent-sized supermarket and an ATM in its central diamond.

Accommodation
At the time of writing there was no hostel accommodation in Killorglin. Campers can push on to the excellent site at Glenbeigh along the next stage. For indoor accommodation, however, Killorglin has a smattering of small hotels and B&Bs. Try Laune Bridge House (0877 447147, www.launebridgehouse.com) for bed and breakfast. It is a 100m or so past the river bridge on the road to Killarney.

STAGE 5
Killorglin to Portmagee

Start	Killorglin
Distance	65.8km
Ascent	1019m
Terrain	Hilly
Summit	150m at 17km

West of **Killorglin** mountains loom up on three sides, and patches of bog and dense pockets of woodland emphasise that upland landscapes dominate the Iveragh Peninsula. The valley-foot town of **Glenbeigh** has a distinctly Scottish feel. The scenery remains grand from here, but by **Cahersiveen** (there are many spellings) the landscape takes second place to history and prehistory.

The first site of historical interest is the former **Caheersiveen Royal Irish Constabulary Barracks**, which towers over the entrance to the town. Now a heritage centre (www.oldbarrackscahersiveen.com), it is a goldmine for local history. The fortress-like barracks, built between 1870 and 1875, show the strategic importance of the nearby Valentia Island telegraph station.

Here you can also find out more about **Daniel 'the Liberator' O'Connell**, who was born nearby, and Monsignor Hugh O'Flaherty – the Scarlet Pimpernel of the Vatican – who is buried in Caheersiveen.

The way to **Valentia Island** is via a short ferry hop from Reenard Point to **Knight's Town**.

The ferry trip is the best place from which to appreciate the grand design of **Knight's Town**. The street layout was planned by Scottish engineer Alexander Nimmo in 1830, and the village was developed in the 1840s.

Transatlantic telegraph cables operated from Valentia Island from 1866, until Western Union International terminated its cable operations in 1966. For more on their history, visit the Valentia Island Heritage Centre.

Out near the coastal radio station on the island's northern tip are the fossil tracks of a tetrapod.

Valentia Harbour

The 385-million-year-old **fossilised trackway** on Valentia Island is the earliest known record of an amphibious creature – probably a salamander-like animal about a metre long – walking on the land.

SKELLIG MICHAEL

Pride of place for this stage must go to the Unesco World Heritage Site of Skellig Michael. Unfortunately you can't cycle there – it's 15km offshore – but Portmagee is the place to pick up a boat trip. This sixth-century Christian monastery perched on a rock face a couple of hundred metres above the Atlantic defies belief. For boats to the Skelligs, try the Sea Quest (066 9476214, www.skelligsrock.com), which leaves at 9am from Portmagee.

Skellig Michael monastery features as 'The first Jedi temple' in the films *Star Wars: The Last Jedi* and *Star Wars: The Force Awakens*.

On the road
This stage takes every opportunity to get away from the Ring of Kerry N70 and the busier parts of the Wild Atlantic Way route. This creates a couple of steep sections, especially leaving Rossbeigh (just after Glenbeigh) and around Kells. On the main roads it is dangerous to stop except in parking areas. Rossbeigh beach is a pleasant place for a break, or there are some viewing areas from the 21km to 25km

mark. The climb along the spine of Valentia Island takes you up to 120m and the climb back from the fossil trackway is about 15 per cent.

Take some cash with you. Although there are ATMs at Cahersiveen, they are thin on the ground after that. The Valentia Island ferry operates continuously from April to October from 8.15am to 10pm. The future of the ferry is in doubt, so check for the latest information.

Accommodation

Portmagee's Skellig connection supports a number of overnight accommodation options, mostly clustered near the bridge and harbour. Skellig Ring House (066 9480018, www.skelligringhouse.com) is modern hostel-type accommodation just through Portmagee. Earlier in the day the Glenross Caravan & Camping Park (066 976 8451, www.campingkerry.com) at Glenbeigh has excellent facilities for touring campers. Caitin's Hostel (25km) is on the main Ring of Kerry route (066 9477614, www.caitins.com). Cahersiveen has the Sive Hostel (066 9472717, www.sivehostel.ie/index.htm) and the Mannix Point Camping & Caravan Park (066 9472806, www.campinginkerry.com).

Options

There is an alternative flatter route across Valentia Island through Chapeltown all the way to Portmagee on the R565. Bear left at the church (48.1km) and it is a further 7.7km to Portmagee.

STAGE 6

Portmagee to Caherdaniel

Start	Portmagee
Distance	45.5km
Ascent	816m
Terrain	Two stiff climbs
Summit	250m at 5km

This stage includes one of the prettiest sections of the Wild Atlantic Way – the climb over the **Coomakesta Pass** (sometimes Coomakista Pass) and round the coast to Caherdaniel. The view from the pass over the crescent-shaped sandy beaches and low rocky isles of **Derrynane Bay** is one of Ireland's most photographed. Early in the day the views across Valentia Island, St Finan's Bay and Ballinskelligs Bay are also outstanding.

It was from **St Finan's Bay** that the monks went to and from Skellig Michael, and when the saw-tooth-shaped rock was abandoned in the 12th century the monks set up a coastal priory at Ballinskelligs.

Further on, **Waterville** is a bright and breezy seaside town.

Silent film star **Charlie Chaplin** liked to take his holidays at Waterville and there is a statue of him on the front.

The lush woodland around **Caherdaniel** is almost tropical, and in this sheltered spot it is hard to resist a swim at the beach.

Daniel O'Connell's ancestral home, **Derrynane House**, is open to the public. Opening hours vary (066 9475113, www.derrynanehouse.ie).
Pressure for Catholic civil rights came to a head when Daniel O'Connell himself was elected as Member of Parliament for Clare in 1828 but as a Catholic was not allowed to take his seat. The following year the Emancipation Act removed anti-Catholic oaths from MPs. O'Connell took his seat in 1830.

The view from the Coomakesta Pass

On the road

Waterville and the Coomakesta Pass are the choice places to stop. The climb up the Coomakesta is a steady four per cent. The service station approaching Waterville is the first decent-sized shop of the day, and there is also a very handy ATM in the village. At the end of the day there is a small shop in Caherdaniel at Freddie's Pub, and also one at the Wave Crest Caravan and Camping Park through the village. The best place for a swim is Derrynane Bay.

Accommodation

The Travellers Rest hostel (066 9475175, www.hostelcaherdaniel.com) is a few metres from the crossroads in Caherdaniel. Just turn left at the end of the stage. The Skellig Lodge/Hostel (066 9479942, www.skelliglodge.com) is at Ballinskelligs (14km). For camping there is a site just through Caherdaniel at the start of Stage 6 – Wave Crest Caravan & Camping Park (066 9475188, www.wavecrestcamping. com). Caherdaniel is one of the quieter stopovers on this route and accommodation is sparse. Local B&Bs include Derrynane Bay House (066 9475404, www. ringofkerry.net) which is 1.2km from the centre of the village along the main road towards Waterville (N70).

Options

Despite the two climbs, this is a relatively fast stage, so consider doubling up with the next stage to Kenmare.

STAGE 7

Caherdaniel to Kenmare

Start	Caherdaniel
Distance	48.2km
Ascent	559m
Terrain	Rolling coastal hills
Summit	13m at 15km

Sneem is a town of contrasts – quiet and reserved on the west side of the river, bustling with coaches, tourists and blaring Irish music on the other. The memorial to former French president General de Gaulle, who was a visitor here, is in the quiet half.

Colourful Kenmare

After Sneem, the sites of note are the Victorian resort hotel at **Parknasilla**, which was much loved by George Bernard Shaw, among others, and the grounds of **Dromore Castle**, which are popular with walkers.

Kenmare is one of the finest Irish small towns. Laid out in the late 17th century, it retains many Georgian town houses.

On the road
The diamond at Sneem, has benches and a shop nearby. Kenmare, at the end of the day, has a decent-sized supermarket (turn left at the central diamond).

Accommodation
Kenmare has as wide a choice of hotel and B&B accommodation as anywhere on the Ring of Kerry. For a extensive list see www.kenmare.com. If you want to camp, the next place beyond Kenmare is the Peacock (064 6684287, www.bearacamping.com), which is 13km along the N71 – see Route 6, Stage 1. For hostel accommodation, in Kenmare there is the Failte Hostel (087 7116092, www.kenmarehostel.com) in a sympathetically adapted Georgian house. Just head up Main Street, turn right at Shelbourne Street and it's 200m on your left. The Greenwood Hostel (064 6689247, www.greenwoodhostel.com) is about 7km back west of Kenmare on the N70 at Templenoe.

Options

From Kenmare you have the choice of heading south along the Wild Atlantic Way or turning north towards Killarney and Tralee to close the loop of Route 5.

At Sneem it is possible to head straight for Killarney (46km away) via Molls Gap – a total of 67km from Caherdaniel. The turn is at 21.4km.

STAGE 8
Kenmare to Killarney

Start	Kenmare
Distance	47.7km
Ascent	840m
Terrain	Long climbs
Summit	240m at 29km

This route through the National Park has fantastic views over the Killarney lakes, including the famous **Ladies View**.

The Gap of Dunloe

Killarney National Park is one of the few places in Ireland to have been **continuously wooded** since the end of the last glaciation.

The **Gap of Dunloe** is a classic notch-through-a-mountain pass, while the wild Black Valley to the south of the pass has some of the grandest mountain scenery in Kerry. The steady climb, followed by a descent along the hairpin road past a string of small lakes, makes this one of the most enjoyable passes in Ireland.

Pony trap rides are popular over the Gap of Dunloe. Look out for pony manure as it's easy to skid on it in the rain.

ALTERNATIVE ROUTE VIA LADIES VIEW

There are two excellent cycling routes from Kenmare to Killarney – either via the Gap of Dunloe as described above, or along the main N71 and through Killarney National Park, taking in Ladies View. If the plan is to continue southwards, but you would like to see Killarney, these two routes combined make a pleasant, lightly loaded, return day trip from Kenmare. Killarney can be busy, so a day trip means enjoying the scenery surrounding the town and avoiding some of the central bustle.

Either route can be done in either direction, the only hitch being the one-way system operating for bikes in the national park from Muckross House (5.6km) to the Meeting of the Waters (11.9km). This makes the national park/N71 route work better if coming from Killarney to Kenmare, so route cards are included for Kenmare to Killarney via the Gap of Dunloe (Stage 8) and Killarney to Kenmare via Ladies View.

The alternative national park/main road route has fantastic views over the Killarney lakes, including the famous Ladies View. The lakeside cycleway through the park is also delightful, and there is a chance to visit a couple of historic buildings. Muckross Abbey is a 15th-century Franciscan foundation, while nearby Muckross House is one of Ireland's leading stately homes. A route card for this route – north to south, from Killarney to Kenmare – is included at the end of the stage route cards in this chapter in case you fancy a two-day tour of the National Park from Kenmare.

On the road
The one-way system for cycles in the national park goes anticlockwise around Muckross Lake. Both routes are shop-free apart from cafés at Ladies View and the northern end of the Gap of Dunloe. There is a large supermarket opposite

the tourist information centre in Killarney. The central car park here also has a public toilet right over in the far corner. O'Sullivan Cycles (064 6631282, www. osullivanscycles.com) is on High Street in the heart of town.

Accommodation

Killarney has the array of hotel and bed and breakfast accommodation you would expect, but things do fill up during the summer. See www.killarney.ie for a comprehensive list of places to stay. The Killarney International Hostel (064 6631240, www.anoige.ie) is an An Óige hostel about 5km out of town towards the Gap of Dunloe. Look for the R563 turn to Dingle off the N72, and the hostel is a few hundred metres down there. Close by at 41km is the Fossa Holiday Hostel (064 6631497, www.fossacampingkillarney.com), which is also a campsite. For centre-of-town options, try one of the many independent hostels, such as the Railway Hostel (064 6635299, www.killarneyhostel.com). The Flesk Caravan & Camping Park (064 6631704, www.killarneyfleskcamping.com) has good facilities and is close to the town centre on the N71.

Options

Killarney station has half-a-dozen services a day to Tralee if you need to skip the final stage and to Dublin (with a change at Mallow).

STAGE 9
Killarney to Tralee

Start	Killarney
Distance	31.0km
Ascent	414m
Terrain	A steady hill climb
Summit	170m at 22km

After the rigours of southwest Kerry, the run back to Tralee from **Killarney** is a breeze. The trip is also a very pleasant one, with some fine views from the climb over the hills to the north of Ballyfinnane.

On the way out of Killarney there is a final chance to gaze back over the lakes and woods from Agadhoe Heights (2km), with its remains of a round tower and castle.

Tralee

The **Ballyfinnane Hill Climb** of 1903 was won by the Honourable Charles Stewart Rolls, of Rolls-Royce fame. There is a memorial by the road.

The climb to the north of **Ballyfinnane**, along the flank of the Slieve Mish mountains, is not too taxing. Devonian rocks make a brief re-appearance on the summit plateau, and with them bog, gorse and heather also emerge briefly, before a descent to the green crescent of fertile pastures surrounding **Tralee**.

On the road
There is just a very short section on the main N22 north out of Killarney but after that the roads are very quiet. There are no shops at all on this stage until Tralee.

Accommodation
See Stage 1A.

ROUTE 5 ROUTE CARDS

Stage 1 Tarbert to Tralee			
0.0			At turn to ferry (small parking area next to shop), continue straight on R551 Ballybunion
0.1	0.1	→	'Coastal Drive'
		✪	Shannon Boating Tragedy memorial
7.3	7.2	⇨	Lislaughtin Abbey (0.4km return)
8.7	1.4	→	'R551 Ballybunion'
8.9	0.2	ATM ♦	Medium-sized shop
11.1	2.2	←	'Lissellton'
13.9	2.8	△ (90)	3–4% climb
14.6	0.7	↑	At crossroads
16.8	2.2	△ (115)	Views to coast
18.3	1.5	←	At T-junction
19.9	1.6	♦ →	Shops on right at Lisselton Crossroads (see note in text)
20.0	0.1	→	'R553 Ballybunion'
20.1	0.1	←	'Ballyduff'
23.6	3.5	←	'R551 Tralee'
27.4	3.8	→	'Coast road'
30.5	3.1	⇨	To Kilmore Strand (2km)

Stage 1 Tarbert to Tralee			
35.6	5.1	♦	Small shop
42.4	6.8	←	At crossroads
42.7	0.3	△ (85)	'Wow' moment as view opens up along strand
43.4	0.7	→	'Ballyheige'
44.4	1.0	⇨ ✪ ♦ WC	To Ballyheige village and beach (1.5km return)
50.8	6.4	→	'Banna Strand' (for shortcut carry straight on)
52.2	1.4	▲	Sir Rogers Caravan & Camping Park
		↑	Carry straight on to beach
52.6	0.4	WC	
52.8	0.2	↑ ↓	Turn around at car park, short walk to beach
53.4	0.6	→	Back at junction
53.7	0.3	↗	Bear right at fork
54.3	0.6	↗	Bear right at fork, Casement memorial is on left
56.4	2.1	✪	Pass Rahanane castle
59.2	2.8	←	At T-junction
59.8	0.6	✪	Church and IRA memorial
60.0	0.2	←	At Ardfert – have to turn, one-way

Stage 1 Tarbert to Tralee			
60.2	0.2	→	'Ardfert Cathedral'
60.3	0.1	✿	'Ardfert Cathedral'
		→	Just after cathedral
60.4	0.1	↑	'R551 Tralee'
67.1	6.7	O ↑ ♦	Grocery store on corner
68.0	0.9	♦	Shop
68.8	0.8	↑	'Town centre', at lights
69.0	0.2	→	'Town centre', at lights
69.1	0.1	←	One way – Kirby's Brouge Inn opposite
69.2	0.1	←	On to the Mall
69.4	0.2	→	'Denny Street', in front of AIB Bank
69.6	0.2	WC	In park on left
		←	At Kerry Musem
69.7	0.1		Arrive tourist information (round side of museum)

Stage 2 Tralee to Dingle			
0.0			Outside tourist information, follow one-way
0.2	0.2	←	One-way
0.4	0.2	←	'(N86) An Daingean'

Stage 2 Tralee to Dingle			
0.7	0.3	O →	'N86 An Daingean'
2.7	2.0	←	Road swings left across bridge
2.8	0.1	↑ ⇨	Blennerville Windmill on right
3.2	0.4	ATM ♦	Service station has good shop
11.7	8.5	✿ ⇨	Derrymore Strand 600m
15.2	3.5	⇦	Alternative route to Dingle via N86 (34.5km)
21.0	5.8	♦ ▲ ⇨	Food store on left; turn right for Anchor Caravan Park (1.2km),
23.4	2.3	⇨	Castlegregory 2km
27.1	3.7	✿ ⇨	Stradbally Strand
28.6	1.5	✿ ⇨	Gowlane Strand
30.4	1.8	▲ ⇨	'Brandon Point'; turn here for hostel at Cloghane
35.6	5.2	⇨	'Brandon Point', the pass starts here (73m)
40.9	5.3	△ (413)	Connor Pass summit
47.9	7.0	↑	Now in Dingle, first crossroads (slightly staggered)
48.2	0.3	O ↑	'Slea Head Drive'
48.4	0.2	← WC	'Slea Head Drive', WC on left

Stage 2 Tralee to Dingle			
48.5	0.1	←	Turn into quay-side area by Dingle tourist information

Stage 3 Tour of the Dingle Peninsula			
0.0		←	From car park exit on Dingle quay, next to tourist informa-tion, turn left
1.0	1.0	← ○ ▲ ⇧	'Slea Head Drive'. Rainbow Hostel, straight on in a few hundred metres
1.3	0.3	ATM ♦	Good shop in service station
7.4	6.1	⇦ ✪ WC	Ventry Strand 100m
10.1	2.7	♦	Small shop
11.2	1.1	✪	Celtic and Prehistoric Museum
12.2	1.0	△ (50)	Steady climb, don't forget to look back
13.0	0.8	✪	Dunbeg Fort (left)
		✪	Famine cottages (right)
13.9	0.9	✪	Beehive Huts, also photo opportunity down coast
15.1	1.2	✪	Parking
15.4	0.3	✪	Parking

Stage 3 Tour of the Dingle Peninsula			
16.4	1.0	✪	Now round-ing Slea Head. Parking and information board about birdlife
16.7	0.3	✪	Cliff-side section of road ends, views of Blaskets ahead
17.5	0.8	✪	Parking
18.5	1.0	⇦ ✪	Swimming beach – Coumeenoole Strand, where *Ryan's Daughter* was partly filmed
20.2	1.7	⇦ ↑	At crossroads, left goes to Dunquin pier
21.7	1.5	⇦ ✪	To Krugers – westernmost pub in Europe (100m)
22.3	0.6	↑ ▲	At crossroads, Dunquin Hostel on right
28.6	6.3	⇦	To beach at Smerwick Harbour (c7km return)
28.8	0.2	▲ ♦	Small shop and Black Cat Hostel
29.3	0.5	✪	Ballyferriter – couple of places offer food
29.7	0.4	✪	Local history museum

Stage 3 Tour of the Dingle Peninsula			
30.8	1.1	↖	'R559 An Daingean' (right goes to Ventry – Ceann Tra)
31.3	0.5	⇦ ✪	To Wine Strand (c1km)
		♦	Pub has small shop and serves food
33.3	2.0	←	'Gallarus, Slea Head Drive'
34.5	1.1	▲ ✪ ⇨	Gallarus campsite on corner, Gallarus Oratory visitor centre (50m on right)
36.1	1.6	← ✪	'Baile na nGall' L5006, access to beach just before turn
37.0	0.9	♦	Shop
37.1	0.1	⇦ →	At T-junction, left leads to pretty harbour and beach at Ballynagall (100m)
37.6	0.5	✪	Raidió na Gaeltachta
39.2	1.6	←	T-junction
40.2	1.0	⇦	Road leads to small quay
41.1	0.9	←	'Slea Head Drive'
45.1	4.0	⇦ →	'An Daingean', left leads to Brandon Creek (2km return)
48.4	3.3	←	'Slea Head Drive'

Stage 3 Tour of the Dingle Peninsula			
49.9	1.5	△ (115)	Fine views on ascent
56.1	6.2	O ↑	Back on outskirts of Dingle
57.1	1.0		Back at Dingle tourist information

Stage 4 Dingle to Killorglin			
0.0		→	From car park entrance by quay, next to tourist information centre, turn right
0.1	0.1	→	First junction
0.3	0.2	O →	'N86 Tralee'
8.8	8.5	→	Leave N56 just past bridge at Lispole; take care – steep climb follows
10.9	2.1	↑	Road joins from left
		↑	Carry straight on when road swings left
11.1	0.2	→	Rejoin main road opposite O'Sullivan's pub – poor visibility, take great care
12.5	1.4	←	'Baile an Bhogaigh' L1224
12.6	0.1	↗	Take right fork

Stage 4 Dingle to Killorglin			
13.7	1.1	↑	Odd crossroads – just keep in a straight-on direction
16.8	3.1	→	At T-junction in Annascaul
		←	At N86
16.9	0.1	♦ →	Small shop
17.0	0.1	✪	Tom Crean Memorial Gardens on right
18.1	1.1	←	'R561'
23.7	5.6	✪	Views of Inch Island from car park
23.8	0.1	✪	Access to Inch beach and takeaway, fast section beside water follows
33.7	9.9	♦	Shop in service station
44.1	10.4	♦ →	'N70 Killorglin', shop on corner, at Castlemaine
44.7	0.6	→	'N70 Killorglin'
47.4	2.7	←	At Milltown, follow N70, swings left
		♦	Shop
		⇧ →	'Killorglin N70', straight on to Killarney 18km
47.5	0.1	♦	Shop
48.0	0.6	← ○	'Knockavota'

Stage 4 Dingle to Killorglin			
50.0	2.0	✪	Views down Dingle Bay to Inch
51.9	1.9	←	At T-junction, rejoining N70
52.6	0.7	⇦ ▲	Laune Valley Farm Hostel
53.9	1.3	○ →	'Ring of Kerry'
54.1	0.2	✪	O'Shea's Cycles
54.2	0.1	↑	'Town centre', at crossroads, note Bianconi Inn opposite
54.3	0.1	ATM	Arrive Killorglin diamond

Stage 5 Killorglin to Portmagee			
0.0			From the diamond, take Langford Street (upper left corner by Fish Shop)
0.8	0.8	→	'Glenbeigh'
8.4	7.6	✪	Fine view of mountains ahead
9.2	0.8	↑	At crossroads with N70
10.3	1.1	←	At T-junction
10.7	0.4	→	'Glenbeigh (back on N70)'
13.1	2.4	▲	Glenross Caravan and Camping Park
13.7	0.6	♦	Shop at Glenbeigh

Stage 5 Killorglin to Portmagee			
13.9	0.2	♦	Supermarket in service station
14.1	0.2	→	'Rossbeigh'
14.4	0.3	→	'R564 Rossbeigh' (just after a small bridge)
14.7	0.3	✿	Small rest area on left
16.5	0.8	✿ WC	Rossbeigh beach
16.8	0.3	↖	At fork
17.9	1.1	△ (145)	Steep climb to here
18.3	0.4	↑	At cross roads
19.3	1.0	♦ →	'Cahersiveen' – on N70, shop on corner
21.7	2.4	✿	Viewing area on cliffs
22.2	0.5	✿	Viewing area on cliffs
22.8	0.6	✿	Rail tunnel on cliff to left
24.0	1.2	✿	On-road cycleway for 1km
24.2	0.2	✿	Viewing area
25.0	0.8	✿	Gleensk viaduct on left
25.7	0.7	▲	Caitins Hostel and Bar
26.8	1.1	→	'Kells'
28.5	1.7	↗	Take right fork, left signed 'Kells PO'
31.0	2.5	→	At T-junction (N70)

Stage 5 Killorglin to Portmagee			
31.1	0.1	←	Continue on small road parallel to N70
34.3	3.2	→	Unsigned, but 'Rock Walk' is signed to left
34.9	0.6	↑	'Dooneen', at crossroads
38.3	3.4	→	At T-junction
38.8	0.5	↖	Left fork
41.3	2.5	✿	Fabulous Arts and Crafts-style chalet in poor repair
41.4	0.1	←	At T-junction
42.1	0.7	✿	Cross bridge – note old rail bridge to left
42.4	0.3	✿	The Old Barracks heritage centre
42.5	0.1	WC	
42.6	0.1	→ ⇦ ▲ ✿	At crossroads, tourist information on right; Sive Hostel (100m) and O'Connell birthplace (1.5km) to the left
42.7	0.1	♦ ATM	Shops and pharmacy down main street
43.5	0.8	✿	Casey's Cycles
43.6	0.1	ATM ♦	Large supermarket

Stage 5 Killorglin to Portmagee			
44.2	0.6	⇨ ▲	Mannix Point Camping and Caravan Park (c600m), turn just before observatory
44.8	0.6	→	'Valentia Island ferry'
47.6	2.8	↑	Arrive ferry quay at Renard Point
47.7	0.1	⇦ →	On leaving ferry at Knightstown, turn right at T-junction in front; go left to transatlantic cable station (400m)
47.8	0.1	←	At clock
47.9	0.1	♦	Small food shop
48.1	0.2	⇦ →	Just before Church of Ireland church; bear left for lowland route by R565
48.3	0.2	✿	Valentia Island Heritage Centre
48.9	0.6	↑ ⇨	At crossroads; Glanleam House to right (1.4km)
50.9	2.0	→	'Dohilla', at crossroads, to visit tetrapod tracks
52.8	1.9	↑ ↓	Turn around at tetrapod car park (200m walk to tracks)

Stage 5 Killorglin to Portmagee			
54.7	1.9	→	Back at crossroads to slate quarry and grotto
56.0	1.3	↑ ↓	Turn at quarry and grotto
57.3	1.3	→	Back at crossroads
57.4	0.1	→	Unsigned
59.1	1.7	↑ ⇨ ✿	Geokaun Mountain and Fogher Cliffs (1.3km, entry fee)
60.2	1.1	↑	At crossroads
63.0	2.8	← ✿	Memorial to landing of first transatlantic cable is in field on right
64.7	1.7	→	'Portmagee '
65.0	0.3	✿	Skellig Experience Visitor Centre
65.6	0.6	→	'Skellig Ring', WC on corner
65.8	0.2		Arrive Portmagee, lost at sea memorial

Stage 6 Portmagee to Caherdaniel			
0.0			Portmagee car park, lost at sea memorial. Head away from bridge
		←	Road swings left
0.4	0.4	▲	Skelling Ring House

Stage 6 Portmagee to Caherdaniel			
2.6	2.2	✪	Coffee shop and walk to 'most beautiful cliffs in Kerry'
4.5	1.9	△ (250)	Views over St Finian's Bay and to Skelligs
7.6	3.1	↖	Road swings left
8.4	0.8	↖	'Cahersiveen', road swings left
10.7	2.3	△ (110)	
10.8	0.1	→	Unsigned road
16.1	5.3	↑	'Strand'
16.4	0.3	▲	Skellig Lodge & Hostel
16.6	0.2	←	'R556 Baile an Scellig'; straight on to beach and WC, right to priory
17.1	0.5	♦	Ballinskelligs post office
17.9	0.8	→	Just before gallery with thatched roof
18.3	0.4	↑	At crossroads, main road swings left, but keep heading straight on
20.5	2.2	→	At crossroads
21.2	0.7	⇨	To beach (500m)
25.8	4.6	→	'N70 Kenmare'
27.6	1.8	♦	Medium-sized shop in service station

Stage 6 Portmagee to Caherdaniel			
		↗	N70 swings right. (Straight on is good alternative but closed at time of writing.)
30.4	2.8	WC	
		⇦ ♦	Waterville tourist information and WC here, shops up street on left
30.6	0.2	✪	Charlie Chaplin statue
31.5	0.9	→	'Kerry Way'
33.6	2.1	←	Gentle climb back to main road
34.3	0.7	→	Onto N70 – careful, poor visibility, start of climb to Coomakesta Pass
38.6	4.3	△ (210)	Car park at top of pass (on right), fantastic view
		↑	Continue towards Caherdaniel
41.3	2.7	→	'Ring of Kerry Cycleway'
41.9	0.6	✪	Enter Derrynane Historic Park
42.6	0.7	← ⇧	Turn left – straight on would take you to beach

Stage 6 Portmagee to Caherdaniel

43.4	0.8	← ✪ ⇨	Turn left – right takes you to Derrynane House (600m return)
43.6	0.2	✪	Ogham stone by road
45.5	1.9	♦	Arrive Caherdaniel crossroads, Freddie's Bar on right has food and shop

Stage 7 Caherdaniel to Kenmare

0.0			Caherdaniel crossroads, go south, 'Sneem'
1.6	1.6	▲ ♦	Wave Crest Caravan & Camping Park has shop
2.5	0.9	⇨	To beach
6.2	3.7	⇦	Staigue Fort (approx 4km and 150m climb)
6.6	0.4	♦	Small shop in service station at Castle Cove
14.9	8.3	△ (130)	3-4% climb
21.0	6.1	✪ ♦	Sneem central diamond/green – note General de Gaulle memorial, also shop

Stage 7 Caherdaniel to Kenmare

21.4	0.4	⇦ ↑ ATM	'N70 Kenmare', Mace shop has ATM, left here will take you to Killarney (c45km)
24.5	3.1	✪	Parknasilla resort
30.2	5.7	✪	Lough Fadda has rather forlorn picnic table
32.9	2.7	✪	Fine section along water starts
35.3	2.4	✪	Cross river gorge (Blackwater River)
39.6	4.3	✪ ⇨	Dromore Castle (1.5km)
40.5	0.9	⇨	Turn to Coss Strand
41.0	0.5	✪	Pat Spillane's Bar, Templenoe
47.5	6.5	→	'Town Centre', at T-junction, Kenmare
47.6	0.1	♦	Supermarket in service station
48.2	0.6		Arrive Kenmare central park, tourist information on right

Stage 8 Kenmare to Killarney

0.0			Kenmare, outside heritage centre/ tourist office, cycle north
0.6	0.6	←	'N70 Cahersiveen'

Stage 8 Kenmare to Killarney			
5.8	5.2	→	'Rossacoosane'
10.3	4.5	△ (200)	Climb levels out onto open moor
12.6	2.3	→	'Killarney'
14.1	1.5	✿	Barfinnhy Lake has picnic table
14.9	0.8	←	'Black Valley Hostel', carry straight on for a few metres for fine view
17.6	2.7	→	'Hillcrest Farmhouse'
22.2	4.6	✿	Pass rapids on Owenreagh River
25.2	3.0	⇨	To Lord Brandon's Cottage (c1km)
26.4	1.2	▲	Black Valley Hostel
27.0	0.6	→	First turn past hostel
29.1	2.1	△ (240)	Head of the Gap of Dunloe
35.2	6.1	▲	Kate Kearney's Cottage Café
36.8	1.6	→	'Killarney'
40.7	3.9	→	'N72 Killarney'
41.3	0.6	▲	Fossa Caravan & Camping Park and Hostel
41.6	0.3	▲	Beech Grove Caravan & Camping Park
44.0	2.4	♦	Good shop in Esso station

Stage 8 Kenmare to Killarney			
45.8	1.8	○ →	'Town centre'
46.9	1.1	↑	'Town centre parking' (left also goes into town)
47.6	0.7	←	'Tourist office'
47.7	0.1	← WC	Turn into car park by tourist office

Stage 9 Killarney to Tralee			
0.0			Killarney tourist information centre, from car park entrance go north
0.1	0.1	→	At T-junction (New Street)
0.3	0.2	←	One-way (High Street)
0.6	0.3	↑	'All routes N22 Tralee'
1.4	0.8	♦	Supermarket
1.5	0.1	○ ↑	'N22 Tralee'
2.2	0.7	←	'Aghadoe'
2.6	0.4	⇦	To Aghadoe church and round tower (5km return)
7.5	4.9	↑	At crossroads
10.1	2.6	↑	At crossroads
11.4	1.3	↑	At crossroads
14.2	2.8	→	'R561 Farranfore'
14.4	0.2	←	'Ballyfinnane'

Stage 9 Killarney to Tralee				
18.2	3.8	↑		'Tralee', at Ballyfinnane crossroads
19.8	1.6	✪		Ballyfinnane Hill Climb Monument
21.9	2.1	△		Windy summit plateau
22.1	0.2	↑		At crossroads
23.9	1.8	←		Road veers left
25.9	2.0	↑		Cross N70
27.2	1.3	→		At crossroads
29.5	0.8	✪		Level crossing
29.7	0.2	○ ↑ ▲ ⇨		R551 town centre, turn right here for Woodlands camping
30.1	0.4	↑		At lights
30.2	0.1	▲		Jim Caball Himself cycle shop on right
30.3		↑		Town Centre
30.4	0.2	→		Killarney N21 (just past orange Brogue Inn)
30.5	0.1	←		Into Bridge Street
30.7	0.2	→		Tourist Office
30.9	0.2	←		Museum in front
31.0	0.1			Arrive tourist information

Killarney to Kenmare via Ladies View				
0.0				Killarney tourist office, Beech Road, turn right out of car park
0.1	0.1	←		'N71 Kenmare', at T-junction
0.3	0.2	○ →		'N71 Kenmare' – big roundabout
0.5	0.2	○ ↑		Mini-roundabout
0.6	0.1	✪ ⇨		Ross Castle (c3km)
1.0	0.4	♦		Shop in service station
		⇦ ▲ ↑		At lights, left leads to White Bridge Caravan and Camping Park (c2.5km)
1.7	0.7	→		Cross road, join cycleway parallel to road by phone boxes; stay on road if going to caravan park
2.4	0.7	▲		Killarney Flesk Caravan & Camping Park
2.6	0.2	♦		Shop at service station
3.3	0.7	✪		Cycleway enters national park
3.8	0.5	↗		Unsigned
4.6	0.8	✪ ↑		'Muckross House', Muckross Abbey on left

Killarney to Kenmare via Ladies View			
5.6	1.0	→ ⇧ ✪	'Meeting of the Waters', Muckross House straight on
9.2	3.6	✪	Brickeen Bridge
10.3	1.1	✪ ⇨	Dinnis Cottage and Meeting of the Waters
11.9	1.6	→	At car park
		→	Join N71
14.0	2.1	✪	Five Mile Bridge – good lake views
15.9	1.9	✪	Alongside Upper Lough
16.6	0.7	✪	Through rock arch, steady climb follows

Killarney to Kenmare via Ladies View			
19.0	2.4	△ (110)	Galway's Bridge
19.8	0.8	✪	Ruined, turreted lodge
20.1	0.3	✪ ♦	Ladies View Cafe
20.3	0.2	✪ ♦	Real Ladies View
21.6	1.3	✪	Best view
26.3	4.7	↖	'N71, Kenmare', Avoca café and shop on corner at Moll's Gap
35.7	9.4	♦	Shop in Esso station
36.3	0.6		Arrive Kenmare central park, tourist information on right

ROUTE 6 THE FUCHSIA COAST

The coast becomes wilder towards the tip of the Beara peninsula (Stage 1)

Start	Kenmare
Finish	Cork City
Distance	359.3km
Ascent	6107m

Southwest Ireland's characteristic pattern of narrow bays and long headlands continues along the Wild Atlantic Way south of Glengarriff. The Beara Peninsula, with its wild rocky western tip and the warm waters of Bantry Bay to the south, is particularly appealing. The Mizen Peninsula has the added attraction of having Ireland's most southwesterly point at Mizen Head.

After the peninsula hopping, the stretch of South Cork from Schull through to the official end of the Wild Atlantic Way at Kinsale makes a pleasant change. The coast east to Cork is wildly fissured, with small villages clustering around narrow harbours. Two of the most idyllic are brightly painted Unionhall, and Glandore (just after) which nestles between tumbling woodlands and the water.

Kinsale is one of Cork's most popular visitor towns – and deservedly so. This is a fitting terminus for the official Wild Atlantic Way. Cork city, although less attractive, still has its fair share of fine buildings and is a further day ahead along rolling country roads.

BETTER BY BIKE

This cycling route from Kenmare to the end of the Wild Atlantic Way at Kinsale tries to keep distances reasonable along a very indented coast where the miles clock up and the hills turn them into long ones. The described route skips the slow run out to Sheep's Head, south of Bantry, and ignores some of the return trips the Wild Atlantic Way

makes to the coast south of Skibbereen and Clonakilty. The route described also tries to keep away from the main roads which become busy, particularly east of Skibbereen.

GETTING TO THE START

Kenmare does not have great transport connections, making cycling the

FUCHSIAS

From late spring until the shoulder of winter, bright red and purple flowers emblazon the hedgerows of Kerry and Cork. The wild fuchsia is not native to Europe, and is of doubtful environmental benefit – back in native Chile, fuchsias support pollinating hummingbirds; here the plant is of limited value to local insects. Nevertheless, West Cork has taken the visitor to heart, even using it, rather appropriately, in tourist branding. The fuchsias flourish alongside other ornamentals, native plants and woodlands, along a coast kept warm and moist by the Gulf Stream.

Route summary table

Stage		Distance	Ascent	Accommodation available	Places with shops/other facilities en route
1	Kenmare to Allihies	76.1km	1399m	Eyeries	Ardgroom
2	Allihies to Glengarriff	57.6km	880m	Garranes, Berehaven, Adrigole	Castletownberehaven
3	Glengarriff to Schull	94.5km	1462m	Eagle Point, Bantry, Barley Cove	Bantry, Durrus
4	Schull to Clonakilty	61.1km	1085m	Skibbereen, Glandore, Ownahinchy	Skibbereen
5	Clonakilty to Kinsale	44.8km	753m	Timoleague, Garrettstown	Timoleague, Garrettstown
6	Kinsale to Cork City	25.2km	528m		Ballinhassig
Total		**359.3km**	**6107m**		Portnoo

easiest way to get to the start of this route. Starting at Killarney adds an attractive day's riding to the start of this route.

By rail/bus

The closest railway station is 35km away at Killarney, see Route 5, Stage 8.

WHEN TO GO

Any time from spring to autumn.

ACCOMMODATION

Accommodation is thin on the ground on for the first three stages of this tour – with exceptions around Glengarriff and Bantry, but you should still be able to find something to suit your budget. From Schull onwards the choice improves although there are very few hostels. There are, however, some excellent camp sites along the coast.

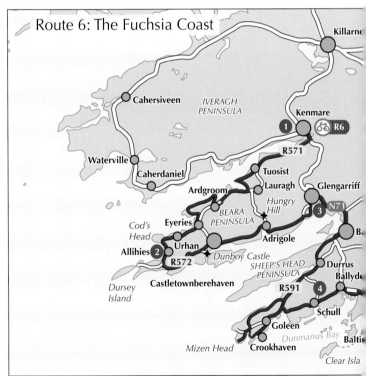

Route 6: The Fuchsia Coast

Killarne

Cahersiveen

IVERAGH
PENINSULA

Kenmare

1 🚲 **R6**

R571

Waterville

Caherdaniel

Tuosist

Lauragh

Glengarriff

Ardgroom

Hungry
Hill

3 N71

Cod's
Head

Eyeries

BEARA
PENINSULA

Allihies **2**

Urhan

Adrigole

B.

R572

Dunboy Castle

SHEEP'S HEAD
PENINSULA

Durrus

Ballyd

Dursey
Island

Castletownberehaven

R591

4

Schull

Goleen

Dunmanus Bay

Balti

Mizen Head

Crookhaven

Clear Isla

Author riding along the north side of the Mizen peninsula (Stage 3)

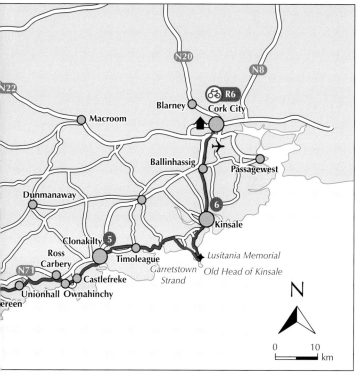

Looking towards the Old Head of Kinsale from Garretstown Beach (Stage 5)

MAPS

The OSI 1:250,000 Ireland South sheet covers the whole of Route 6. For 1:50,000 coverage, the following sheets from the OSI Discovery series are needed: 85 Cork Kerry, 84 Cork Kerry, 88 Cork, 89 Cork, 87 Cork. About 1km of the route leaving Kenmare is on sheet 78 Kerry – but it is barely worth buying this unless required for another route.

OPTIONS

Shortcuts are possible across all the peninsulas. If flying out of Cork, there is no need to head right into Cork City, as Stage 6 passes within 10km of the airport.

ONWARDS

For a circular route back to Kenmare consider going east from Cork to Youghal, then north and west to Killarney via the Blackwater Valley.

STAGE 1
Kenmare to Allihies

Start	Kenmare
Distance	76.1km
Ascent	1399m
Terrain	Tiring, short sharp climbs
Summit	100m at 68km

This is a hard but rewarding day. All the peninsulas show a marked transition from a relatively protected climate and lush vegetation at their eastern end, towards a rocky, exposed western tip, but it is on the **Beara Peninsula** that this change is the most abrupt and dramatic. The last sign of lush woodland is around **Lauragh** where Derreen Garden (open year round, 10am–6pm 064 6683588, www. derreengarden.com) is known for its subtropical plants. To the west is a land of open coasts and small harbours and wave-scoured headlands.

The open headlands provide dramatic backdrops for both the **Ballycrovane Ogham Stone** and the **Hag of Beara**, just before Eyeries.

According to legend this rock is the remains of the ancient Hag of Beara, awaiting the return of her husband

The **Hag of Beara** is one of the oldest and most powerful of mythical beings associated with Ireland, said to have lived seven lives before being turned to stone here, waiting for her husband Manannan, God of the Sea, to return to her.

Ogham is a primitive script that probably dates from the fourth century. It reads vertically and the letters of the alphabet are represented by a series of lines, commonly carved along the edge of a rock or stone. The Ballycrovane stone is the tallest one in Europe.

On a dull day the bright yellow, pink, red and green houses of **Eyeries** (59km) glow optimistically in a landscape of grey water and grey rock. When the sun shines the water sparkles and the small coves invite swimmers.

After crossing a col in the lee of **Cod's Head**, the coast road enters some of the most dramatic scenery in Ireland. Grey stone hills with tortuously folded rocks plunge down into the open Atlantic. Abandoned copper workings dot the mountains here.

Allihies, like Eyeries before it, is painted brightly, as if to ward off the some-times bleak landscape. Here a warm hostel and a fine beach await. There is also the Allihies Copper Mine Museum (027 73218, www.acmm.ie) in a restored non-conformist chapel just through the village.

On the road
The best shop on the stage is at **Ardgroom**. Take cash with you from Kenmare. There is no ATM until Castletownberehaven, 19km along Stage 2. As noted above, be prepared for this stage to be more tiring than the relatively small climbs sug-gest. There is a supermarket in Allihies at the end of the day.

Accommodation
Kenmare has as wide a choice of hotel and B&B accommodation as anywhere on the Ring of Kerry. For an extensive list see www.kenmare.com. For hos-tel accommodation in Kenmare there is the Failte Hostel (087 7116092, www.kenmarehostel.com). Just head up Main Street, turn right at Shelbourne Street and it's 200m on your left.

Accommodation is limited in the area around Allihies but in the heart of town you will find the Seaview Guest House (02 773004, www.allihiesseaview.com). If you wish to shorten the day, there is B&B accommodation around Eyeries.

Allihies Hostel (027 73107, www.allihieshostel.net) is right in the heart of the village. Earlier in the day there is camping and budget accommodation at Beara Camping (13.8km, 064 6684287, www.bearacamping.com) – but take supplies as there is not much around here. Further on is an independent hostel at Glanmore Lake (28km, 064 6683181) a couple of kilometres off the route.

Creeveen Lodge Caravan and Camping Park (064 6683131, www.creveenlodge.
com) is in the same area. See Options for directions.

Options
It is possible to complete Kenmare to Glengarriff in one day (and save about 71km)
by following the Healy Pass across the peninsula from Lauragh to Adrigole. For
this option, turn left at 27.8km, then right after about 300m and onto the R574.
Creeveen Lodge camping is a further 1.5km down this road. The pass summits at
about 300m and you rejoin the route card at 35.6km on Stage 2. This gives a total
distance for Kenmare to Glengarriff of about 63km. An earlier turn to the Healy
Pass (at 16.5km) saves another 4km, but involves an extra climb to about 170m.

STAGE 2
Allihies to Glengarriff

Start	Allihies
Distance	57.6km
Ascent	880m
Terrain	A few easy climbs
Summit	120m at 46km

From **Allihies** the terrain becomes gentler, but not without a final flourish climbing over the spine of the peninsula through the Bealbarnish Gap (4km). The turn
for **Dursey Island** – one of the 'Discovery Points' on the Wild Atlantic Way – is
just over this summit. The island is reached by a cable car slung over a swirling
tidal race.

Approaching the bustling port of **Castletownberehaven** there is a chance to
see **Dunboy Castle** and Puxley's Mansion.

Dunboy Castle was the scene of the 1602 Siege of Dunboy, in which the
English broke O'Sullivan Bere rule over the peninsula.

Castletownberehaven, now a busy fishing port, was one of the Irish Treaty
Ports, not abandoned by the British until 1939.

Glengarriff nestles at the base of the Beara peninsula

East of the town a grey rockface starts to loom over the road – this is the **Hungry Hill** from the Daphne du Maurier novel of the same name. The hill is the highest peak in the spine of the peninsula. In the novel, the Puxleys, who grew rich from the Beara copper mines, are called the Brodricks, and **Puxley's Mansion** is Clonmere. The Mansion, once an atmospheric ruin, was subjected to a failed hotel development at the height of Ireland's property boom – and is now boarded up.

Glengarriff, an attractive town that shows its resort pedigree through the fine 250-year-old Eccles Hotel commanding the mountain-backed bay. Garinish Island, with its Italianate gardens and lush subtropical vegetation, is worth a visit.

On the road
Castletownberehaven has shops, an ATM and a central square in which to sit down for a break. The small quay near Puxley's Mansion/Dunboy Castle is also pleasant. There is no ATM in Glengarriff.

Accommodation
There is camping on the way into town at Glengarriff Caravan and Camping Park (027 63154, open March to October). For details of other accommodation, enquire at the tourist office (027 63084) or see www.glengarriff.ie. The town has

a good selection of B&Bs and hotel accommodation. Glengarriff once had two operating hostels, but both were closed at the time of writing.

Early on the stage (11km) is Garranes Hostel (027 73032, www.dzogchenbeara.org). For camping, a short way east of Castletownberehaven you will find the Berehaven Camper and Amenity Park (027 70700, www.berehavengolf.com/camping at 23km). Adrigole has the Hungry Hill Lodge Hostel and campsite (027 60228, www.hungryhilllodgeandcampsite.com).

Options

Consider pushing on to Bantry to take some of the sting out of Stage 3.

It is possible to skip the side road at 48.0km and stay on the R572 into Glengarriff (rejoining the route card at 53.7km), saving 4km and some short climbs but missing some pretty coastline. The trip out to the Dursey Island cable car would add about 16km to the stage. Check www.durseyisland.ie for the latest operating information.

STAGE 3

Glengarriff to Schull

Start	Glengarriff
Distance	94.5km
Ascent	1462m
Terrain	Coastal hills
Summit	160m at 24km

This stage heads to Ireland's far southwestern tip at Mizen Head, and it is common to meet groups of cyclists on the Malin to Mizen (or Mizen to Malin) length-of-Ireland run – usually done in a week or so.

The town of **Bantry** is a fine traditional market town, with winding narrow streets and an open square by the harbour. Memorials in the square and around town commemorate the invading French fleets of 1689 and 1796, and there is more about the fleets at nearby Bantry House & Garden (open daily 10am–5pm April to October, 027 50047, www.bantryhouse.com).

During the Second World War years ('the Emergency' in Ireland) the Second Cyclist Squadron of the Irish Army was stationed at **Bantry House**. This fine

Mizen Head

18th-century pile has some grand authentic interiors and the gardens are also of interest.

The south side of **Dunmanus Bay** has a couple of tumbling tower-house castles. Dunmanus Castle is the best preserved of the O'Mahony castles that dot the Mizen, and it guards a pretty harbour of the same name.

Mizen Head has a visitor centre (028 35115, www.mizenhead.net), and you pay €7.50 to walk right out to the lighthouse, but it is a spectacular spot (open daily March to October, weekends only in winter, closing time varies from 4pm in winter to 7pm in high summer). Just round the corner, **Crookhaven** is a picturesque harbour village in a long, narrow rocky cove.

A little further round the south coast, Barley Cove is a fine swimming beach also notable for the fine machair grasslands behind the foreshore.

At the end of the day, **Schull** is the first decent-sized town since Bantry.

On the road

Bantry is the biggest town in the area. As well as general stores and ATMs, Nigel's Bicycle Shop (027 52 657) is on the way into town from the north. Wolf Tone Square has benches, and even public toilets nearby. Durrus has a fine shop, and the local cheese, Durrus Gold, is an excellent traveller.

Accommodation

Schull now has camping a few hundred metres from town at Summerfield Campsite/B&B (086 7252031, www.campinginschullsummerfield.com). Take the first turn on the right after entering town (from the west), signed 'Colla'. Check www.schull.ie for the latest on accommodation in the Schull area but the village is a popular destination and supports a hotel, the Schull Harbour Hotel (028 28801, www.schullharbourhotel.ie) and a handful of B&Bs.

Earlier in the day are the excellent waterside facilities at Eagle Point Camping (11km, 027 50630, www.eaglepointcamping.com) some 6km before Bantry. Bantry town has B&B and hotel accommodation (see www.bantry.ie for an up-to-date list) but beware of festival weekends (see the same site for dates) when the town can fill up. The closest site to Mizen Head is Barley Cove Holiday Park (72km, 028 35302, www.barleycoveholidaypark.ie, open June to September).

Options

There are a few shortcuts across the Mizen to Schull, at 32.3 and 36.2km, giving total distances, Glengarriff to Schull, of approximately 42km and 46.km respectively.

STAGE 4
Schull to Clonakilty

Start	Schull
Distance	61.1km
Ascent	1085m
Terrain	Gentle coastal hills
Summit	100m at 40km

To the east of Schull it is necessary to stay some distance inland at times to keep the distances down. The cycling is nonetheless pleasant, the roads are not too busy, and the interest starts to pick up approaching Skibbereen.

This area was one of the worst affected by the **Great Famine** of 1845–9. The famine is one of the watersheds in Irish history. Find out more at the Skibbereen Heritage Centre (028 40900, www.skibbheritage.com), which is open 10am–6pm daily from mid-May to late September.

By the slate-roofed waterside village of **Unionhall** the coast has settled into a pattern of inlets snaking into low coastal hills. Glandore, across the inlet from Unionhall, with its tiny harbour and beach hemmed by wooded slopes, is straight off a holiday postcard. Just past here, the Drombeg Stone Circle is a well-visited megalithic site. Further on, Ross Carbery, now bypassed by the highway, is a classic hilltop market town.

Ownahinchy (Ownahincha) has a bathing beach. The castellated Gothic outline of Castlefreke is in private hands, but nearby Rathbarry is one of the finest estate villages in Ireland.

Clonakilty is a bright and bustling market town. Irish patriot Michael Collins was born here, and in the centre of town there is a statue of him overlooking an elegant garden square.

Michael Collins was a charismatic Irish revolutionary who also showed organisational and political skills in his role as minister for finance in the First Dáil (parliament) of 1919. Find out more at the Michael Collins Centre (023 8846107, www.michaelcollinscentre.com), about 5.5km along Stage 5. Michael Collins was killed in the civil war that followed the Anglo-Irish Treaty.

Ownahinchy strand

Michael Collins looks out on Clonakilty

On the road

The best place to shop before Clonakilty is the supermarket at Schull. Skibbereen also has plenty of shops and ATMs. By the harbour in Unionhall is a good halfway point for a break. Ownahinchy is the best beach on the stage.

This stage finishes with a loop through the town centre. And a short detour up the hill into Ross Carbery is also rewarding. Clonakilty has a cycle shop – MTM Cycles is on Ashe Street (023 8833584).

Accommodation

This holiday coast is well provided with campsites, but the hostel situation is not great. Meadow Camping (028 33280) is close to Glandore (39km). O'Riordan's Caravan Park (023 8848216) is by the beach at Ownahinchy.

Clonakilty is one of those towns where hostels appear sporadically, so check www.clonakilty.ie for the latest information. Clonakilty is a hardworking market town and local hub which supports a number of B&Bs, guesthouses and hotels. The route passes the tourist information office (023 8833226), opening hours vary. The Desert House Caravan and Camping Park (023 8833331) overlooks the bay and is only a couple of kilometres from Clonakilty – carry straight on at 0.4km on Stage 5. The Russagh Mill Hostel (028 22451, www.russaghmillhostel.com), a couple of kilometres outside Skibbereen on the Castletownshend road, also has camping – turn right at 23.5km and follow R596 Castletownshend signs. On the same road is the Hideaway Camping and Caravan Park (028 22254).

Options
If you are stopping mid-stage, Skibbereen is the best choice for accommodation. There are a couple of hotels in town and a choice of B&Bs. From Skibbereen you could head south to Baltimore (13km) where you can catch a ferry to Cape Clear Island (028 39159, www.cailinoir.com).

STAGE 5
Clonakilty to Kinsale

Start	Clonakilty
Distance	44.8km
Ascent	753m
Terrain	Gentle coastal hills
Summit	135m at 6km

One of the highlights of the start of the stage is the airy ridge road leaving **Clonakilty** with views back as far as the Beara Peninsula. The route soon passes the Michael Collins Centre (023 8846107, www.michaelcollinscentre.com) and soon after this is **Timoleague**, with its 13th-century Franciscan friary set alongside tidal flats at the head of a protected estuary.

> The original monastic settlement at Timoleague was founded by **St Mologa** in the sixth century. He also brought beekeeping to Ireland.

Garranefeen Strand has well-developed saltmarsh and dune systems, but after here the stage leaves the shore for a while until the approach to one of the scenic highpoints of the south coast – the **Old Head of Kinsale**. The head itself, a 5km long promontory of slates and grits, is probably most impressive from the fine beach at **Garrettstown**, but the ride out to near the end is worthwhile for the sense of space and the views along the coast. The very tip of the head is a private golf course, but the ruined castle, a signal tower and the **Lusitania Memorial** are all before the gates.

The Cunard liner **RMS Lusitania** was torpedoed about 13km off the Old Head of Kinsale by a German U-boat in May 1915. Of the 1959 passengers and crew, 1198 died.

Kinsale is a beautifully situated historic port town that has maintained a traditional core. The Battle of Kinsale in 1601 had far-reaching consequences in Irish history. In the historic centre, Desmond Castle is a fine example of an urban tower-house. The Wild Atlantic Way officially ends at Kinsale.

On the road
One or other of the beaches at Garrettstown is a good point to take a break. There is a small shop nearby, but it is better to pick something up at Timoleague, which has a shop at the service station, or even before leaving Clonakilty. There are no shops between Garrettstown and Kinsale. At the end of the day Kinsale has a choice of shops, including a supermarket in the middle of town. There are also plenty of ATMs.

Accommodation
Dempsey's Hostel (021 4772124, www.dempseyhostel.com) is on the R600 towards Cork, about 700m from the centre of Kinsale. You can also pitch a tent in the garden there. The town is a popular getaway for well-heeled Cork dwellers

Kinsale Harbour

and the riverside area, in particular, is packed with overnight accommodation options. Summer prices are, however, on the high side. See www.kinsale.ie for a selection.

The nearest campsite to Kinsale is at the Garrettstown Holiday Park (021 4778156, www.garrettstownhouse.com), which is about 14km away. Pad Joe's pub in Timoleague offers hostel-style accommodation (023 8846125).

Options
Combining this stage with Stage 6 makes it is possible to ride Clonakilty to Cork in a long day (70km).

STAGE 6
Kinsale to Cork

Start	Kinsale
Distance	25.2km
Ascent	528m
Terrain	Undulating with one steep climb
Summit	150m at 16km

This old route from **Kinsale** to Cork gives a taste of what many Irish main roads were like until not very long ago. The former highway rolls over hill and dale. Trees and hedgerows crowd in, while a patchwork of green pasture and yellow wheatfields spreads to the low hills on the horizon.

The road passes through the sites of the English and Irish encampments in the lead up to the **Battle of Kinsale** in 1601. The English forces were camped on a ridge immediately north of the town (2km). The Irish forces occupied a ridge further towards Cork (6km) as they sought to assist Spanish forces besieged in Kinsale town. Defeat at the Battle of Kinsale heralded the end of the old Gaelic order in Ireland. Hugh O'Neill, Earl of Tyrone, headed back to Ulster, while 'Red' Hugh O'Donnell left for Spain.

The southern approach to Cork City is guarded by a line of low Old Red Sandstone hills. The climb up from **Ballinhassig** is close to 20 per cent, making

Cork City

it the steepest in this guidebook. The entry into Cork from this side is through charmless housing estates, but the route is easy to follow into the heart of the city.

Cork City itself has some fine public buildings and elegant shopping streets. Tourist attractions include ringing the famous Bells of Shandon at St Anne's Church, and visiting the 19th-century Gothic Cork City Gaol, now a heritage centre.

On the road

This is a surprisingly hilly route. The only shop on route is at Ballinhassig. If heading onwards past Cork, the city is the place to resupply and organise any bike maintenance you might need. There is a choice of cycle shops. Kilgrews Cycle Centre (021 4276255, www.kilgrewscycles.ie) is in the central area of the city. Just head north up Grand Parade/Corn Market and look for Kyle Street on the left just before the river. There is any number of outdoor equipment suppliers, including the Outdoor Adventure Store on Paul Street (021 4276382, www.oasoutdoors.co.uk). The tourist office (021 4255100), on Grand Parade, is closed on Sundays.

Accommodation

Cork has a five-star An Óige hostel (021 4543289, www.anoige.ie) about 1km to the west of the city centre, near University College Cork. There is an active independent hostel scene. Kinlay House (021 4508966, www.kinlayhousecork.ie) advertises bike storage. Cork, as the Republic of Ireland's second largest city, draws in a cluster of hotels, including major international chains. A look at www.cork.ie will show you the wide

Saint Fin Barre's Cathedral, Cork is the first major building by notable Victorian architect William Burges

range of hotel and B&B accommodation in and around the city.

For camping, Blarney Caravan & Camping Park (021 4516519, www.blarneycaravanpark.com) is about 9km to the northwest of the city. It is possible to get there, avoiding the main roads, by picking up Blarney Road, off Shandon Street, just north of the river, and then following this small road out of the city. Take the right fork at Cloghan crossroads, which is about 500m after the last industrial estate. The campsite is signed from Blarney.

Options

If you are heading straight to Cork airport, it is on the south side of the city. From this stage at Ballinhassig (13.4km) follow the R613 east and then the R600. It is about 9km.

Stage 1 Kenmare to Allihies

0.0			Kenmare, the Square, by central park area next to visitor information sign, follow N71 Glengarriff
0.3	0.3	→	'N71 all routes', at top of Main Street
0.5	0.2	← ▲	'Glengarriff 27', Failte Hostel on this corner
1.4	0.9	→	'Castletownbere R571', just over bridge
7.6	6.2	♦	Small shop
13.8	6.2	▲	Beara Camping and The Peacock hostel
13.9	0.1	⇦ ✪	Gleninchaquin Park (c7km)
16.5	2.6	⇧ →	'R573 Castletownbere', straight on to the Healy Pass
18.6	2.1	✪	Waterfall
22.8	4.2	✪	Can get down to stony beach
24.5	1.7	✪	Killmakillioge Quay
27.3	2.8	✪ ⇨	Derreen Garden

Stage 1 Kenmare to Allihies

27.8	0.5	⇦ ▲ →	'Castletownbere R571', turn left for Creveen Lodge Caravan and Camping about 2km
28.8	1.0	⇦ ▲	An Óige Hostel at Glanmore Lake about 2km
31.5	2.7	✪	By inlet – rock and water landscape
35.1	3.6	✪	Co Cork boundary
36.7	1.6	↖	'Beara Way cycle route'
36.8	0.1	↗	Bear right at fork
38.7	1.9	→	Turn right into Ardgroom village
38.9	0.2	← ♦	'L4911 Ring of Beara', shop on corner
42.3	3.4	←	Road swings left at small harbour
42.7	0.4	↗	Road swings right
42.9	0.2	↖ ✪ ⇨	Road swings left, right leads to beach
43.3	0.4	△ (70)	Few sharp climbs, views along coast
44.1	0.8	✪ ⇨	To Luas pier
44.7	0.6	→	'Ring of Beara'

Stage 1 Kenmare to Allihies

47.0	2.3	→	'Ring of Beara', at T-junction
52.8	5.8	↑	'Ring of Beara', at crossroads
54.6	1.8	✪	Hag of Beara
56.4	1.8	✪ ⇨	Ballycrovane ogham stone, about 150m on left, small entry charge
56.8	0.4	→	'Ring of Beara'
59.6	2.8	♦	Small shop at Eyeries
59.9	0.3	♦	Shop and café
60.2	0.3	→	'R571 Castletownbere-haven'
60.8	0.6	→	'R575 Allihies'
64.2	3.4	✪ ⇨	To beach, 100m
64.9	0.7	▲	Shop and hostel at Urhan
67.7	2.8	←	'R575 Allihies'
68.3	0.6	△ (100)	Stiff climb – views to Kerry Heads and lonely road along coast
68.7	0.4	✪	Mass rock
70.7	2.0	△ (95)	Views south to Sheep's Head Peninsula
71.7	1.0	✪	As far west as we go
73.1	1.4	✪	Parking area, benches

Stage 1 Kenmare to Allihies

73.9	0.8	✪	Harbour at foot of massive hills of exposed grey rock
74.2	0.3	✪	Massively folded rocks
74.6	0.4	✪	Copper workings all around
74.8	0.2	← ○	'Allihies', beach is straight on about 2km
76.1	1.3	▲ ♦ WC	Arrive Allihies, hostel on left, WC on right, supermarket 100m further on

Stage 2 Allihies to Glengarriff

0.0			From centre of Allihies, by hostel across from WC, head south
0.1	0.1	♦	Supermarket
0.4	0.3	✪	Allihies Copper Mine Museum
1.1	0.7	✪ ⇨	Turn right for sandy cove (1.3km return)
3.9	2.8	✪	Parking area, bench view of coast
4.1	0.2	△ (110)	Bealbarnish Gap
4.3	0.2	✪ ⇨	Leads to Dursey Island (c8km)
11.3	7.0	▲	Garranes Hostel

Stage 2 Allihies to Glengarriff

12.1	0.8	△ (110)	Top of long, gentle climb, views east along coast
16.8	4.7	✪ ⇨	Dunboy Castle and Puxley Mansion (2.5km) return
19.6	2.8	✪	Centre of Castletownbere-haven – benches
19.8	0.2	▲ ♦ ATM	Supermarket has ATM, hostel on left
20.1	0.3	✪	Timothy Harrington statue
20.9	0.8	✪	Anchor in park from French Fleet of 1796
21.9	1.0	♦	Shop at service station; Bike n Beara bike shop
23.9	2.0	▲	Berehaven Camper & Amenity Park
26.6	2.7	✪	Hungry Hill looms over road
35.3	8.7	▲	Hungry Hill Lodge & Camping Site – register at pub
35.5	0.2	♦	Shop
35.6	0.1	⇦	'R574 Healey Pass'
37.0	1.4	✪ ⇨	Road to beach and pier (500m)
39.5	2.5	✪ ⇨	To beach
40.5	1.0	✪ ⇨	To beach

Stage 2 Allihies to Glengarriff

40.8	0.3	♦	Small shop in service station
46.4	5.6	△ (130)	Views over Bantry Bay
48.0	1.6	→	'L4926 Seal Harbour' (can continue on main road)
48.4	0.4	← ⇧	Turn left, continue straight on for Seal Harbour (600m) – turn is easy to miss, behind rock!
52.0	3.6	✪	View over Garinish Island
53.2	1.2	←	Road swings left
53.7	0.5	→	Rejoin R572
55.1	1.4	▲	Two camping parks – O'Shea's and Glengarriff
57.3	2.2	→	'Bantry' at T-junction in Glengarriff
57.6	0.3	WC ✪	Tourist information

Stage 3 Glengarriff to Schull

0.0			Glengarriff tourist information office – head east on N71 towards Bantry
0.2	0.2	✪	Park with benches
0.5	0.3	✪	Glengarriff pier – ferries to Garinish Island

Stage 3 Glengarriff to Schull			
0.6	0.1	♦	Shop in service station
1.3	0.7	✪ ⇨	Beach
9.3	8.0	✪	Cross River Coomhola as it enters Bantry Bay
11.0	1.7	♦ ⇨ ▲	shop in service station on left, turn right for Eagle Point Camping
16.0	5.0	♦	Shop in service station
17.0	1.0	♦	Small shop
17.1	0.1	♦	Nigel's Bicycle Shop
17.5	0.4	⬉ WC	Follow one-way system into Bantry
17.6	0.1	✪	Tourist information on left – now in Wolfe Tone Square
		→	'N71 Skibbereen'
		✪ ATM♦	Square has benches, ATM across road, shops back in town
17.8	0.2	WC ATM	Shops and ATM on left
18.1	0.3	♦	Shop in service station
18.8	0.7	✪	Entrance to Bantry House on left

Stage 3 Glengarriff to Schull			
19.9	1.1	→	'Killcrohane' (second of two turns close together)
22.5	2.6	←	'Sheep's Head Way, Durrus'
22.8	0.3	←	'Sheep's Head Way, Durrus'
24.4	1.6	△ (160)	Very steep climb – fine views over Bantry Bay
26.1	1.7	←	Just after bridge
26.7	0.6	⬈	Road swings right
26.8	0.1	⬉	Road swings left
28.9	2.1	←	At crossroads, turn over stone bridge
29.9	1.0	♦ →	At T-junction in Durrus, store opposite
		↑	'R591 Crookhaven'
32.3	2.4	⇦	Shortcut to Ballydehob (8km) or Schull (10km)
35.5	3.2	✪	Castle on right
36.2	0.7	⇦	Shortcut to Schull (10km)
43.9	7.7	→	Unsigned turn by empty farmhouse
45.2	1.3	✪	Dunmanus harbour
45.5	0.3	✪	Castle

Stage 3 Glengarriff to Schull

52.5	7.0	△ (150)	Fine views along coast
57.9	5.4	↑	At crossroads
58.9	1.0	→	'Mizen Head'
59.4	0.5	⇦	To Barley Cove (1km)
60.9	1.5	←	'Mizen Head'
64.8	3.9	↑↓	Mizen Head car park, turn around, retrace steps
68.7	3.9	→	At T-junction
70.2	1.5	→	'Crookhaven'
70.9	0.7	⇦ ✪	Beach – fine machair behind Barley Cove
72.8	1.9	▲	Barley Cove Holiday Park
73.2	0.4	← ⇨	'Schull', for Crookhaven turn right (c2km)
74.9	1.7	✪	Past mineral-loading chutes
79.0	4.1	↑ ♦	'Schull', at cross-roads in Goleen, shops and greengrocer
84.0	5.0	✪	Lagoon at Toormoor
85.2	1.2	♦	Small shop
86.8	1.6	✪	Altar wedge tomb
94.2	7.4	▲ ⇨	Turn for Summerfield Camping

Stage 3 Glengarriff to Schull

94.4	0.2	♦	Supermarket (car park entrance is back near bank)
94.5	0.1		Finish by turn to pier

Stage 4 Schull to Clonakilty

0.0			Schull – by turn to pier, continue east on R591
7.6	7.6	↑	'N71 Skibbereen', at crossroads, in Ballydehob
7.7	0.1	✪	Statue to Danno O'Mahony, 1935-6 Heavyweight All In Wrestling Champion
7.9	0.2	♦	Shop
		WC	Roadside park
8.0	0.1	✪	Cross bridge; note fine viaduct on former Schull & Skibbereen railway line
9.2	1.2	→	'Skeaghanore West' (take care, poor visibility behind)
10.4	1.2	↑	At crossroads
10.7	0.3	↑	Continue ahead as road swings right
11.6	0.9	↑	At crossroads
12.5	0.9	↑	At crossroads

Stage 4 Schull to Clonakilty

12.6	0.1	✪	Ruined church
13.0	0.4	↖	After bridge take left fork
14.0	1.0	→	Onto N71
14.6	0.6	✪	Layby has views to Fastnet and Turk Head
17.1	2.5	←	'Letterscanlan'
17.4	0.3		Road bends sharp right
18.0	0.6	△ (70)	
19.0	1.0	↑	Up hill, signed 'Cycle Route 3'
19.5	0.5	△ (70)	Views over river
19.9	0.4	↗	Take right fork
20.9	1.0	←	On to N71
21.7	0.8	✪	Abbeystrowry famine graveyard on left
21.9	0.2	→	'Baltimore'
22.1	0.2	↖	Road swings left
23.0	0.9	✪	Skibbereen Heritage Centre
		↑	'Castletown-shend'
23.1	0.1	♦	Shop
23.3	0.2	↖	Bear left with one-way system
23.4	0.1	ATM	
23.5	0.1	⇦	North Street, tourist information – turn right here for Castletownshend road

Stage 4 Schull to Clonakilty

		↑	Pass to left of post office
23.6	0.1	↖	At police station take left fork
24.4	0.8	↗	Road swings right, ignore turn to left
26.4	2.0	→	Signed 'Cycle Route One'
27.2	0.8	↑	'Cycle Route One', ignore right fork
28.3	1.1	←	At cross roads
28.9	0.6	↗	'Unionhall'
30.8	1.9	↗	Bear right
31.4	0.6	✪	Picnic area
32.6	1.2	△ (80)	
32.8	0.2	←	Road swings left, descend into Unionhall
33.7	0.9	⇨	Right goes to Reen pier (c3.5km)
33.9	0.2	WC	In Unionhall
34.3	0.4	♦	Shop
		↑	'Glandore, Leap'
34.5	0.1	←	'Glandore, Leap', good view from causeway
34.6	0.1	→	'Glandore'
35.6	1.0	→	'Glandore', after bridge
37.1	1.5	→	Road swings right in Glandore village

Stage 4 Schull to Clonakilty			
37.3	0.2	WC	
37.7	0.4	✪	Steps to beach
39.0	1.3	▲	The Meadow Camping Park
39.9	0.9	⇨	Drombeg Stone Circle (0.8km)
40.0	0.1	△ (100)	At Drombeg
44.2	4.2	⇧ →	'Clonakilty', Rosscarbery village centre is straight on
46.3	2.1	♦	Shop in service station
46.6	0.3	→	'R598 Ownahinchy'
47.7	1.1	✪ WC	Beach
48.0	0.3	▲	O'Riordan's Caravan Park
48.2	0.2	←	'L8025 Rathbarry', keep an eye out for Castlefreke through trees
50.2	2.0	←	'R598 Rathbarry', at T-junction
50.4	0.2	→	At this junction initially bear right then look straight ahead for the road signed 'Sprigging School' and take that with the post office immediately on your right side.
50.7	0.3	✪	Small picnic area

Stage 4 Schull to Clonakilty			
		✪	Sprigging School
50.9	0.2	✪	Estate church
53.2	2.3	↑	'Clonakilty'
54.2	1.0	△ (70)	
56.5	2.3	↑	'Duneen', at crossroads
57.5	1.0	←	'Clonakilty', at crossroads
59.6	2.1	→	'N71 Cork'
59.8	0.2	↗	At Clonakilty town pump bear right
60.0	0.2	♦ ATM	Supermarket
		←	Unsigned
60.1	0.1	↑	At crossroads
60.2	0.1	←	At crossroads, tourist information in front
		♦	MTM Cycles
60.3	0.1	↑	Just after small park and memorial
60.5	0.2	←	At crossroads
60.6	0.1	↑ ✪	At crossroads, Michael Collins statue on right, followed by park
60.7	0.1	←	'N70 Cork', at end of square
60.9	0.2	←	Back on main road near pump
61.1	0.2		End at corner with Croppy Quay

Stage 5 Clonakilty to Kinsale			
0.0			On N71, at Croppy Quay, head east
0.4	0.4	O →	'Ring'
		←▲O	Immediately left, carry straight on for Desert House Caravan & Camping Park
2.5	2.1	→	At T-junction
3.8	1.3	←▲⇧	'Michael Collins Centre', continue straight on for Sextons Caravan & Camping Park (3.1km)
4.8	1.0	↑	'Michael Collins Centre' at crossroads
5.5	0.7	✪	Michael Collins Centre
5.8	0.3	△ (135)	Last views of hills of Beara Peninsula
8.5	2.7	↖	Continue ahead as road swings to right
9.0	0.5	→	At T-junction, descend into Timoleague
9.7	0.7	→	At bottom of hill
		✪	Monument to St Mologa
		←	'Franciscan friary, Abbey Street'
		▲	Pad Joe's Hostel on left

Stage 5 Clonakilty to Kinsale			
9.8	0.1	↑	Continue straight on as road swings right 'Abbey'
9.9	0.1	✪	Timoleague Abbey
		←	Continue past abbey and turn left
10.1	0.2	WC	Also has tap for water bottles
10.3	0.2	→	'Kinsale R600'
10.5	0.2	→	'Kinsale'
14.5	4.0	✪	Picnic area
16.9	2.4	✪	Picnic area
18.7	1.8	✪	Access to Garraneteen Strand
19.9	1.2	→	'R600 Ballinspittle'
23.7	3.8	→	'L3222 Garrettstown'
24.4	0.7	↑	At crossroads
27.3	2.9	✪	Views of open ocean to south and west... forever
27.8	0.5	→ ⇐ ▲	'Old Head R604', Garrettstown Holiday Park on left (c1km)
27.9	0.1	✪	Beach
28.3	0.4	WC	
29.0	0.7	♦	Small shop

Stage 5 Clonakilty to Kinsale			
29.3	0.3	✪	Beach – careful of sand blown over road
30.0	0.7	→	'Old Head L3233'
32.5	2.5	✪ ⇨	To Old Head castle and golf club (200m), Lusitania memorial and signal tower on left
34.9	2.4	→	'Kinsale'
38.7	3.8	→	'L3224 Sandycove'
39.4	0.7	↖	Take left fork
41.7	2.3	↑	Continue straight on over bridge
42.2	0.5	←	At T-junction
		→	'R600 Kinsale'
43.1	0.9	→	At end of bridge, road swings right
44.2	1.1	→	Follow R600
44.6	0.4	✪	Small park
44.7	0.1	WC	
44.8	0.1		Arrive Kinsale tourist office

Stage 6 Kinsale to Cork			
0.0			Opposite tourist office, outside Temperance Hall, go NW down road between Temperance Hall and Methodist church
0.1	0.1	←	At crossroads, pass to left side of Market Hall – note fish weathervane on roof
0.2	0.1	→	Police station on your left just after turn
0.4	0.2	✪	Desmond Castle
1.1	0.7	↑	At crossroads
1.3	0.2	→	At T-junction join R607
2.0	0.7	✪ →	'Brownsmills, L3203', English camp was in this area – see sign on right
2.5	0.5	✪	Oysterhaven Creek – ships supplied English from here, sign
5.2	2.7	△ (80)	Look back to Ardmartin Ridge – held by the English
6.1	0.9	✪	O'Neill set off west from here to flank the English
8.2	2.1	△ (115)	Steady climb to this point

Stage 6 Kinsale to Cork			
8.8	0.6	↑	At crossroads
10.7	1.9	↗	'Cork'
13.4	2.7	→	At T-junction in Ballinhassig
		← ♦ ⇧	Take road immediately to left side of shop, straight on to airport (9km) via R613 and R600
14.1	0.7	✪	Very steep climb – 20%
16.1	2.0	△ (150)	Views of Cork, ahead
16.6	0.5	→	At T-junction
18.9	2.3	△ (140)	By TV transmitter climb – 7% in places
21.3	2.4	O ↑ ♦	'South Ring', shop on left
21.8	0.5	↑	At lights
22.3	0.5	↑	'The Lough', at lights
23.0	0.7	↑	At lights
23.8	0.8	↑	'City centre'
23.9	0.1	↗	Road swings right
24.0	0.1	←	'City centre'
24.1	0.1	→	'City centre', at lights
24.2	0.1	←	'City centre', at lights, cathedral on corner
		✪	St Finbarr's Cathedral on right
24.3	0.1	↑	Straight on at lights
24.5	0.2	→	'An Lár', now at Wandesford Quay
24.6	0.1	←	Cross bridge
24.7	0.1	→	At lights, pass in front of court building
25.0	0.3	→	At lights, enter Grand Parade
25.2	0.2		Arrive Cork tourist office

APPENDIX A
Useful contacts

The Wild Atlantic Way
(official driving route)
www.discoverireland.ie/
wild-atlantic-way

Travel
Ferry
Brittany Ferries
www.brittanyferries.com
Ireland 021 4277801
UK 0330 1597000
France 02 98 244 701

Irish Ferries
www.irishferries.com
Ireland 0818 300400
UK 03717 300400

P&O Ferries
www.poferries.com
UK 01304 448888
Ireland 01 6869467

Stena Line
www.stenaline.com
UK 03447 707070
Ireland 01 9075555
France 02 334 32387
(for Cherbourg–Rosslare services only)

Rail
Irish Rail
www.irishrail.ie
01 8366222

Translink (Northern Ireland)
www.translink.co.uk
028 9066 6630

Buses
Bus Éireann
www.buseireann.ie
0818836611, or +35318366111
outside Ireland

Translink (Northern Ireland)
www.translink.co.uk
028 9066 6630

Visas
Republic of Ireland visa information
www.dfa.ie/travel/visas

Northern Ireland visa information
www.gov.uk/check-uk-visa

Accommodation
Hostels
Independent Holiday Hostels of Ireland
(IHH)
www.hostels-ireland.com

An Óige (Irish Youth Hostel Association)
www.anoige.ie
04 044 5342

Hostelling International Northern Ireland
www.hini.org.uk
028 9032 4733

Camping
Camping Ireland
www.campingireland.ie

Coillte (forests in the Republic of Ireland)
www.coillte.ie

Bed and breakfast
B&B Ireland
www.bandbireland.com
071 98 22222

Emergencies

Crime

Emergency numbers for police, fire and ambulance are 999 or 112 (all of Ireland). For non-emergency police matters, contact the nearest Garda station, or in Northern Ireland, police station.

In the Republic, the nationwide free Irish Tourist Assistance Service aims help with the practical and emotional aftermath of crime (www.itas.ie, 01 6669354).

Healthcare

In the Republic, the local Health Service Office (www.hse.ie) will have numbers for GPs contracted under the Primary Care Reimbursement Services (PCRS) scheme. See 'Health and Safety' in the introduction for more information.

APPENDIX B

Glossary

Anglicised placenames and their Irish equivalents

English	Irish	meaning
Aran Islands	*Oileáin Árann*	
Ardfert	*Ard Fhearta*	the hill of miracles (or the high place of St Erc)
Achill Island	*Oileán Acla*	
Ballina	*Béal an Átha*	mouth of the ford
Ballyshannon	*Béal Átha Seanaidh*	the mouth of Seannach's ford
Bantry	*Beanntraí*	(the place of) Beann's people
Belmullet	*Béal an Mhuirthead*	mouth of the Mullet (peninsula)
Bundoran	*Bun Dobhráin*	mouth of the little water
Caherdaniel	*Cathair Dónall*	Dónall's stone ringfort
Cahersiveen	*Cathair Saidhbhín*	little Sadhbh's stone ringfort
Clifden	*An Clochán*	stepping stones/causeway
Clonakilty	*Cloich na Coillte*	stone (building) of the woods
Cork	*Corcaigh*	marsh
Dingle	*Daingean Uí Chúis/ An Daingean*	the stronghold of Clan Ó Cúis/the stronghold

English	Irish	meaning
Donegal	*Dún na nGall*	the fort of the foreigners (Vikings or Scots)
Doolin	*Dúlainn*	possibly from dubh linn – dark pool – or dubh lann – dark land
Ennis	*Inis*	island (Inis is short for Inis Cluain Ramh Fhada – island of the long rowing meadow)
Galway	*Gaillimh*	stony (after the Gaillimh river)
Glencolumbkille	*Gleann Cholm Cille*	valley of Colm Cille (St Columba)
Glenveagh	*Gleann Bheatha*	valley of the birches
Inishbofin	*Inis Bó Finne*	the island of the White Cow (the White Cow was an ancient Celtic deity)
Kenmare	*Neidín/Ceann Mara*	the little nest/promontory of the flood tide
Kerry	*Ciarraí*	(the place of) Ciar's people
Kilkee	*Cill Chaoi*	the church of Caoineadh Ita (the lamentation of St Ita)
Killarney	*Cill Airne*	the church of St Airne
Killybegs	*Na Cealla Beaga*	small cells (associated with a monastic settlement)
Kilrush	*Cill Rois*	church of the wooded height
Kinsale	*Cionn tSáile*	headland of the tide
Lahinch	*An Leacht*	memorial cairn
Letterkenny	*Leitir Ceanainn*	hillside of the O'Cannons
Mayo	*Maigh Eo*	plain of the yew
Schull	*An Scoil*	the school
Skibbereen	*An Sciobairín*	little boat harbour
Sligo	*Sligeach*	place of splintered rocks
River Shannon	*an tSionainn*	named after Sionna, a Celtic deity (her name means 'wise one')
Tarbert	*Tairbeart*	isthmus
Tralee	*Trá Lí*	the beach/strand of the River Lee

Elements of Irish placenames

Irish element	anglicised	meaning
ard	ard	high/height
baile	bally	town
beag	beg	little
béal	bel, bell	mouth/river mouth
bun	bun	foot/bottom/river mouth
carraig	carrick	rock
cathair	cahir, caher	stone ringfort
cill	kill	church
clár	clare	level ground
coill	kill	woodland
dún	dun, down	fort
droim/druim	drum, drom	ridge
gleann	glen, glan	valley
inis	ennis, inish	island
loch	lough	lake
ros	ros, rush	(wooded) promontory
ráth	rath, rah	earthen ringfort
sean	shan	old
trá	tra	beach

A few Irish phrases

English	Irish	pronunciation
hello (greeting one person)	Dia duit!	jee-uh didge
hello (more than one person)	Dia daoibh!	jee-uh deev
hello (replying)	Dia is Muire duit/daoibh!	jee-us mwir-uh didge/deev
hello (on the road)	Is é do bheatha!	shay do vah
please (to one person)	le do thoil/más é do thoil é	lay-do hull/mas ay do hull ay

English	Irish	pronunciation
please (more than one person)	*le bhur dtoil/más é bhur dtoil é*	lay woor dull/mas ay voor dull ay
thank you (to one person)	*go raibh maith agat*	gur-a ma o-gut
thank you (more than one person)	*go raibh maith agaibh*	gur-a ma o-giv

Useful words

Irish	English	pronunciation
leithreas	toilet	leh-ris
fir	men	fir
mná	women	m'nah (or mraa in Donegal)
rothar	bicycle	ro-her
sláinte	cheers! (as in a toast)	slawn-che

Signs you might see on the road

Irish	English	pronunciation
aire!	caution	ar-eh
an Ghaeltacht	Irish-speaking area	gale-taght
an lár	centre (as in town centre)	an lar
bealach rothaíochta	cycle route	bya-logh ro-hee-ogh-tuh
bóthar dúnta	road closed	boh-her doon-tuh
brú óige	youth hostel	broo oy-geh
ceantar coisithe	pedestrian area	kyan-ter kosh-ee
géill slí	give way	gayl shlee
go mall	slow	guh moll
ionad campála	campsite	un-ud kamp-all-uh
ná scoitear	no overtaking	naw skutch-er
oifig fáilte	tourist office	ef-ig fol-chuh
óstán	hotel	oh-stawn
trá	beach/strand	tra

APPENDIX C
Deviations from the Wild Atlantic Way driving route

The version of the Wild Atlantic Way (WAW) described in this book, in Routes 1 to 6, is devised to combine the best roads available for quiet and scenic cycling with feasible day stages between refuelling points and stopovers. The details of the diversions from the official (and signed) driving route are outlined below.

Route 1
The WAW officially starts (or finishes) on the border at Muff, not Derry/Londonderry.

Stage 1
At Greencastle, the WAW takes a 9km loop out to Inishowen Head (turn right at the fisheries college) which you may wish to take if you are ahead of schedule. The driving route also takes a more westerly route to Kinnagoe Bay. The route described here is more scenic although the road is narrower and less suited to cars. The preferred cycling route also sticks closer to the coast between Kinnagoe Bay and Culdaff, only returning to the main R238 just before the village.

Stage 2
Between Culdaff and Clonmany the route described here follows the signed WAW apart from a shortcut at Benduff (42.1km) which saves some 3km or so.

Stage 3
The stage from Clonmany to Letterkenny follows the WAW driving route closely as far as Buncrana. The exception is that the road on the north side of the Owenerk river (turn at 15.2km) is quieter and has better views that the road on the other side of the river followed by the WAW. The WAW rather rushes through the area between Buncrana and Letterkenny, sticking to the R238 and then the very busy N13 after Burnfoot. The route described here follows some almost deserted roads close to Lough Swilly and then approaches Letterkenny from the south in a far less hectic route.

Stage 4
From Letterkenny to Portsalon the WAW follows the main coastal roads (the R245, R247 and R246). The route described here finds a quieter way out of Letterkenny, again close to Lough Swilly, as far as Ramelton by which stage the traffic on the main coastal roads is usually a little quieter.

Stage 5
This stage largely follows the WAW to Fanad Head and beyond. But the preferred cycling route is continue westwards at Ballyhiernan Bay and follow some of the very small roads right along the coast and then return to the WAW just before the Mulroy Bay bridge.

Stage 6
At 33.3km the WAW continues along the N56 via Dunfanaghy to Gortahork and then via the R257 to Bunbeg for a total distance from Downies to Bunbeg of some 82km. But inland

from Creeslough you will find some of Ireland's grandest mountain scenery. My preferred cycling route is to turn westwards at Creeslough, across the lower slopes of Muckish mountain, along the the edge of the Glenveagh National Park and past Mount Errigal, Donegal's highest peak. This area includes some of Ireland's finest glaciated landscapes and is a worthy alternative to the coastal route, especially on the sections where the coast road veers well away from the shoreline. It is also 15km shorter.

Stage 7

At 7.0km the WAW continues for a further 300m along the N56, then turns right onto the R259 which it follows along the coast via Burtonport to Dungloe for a further 34km to Dungloe. The route preferred here is to cut across the hills to Dungloe along some very quiet moorland roads which also saves some 20km of riding on main roads. The stage finishes at Portnoo, which is officially a side-trip on the WAW but is worthy of a short stay. The area has some well protected beaches and picturesque inlets.

Stage 8

From Portnoo, the WAW returns straight to the R261 and neglects the quiet backwater of the Rossbeg peninsula. The route here explores the Rossbeg before rejoining the R261 and heading towards Ardara.

Route 2

Stage 1

The WAW between Donegal and Ballyshannon follows the R267 to Rossmore and then the N15 to Ballintra where it turns westward to loop along the R231 to Ballyshannon. There are

Ballyshannon's main street (Route 2, Stage 2)

however some fine country roads along this section of coast so this cycling route finds a quieter way out of Donegal town and sticks closer to the coast to the grand beach at Rossnowlagh. From there a gentle climb over the hills to Ballyshannon offers better views of the coast than the main R231 route.

Stage 2

From Ballyshannon to Sligo town the WAW driving route initially follows the R267 southwards before joining the N15 near Bundoran. The N15 is at best unpleasantly fast and at worst dangerously busy for cycling. The route described here follows a largely parallel path along the network of older roads by the coast and finds a quieter back way into bustling Sligo.

Stage 3

South of Sligo the main Wild Atlantic Way route becomes better suited to cycling. The route described here does take the

Rosserk Friary is one of the finest Franciscan friaries in Ireland (Route 2, Stage 4)

opportunity to get off the main N59 coast road at Beltra (29.3km), some 6km before the official route leaves the highway, before rejoining the WAW route towards Ballina after Dromore beach.

Stage 4

The preferred cycling route from Ballina to Belmullet largely follows the official WAW driving route. However taking some of the quieter roads leaving Ballina, as described here, leads you through some idyllic scenery alongside the Moy estuary. It also takes you close to the ruins of Rosserk Friary and Moyne Abbey. From Belmullet the signed WAW takes you on a 42km loop out to southwest tip of The Mullet, which you may feel inspired to ride if decent weather offers the prospect of views across Blacksod Bay towards Achill Island.

Stage 5

The WAW leaves Belmullet as it arrived, on the R313 before turning into a loop along the coast at Bunnahowen (7.2km). You may wish to extend the route described here by 8km or so by taking that signed loop. I prefer the graded climb over the scenic Tristia bog and into Bangor Erris – where you can rejoin the

WAW – to the undulating coastal road.

As a cyclist it makes sense to join the Great Western Greenway cycleway at Mulranny rather than following the roads into Achill Sound.

Stage 6

The described route on Achill Island follows the WAW.

Stage 7/7A

The Great Western Greenway cycling path follows the old Achill Island railway route all the way to Westport. The WAW takes the N59 road.

Route 3

Stage 1

The WAW will take you straight from Westport to Roonagh, where ferries depart for Clare Island. The route described here makes a minor deviation from the R335 to take in Murrisk Abbey where there are fine views of Croagh Patrick. It also visits the Carrowmore sand cliffs between Louisburgh and Roonagh.

Stage 2

Clare Island is not included on the WAW but offers some worry-free cycling on very quiet roads.

Stage 3

The WAW returns to Louisburgh from Roonagh where it joins one of the larger local coastal roads and zigzags to the R335 onwards to Leenane and further to Tully. Cyclists can save some of the backtracking using the network of small roads to rejoin the R335 at Tawnymackan. Thereafter the described route follows the WAW all the way to Tully.

Stage 4

The WAW turns back on itself at Tully and takes the direct route to Letterfrack. This rather neglects the stunning mountain and coastal scenery around Renvyle, which the route described here explores before rejoining the WAW at Dawros Bridge. After Letterfrack the route described here leaves the N59 before the WAW (at 18.2km) but rejoins the signposted WAW route at Cleggan.

Soon after rejoining the N59 at Letternoosh the WAW turns westwards along the stunning Sky Road in a 13km loop into Clifden. Take that route rather than the straight through route described here if you have good weather and the energy. But it is best ridden without luggage as a gentle outing from Clifden.

Stage 5

Inishbofin is not on the WAW driving route.

Stage 6

From Clifden to Kilkieran the WAW follows the R341, then the R340 along the coast. The route described here cuts out the loop through Ballyconneely and Roundstone by turning at Ballinaboy (3.5km), saving some 19km and also taking in a lovely unfenced road across lake strewn boglands. If you get fine weather,

the official WAW also takes a loop along the coastal road (at 30.9km) to Carna. This adds some 5km to the total distance to Kilkieran. At Casla, a 33-km signed side-trip on the WAW takes you to Coral Strand near Carraroe, and Lettermore Island. You may be able to squeeze this into your itinerary.

Stage 7

The described route follows the WAW right to the doorstep of Galway where it finds a quieter way into town via Claddagh.

Route 4

Stage 1

This stage follows the WAW route to the Aran ferry at Rossaveel, apart from finding a quieter way out of Galway for the first few kilometres.

Stages 2 and 3

Stages 2 and 3 are not on the WAW driving route.

Green-laning on Inisheer (Route 4, Stage 3)

Stage 4

If you are arriving at Doolin from the Aran Islands (the preferred cycling route here), Stage 4 gives you an opportunity to explore some of the WAW northwards to Ballyvaughan and then visit the high Burren, which is not on the WAW, on a lightly loaded day trip. If you are riding from Galway you can follow the route outlined from Galway to Ballyvaughan, along the WAW, and then continue along the signed WAW route to Doolin.

Stage 5

The described route from Doolin to Kilrush follows the signed WAW route apart from taking the coast road at Kilbaha (L2002) for the return trip from Loop Head to Carrigaholt.

Stage 6

The WAW departs the described route at the turn for the Shannon Ferry (9.1km).

Stage 7

The stage from Ennis to Limerick is not on the WAW.

Stage 7A

The stage from Limerick to Tarbert returns you the the WAW at the Tarbert ferry crossing.

Route 5

Stage 1

At Ballylongford, the route described here takes a break from the main road with a climb over low hills to Lisselton (turn at 11.1km), but you may wish to follow the WAW route along the coast and rejoin this stage at Gortagurrane (23.6km on this stage). On the way into Tralee the route described takes advantage of the minor roads around Banna Strand and Ardfert to stay closer to the coast than the WAW. It also skips the detour out to Fenit harbour from Ardfert, to keep the distances down.

Stage 2

From Tralee to Dingle, the WAW follows the route described in this book.

Stage 3

The tour of the Dingle peninsula route described here is identical to the WAW driving route.

Stage 4

From Dingle to Killorglin the WAW driving route follows the main coastal roads, the N86 then the R561 and N70. The N86, in particular, can be busy so the route described here finds some older roads around Lispole and Annascaul. It also leaves the N86 for a while between Milltown and Killorglin.

Stage 5

After Killorglin the WAW follows the 'Ring of Kerry' route along the main coastal roads. The cycling route described here keeps off the main N70 road as much as possible by picking up nearby local roads – in particular when leaving Killorglin and approaching Cahersiveen. The route described here also incorporates a trip along Valentia Island which is a side-trip on the WAW through route.

Stage 6

Between Portmagee and Caherdaniel, the cycling route takes a few opportunities to get away from the main road, leaving the WAW at Keel (8.4km), leaving Ballinskelligs (17.9km), after Waterville (31.5km) and finds a quieter way into Caherdaniel (turn at 41.3km).

Stage 7

From Caherdaniel to Kenmare, this cycling route follows the WAW route.

Stage 8

Stage 7 between Killarney and Kenmare is not on the WAW.

Stage 9

The stage from Killarney to Tralee is not on the WAW.

Route 6

Stage 1

This stage from Kenmare to Allihies follows the WAW apart from leaving the R571 on the approach to Ardgroom (36.7km) and then taking a more coastal route past Ardgroom Harbour and returning to the WAW past Eyeries (60.2km).

Stage 2

This stage follows the WAW driving route as far as the approach to Glengarriff (48.0km) when cyclists may prefer the route described here which explores some of the small beaches close to town.

Stage 3

The route described here follows the WAW as far as the Sheeps Head peninsula. At 22.5km, however, it turns to climb over the peninsula ridge on a road that opens up fine views over Bantry Bay and towards Mizen Head. You may wish to continue on the WAW route to the tip of the peninsula and rejoin the described route at Durrus, but you will miss out on a grand climb. It is also 54km from that turn to Durrus via the WAW, this way is 7.4km.

The other deviation from the WAW is to follow the quieter roads on the north side of the Mizen peninsula by turning off the R591 at 43.9km.

Stage 4

Between Schull and Clonakilty the WAW takes some leg-sapping coastal loops to Roaringwater Bay, Baltimore, Toe Head near Castle Townsend and Galley Head, south of Clonakilty. The route here takes in some of the quieter small coastal roads between Ballydehob and Skibbereen. Also included here, and not on the WAW, is the particularly beautiful section of coast between Skibbereen and Rosscarbery which is close to the direct coastal route but on small traffic-free roads.

Stage 5

Stage 5 marks the final section of the WAW from Clonakilty to Kinsale. The official driving route follows the R600 all the way to Kinsale with just a small deviation away from the main road to take in the Old Head of Kinsale viewpoint. To get away from the main road, the route described here takes an old ridge route from Clonakilty to Timoleague, which has the bonus of the final views back westwards, as far as the Kerry mountains on a clear day. The described route also finds a quieter way between the Old Head of Kinsale and the town, rejoining the WAW just before the bridge over the Bandon river.

Stage 6

The WAW officially finishes (or starts) at Kinsale rather than Cork.

APPENDIX D
Further reading

Geology

Geology and Scenery in Ireland, JB Whittow, Pelican Books, Harmondsworth, 1974. Out of print and, in parts, out of date, but a comprehensive tour of Ireland's geology and landscape for the layman.

Classic Geology in Europe 5: The North of Ireland, Paul Lyle, Terra Publishing, Harpenden, 2003. More technical than the above, and just covering Ulster, but still comprehensible to the average reader and well illustrated.

Wildlife and flowers

Ireland: A Smithsonian Natural History, Michael Viney, Blackstaff Press, Belfast, 2003. A loving account of the Irish landscape that is not overly scientific.

History

Teach Yourself the History of Ireland, FJM Madden, Hodder Education, London. Get the latest edition – it is regularly updated; a comprehensive and easy-to-digest history that is kept bang up to date.

The Concise History of Ireland, Sean Duffy, Gill and Macmillan, Dublin, 2005. Well-illustrated history, particularly good on the 14th century onwards.

Culture

Irish Writing: An Anthology of Irish Literature in English 1789–1939, ed Stephen Regan, Oxford University Press, 2004. Bit heavy in places (like the Connor Pass), but includes some key political writings, travelogues and poetry (including WB Yeats) as well as fiction. Also includes JM Synge's *Riders to the Sea* and an excerpt from *The Aran Islands* (1907) – which may leave you wanting more.

Opened Ground: Poems 1966–1996, Seamus Heaney, Faber and Faber, London, 2007. Maybe a bit big to carry, but peerless poetry, especially when reflecting on an Ulster childhood.

The Collected Stories, William Trevor, Penguin, London, 2003. Wonderful short stories from one of the masters of the art in a very heavy volume that's worth carrying if you want reading matter on the trip.

Spill Simmer Falter Wither, Sarah Baume, Windmill Books, London, 2015. A journey of sadness and beauty which begins and ends on the Irish coast, beautifully written.

City of Bohane, Kevin Barry, Vintage, London, 2012. Uses the setting of an Irish port city in a future with little technology to interrogate modern Ireland.

Miscellaneous

Round Ireland in Low Gear, Eric Newby, Picador, London, 1988. Required reading for anyone mad enough to think of touring Ireland in winter.

APPENDIX E
Calibrating your cycle computer

The distances in this guide were measured with a cycle computer driven by a wheel sensor. These computers calculate distance by multiplying the number of turns of the wheel by the distance the wheel travels for each turn (the circumference of the tyre). If you are using a similar computer, adjusting your cycle computer to the fit in with the calibration in the guide will make it easier to follow the directions.

If you are consistently under- or over-reading compared to the guide you can tweak the wheel diameter setting on your cycle computer using the following formula.

New Wheel diameter (NW) = [Book Distance (BD)/Your Measured Distance (MD)] * Old Wheel diameter (OW)

The longer the distance you choose for this comparison, the more accurate the adjustment will be. Try and do at least 10km, preferably on a well-surfaced road with few turns. Don't use a hilly section as experience shows zig-zagging across the road during climbs can throw distances off considerably.

For example, you have 42-559 (26x1.60) tyres and are using the 'maker's guide' setting of 2010mm tyre diameter. On Route 1, Stage 1, you measure the distance between joining the A2 and the Lough Foyle ferry (30.8km) as 30.4km.

You are under-reading slightly so:

New Wheel diameter (NW) = [BD/MD] * OW

NW = [30.8/30.4] * 2010 = 2036

So you should adjust your wheel diameter to 2036mm to be consistent with the book.

Resettable trip counters
If you choose a cycle computer with a resettable trip counter it makes following the route cards easier. If you divert from the route or take a side trip, you can then re-set the trip counter to correspond with the route card when you return to the route, making it easy to follow subsequent directions.

At the time of writing there were two such cycle computers on the market:

- Ciclo CM2.2: As used for the book. The 'day stage' total can be reset/set to any value at any time.

- VDO M3 WR: Has a separate 'navigator' trip counter that can be reset or adjusted without affecting totals. Also available in a wireless version, the M3 WL.

DOWNLOAD THE GPX FILES

All the routes in this guide are available for download from:

www.cicerone.co.uk/909/GPX

as standard format GPX files. You should be able to load them into most online GPX systems and mobile devices, whether GPS or smartphone. You may need to convert the file into your preferred format using a conversion programme such as gpsvisualizer.com or one of the many other such websites and programmes.

When you follow this link, you will be asked for your email address and where you purchased the guidebook, and have the option to subscribe to the Cicerone e-newsletter.

LISTING OF CICERONE GUIDES

BRITISH ISLES CHALLENGES, COLLECTIONS AND ACTIVITIES

Cycling Land's End to John o' Groats
Great Walks on the England Coast Path
The Big Rounds
The Book of the Bivvy
The Book of the Bothy
The Mountains of England & Wales:
Vol 1 Wales
Vol 2 England
The National Trails
Walking the End to End Trail

SHORT WALKS SERIES

Short Walks Hadrian's Wall
Short Walks in Arnside and Silverdale
Short Walks in Dumfries and Galloway
Short Walks in Nidderdale
Short Walks in the Lake District: Windermere Ambleside and Grasmere
Short Walks in the Surrey Hills
Short Walks Lake District – Coniston and Langdale
Short Walks on the Malvern Hills
Short Walks Winchester

SCOTLAND

Ben Nevis and Glen Coe
Cycle Touring in Northern Scotland
Cycling in the Hebrides
Cycling the North Coast 500
Great Mountain Days in Scotland
Mountain Biking in Southern and Central Scotland
Mountain Biking in West and North West Scotland
Not the West Highland Way Scotland
Scotland's Best Small Mountains
Scotland's Mountain Ridges
Scottish Wild Country Backpacking
Skye's Cuillin Ridge Traverse
The Borders Abbeys Way
The Great Glen Way
The Great Glen Way Map Booklet
The Hebridean Way
The Hebrides
The Isle of Mull
The Isle of Skye
The Skye Trail
The Southern Upland Way
The West Highland Way
The West Highland Way Map Booklet
Walking Ben Lawers, Rannoch and Atholl

Walking in the Cairngorms
Walking in the Pentland Hills
Walking in the Scottish Borders
Walking in the Southern Uplands
Walking in Torridon, Fisherfield, Fannichs and An Teallach
Walking Loch Lomond and the Trossachs
Walking on Arran
Walking on Harris and Lewis
Walking on Jura, Islay and Colonsay
Walking on Rum and the Small Isles
Walking on the Orkney and Shetland Isles
Walking on Uist and Barra
Walking the Cape Wrath Trail
Walking the Corbetts
Vol 1 South of the Great Glen
Vol 2 North of the Great Glen
Walking the Galloway Hills
Walking the John o' Groats Trail
Walking the Munros
Vol 1 – Southern, Central and Western Highlands
Vol 2 – Northern Highlands and the Cairngorms
Winter Climbs in the Cairngorms
Winter Climbs: Ben Nevis and Glen Coe

NORTHERN ENGLAND ROUTES

Cycling the Reivers Route
Cycling the Way of the Roses
Hadrian's Cycleway
Hadrian's Wall Path
Hadrian's Wall Path Map Booklet
The Coast to Coast Cycle Route
The Coast to Coast Walk
The Coast to Coast Walk Map Booklet
The Pennine Way
The Pennine Way Map Booklet
Walking the Dales Way
Walking the Dales Way Map Booklet

NORTH-EAST ENGLAND, YORKSHIRE DALES AND PENNINES

Cycling in the Yorkshire Dales
Great Mountain Days in the Pennines
Mountain Biking in the Yorkshire Dales
The Cleveland Way and the Yorkshire Wolds Way
The Cleveland Way Map Booklet
The North York Moors
Trail and Fell Running in the Yorkshire Dales
Walking in County Durham
Walking in Northumberland

Walking in the North Pennines
Walking in the Yorkshire Dales: North and East
Walking in the Yorkshire Dales: South and West
Walking St Cuthbert's Way
Walking St Oswald's Way and Northumberland Coast Path

NORTH-WEST ENGLAND AND THE ISLE OF MAN

Cycling the Pennine Bridleway
Isle of Man Coastal Path
The Lancashire Cycleway
The Lune Valley and Howgills
Walking in Cumbria's Eden Valley
Walking in Lancashire
Walking in the Forest of Bowland and Pendle
Walking on the Isle of Man
Walking on the West Pennine Moors
Walking the Ribble Way
Walks in Silverdale and Arnside

LAKE DISTRICT

Bikepacking in the Lake District
Cycling in the Lake District
Great Mountain Days in the Lake District
Joss Naylor's Lakes, Meres and Waters of the Lake District
Lake District Winter Climbs
Lake District: High Level and Fell Walks
Lake District: Low Level and Lake Walks
Mountain Biking in the Lake District
Outdoor Adventures with Children – Lake District
Scrambles in the Lake District – North
Scrambles in the Lake District – South
Trail and Fell Running in the Lake District
Walking The Cumbria Way
Walking the Lake District Fells:
Borrowdale
Buttermere
Coniston
Keswick
Langdale
Mardale and the Far East
Patterdale
Wasdale
Walking the Tour of the Lake District

DERBYSHIRE, PEAK DISTRICT AND MIDLANDS

Cycling in the Peak District
Dark Peak Walks
Scrambles in the Dark Peak

ITALY

Alta Via 1 / Alta Via 2 – Trekking in the Dolomites
Day Walks in the Dolomites
Italy's Grande Traversata delle Alpi
Italy's Sibillini National Park
Ski Touring and Snowshoeing in the Dolomites
The Way of St Francis
Trekking in the Apennines
Trekking the Giants' Trail: Alta Via 1 through the Italian Pennine Alps
Via Ferratas of the Italian Dolomites: Vols 1&2
Walking and Trekking in the Gran Paradiso
Walking in Abruzzo
Walking in Italy's Cinque Terre
Walking in Italy's Stelvio National Park
Walking in Sicily
Walking in the Aosta Valley
Walking in the Dolomites
Walking in Tuscany
Walking in Umbria
Walking Lake Como and Maggiore
Walking Lake Garda and Iseo
Walking on the Amalfi Coast
Walking the Via Francigena Pilgrim Route Parts 2 and 3
Walks and Treks in the Maritime Alps

MEDITERRANEAN

The High Mountains of Crete
Trekking in Greece
Walking and Trekking in Zagori
Walking and Trekking on Corfu
Walking in Cyprus
Walking on Malta
Walking on the Greek Islands – the Cyclades

NEW ZEALAND AND AUSTRALIA

Hiking the Overland Track

NORTH AMERICA

Hiking and Cycling the California Missions Trail
The John Muir Trail
The Pacific Crest Trail

SOUTH AMERICA

Aconcagua and the Southern Andes
Hiking and Biking Peru's Inca Trails
Trekking in Torres del Paine

SCANDINAVIA, ICELAND AND GREENLAND

Hiking in Norway – South
Trekking in Greenland – The Arctic Circle Trail
Trekking the Kungsleden
Walking and Trekking in Iceland

SLOVENIA, CROATIA, SERBIA, MONTENEGRO AND ALBANIA

Hiking Slovenia's Juliana Trail
Mountain Biking in Slovenia
The Islands of Croatia
The Julian Alps of Slovenia
The Mountains of Montenegro
The Peaks of the Balkans Trail
The Slovene Mountain Trail
Walking in Slovenia: The Karavanke
Walks and Treks in Croatia

SPAIN AND PORTUGAL

Camino de Santiago: Camino Frances
Coastal Walks in Andalucia
Costa Blanca Mountain Adventures
Cycling the Camino de Santiago
Cycling the Ruta Via de la Plata
Mountain Walking in Mallorca
Mountain Walking in Southern Catalunya
Portugal's Rota Vicentina
Spain's Sendero Historico: The GR1
The Andalucian Coast to Coast Walk
The Camino del Norte and Camino Primitivo
The Camino Ingles and Ruta do Mar
The Camino Portugues
The Mountains of Nerja
The Mountains of Ronda and Grazalema
The Sierras of Extremadura
Trekking in Mallorca
Trekking in the Canary Islands
Trekking the GR7 in Andalucia
Walking and Trekking in the Sierra Nevada
Walking in Andalucia
Walking in Catalunya – Barcelona
Walking in Catalunya – Girona Pyrenees
Walking in Portugal
Walking in the Algarve
Walking in the Picos de Europa
Walking La Via de la Plata and Camino Sanabres
Walking on Gran Canaria
Walking on La Gomera and El Hierro
Walking on La Palma
Walking on Lanzarote and Fuerteventura
Walking on Madeira
Walking on Tenerife
Walking on the Azores
Walking on the Costa Blanca
Walking the Camino dos Faros

SWITZERLAND

Switzerland's Jura Crest Trail
The Swiss Alps
Tour of the Jungfrau Region
Trekking the Swiss Via Alpina
Walking in the Bernese Oberland – Jungfrau region
Walking in the Engadine – Switzerland
Walking in the Valais
Walking in Ticino
Walking in Zermatt and Saas-Fee

CHINA, JAPAN AND ASIA

Hiking and Trekking in the Japan Alps and Mount Fuji
Hiking in Hong Kong
Japan's Kumano Kodo Pilgrimage
Trekking in Tajikistan

HIMALAYA

Annapurna
Everest: A Trekker's Guide
Trekking in Bhutan
Trekking in Ladakh
Trekking in the Himalaya

MOUNTAIN LITERATURE

8000 metres
A Walk in the Clouds
Abode of the Gods
Fifty Years of Adventure
The Pennine Way – the Path, the People, the Journey
Unjustifiable Risk?

TECHNIQUES

Fastpacking
Geocaching in the UK
Map and Compass
Outdoor Photography
The Mountain Hut Book

MINI GUIDES

Alpine Flowers
Navigation
Pocket First Aid and Wilderness Medicine
Snow